STEVO
Looking Back

STEVO
Looking Back

MIKE STEPHENSON

VERTICAL EDITIONS

www.verticaleditions.com

First published in the United Kingdom in 2007 by
Vertical Editions, 7 Bell Busk, Skipton,
North Yorkshire BD23 4DT

www.verticaleditions.com

ISBN 978-1-904091-23-3

Cover design and typeset by HBA, York

Printed and bound by the Cromwell Press, Trowbridge

For my children Craig, Hayley, Alyssa and Kayley.

CONTENTS

FOREWORD

They say a week is a long time in rugby league. In that case, the number of years I've spent working in rugby league must constitute a lifetime! It was way back in 1988 that Stevo and I got together for our first ever commentary. The commentary was for BBC Radio. They were sending me out to Australia to cover the Lions Tour and I was looking for someone to be my side-kick. I had bumped into Stevo a wee while earlier when he personally delivered a letter from a commentator to a female member of the BBC staff soon after the Cricket World Cup. He strayed into the offices of New Broadcasting House on Oxford Road in Manchester one morning. The lady in question wasn't there but such was the alleged importance of the delivery he had to make, he insisted on sticking around until she did show. So we wandered into a local hostelry to while away a couple of hours (I remember that I was buying of course) and we got on like a house on fire. 'Keep me in mind and look me up if ever you come to Aussie,' I vaguely remembered Stevo saying. So when the tickets arrived for Australia the following year I did exactly that! I told the BBC bosses that Stevo and I were the best of mates and, more importantly, that Stevo would work for peanuts. Stevo was in. The Eddie and Stevo commentary team was born. I didn't know then that this many years later we'd still be together!

Two years later I was looking for someone to work alongside me for BSB on the birth of satellite television. We'd tried all sorts of permutations. Some were good, some were bad. Then one day I was in the office in London, browsing through a copy of the *Australian Big League* magazine and suddenly Stevo's face was smiling out at me. He was on his way over to London with a fans' group and the 1990 Kangaroos. BSB had bought the rights to the tour. I wondered whether Stevo would like to do some commentary work on the games. I cleared it with the boss and gave Stevo a call. Stevo will tell you (he says so in this book) that he was sitting by his pool on Sydney's northern beaches sipping a gin and tonic when the phone rang. He was told it was that Eddie bloke from the Old Dart on the other end. Stevo's version is that I then had to get down on one knee and persuade him to join the satellite TV revolution. In truth, he was unemployed and unemployable down under, so he jumped at the chance. His bags were packed before he'd put down the phone! Anyway whichever version you believe, it was the start of a wonderful friendship. In our own small way I like to think we have helped popularise a fantastic sport.

It has been a roller coaster of a ride. We've had our ups and downs. Ask Stevo to tell you about a night we spent in Parkes in New South Wales. Despite this, we are still together after all these years. Just think if I'd shot him way back then I'd have been out now!

In all honesty, the years have flashed by and here is Stevo, looking back over his rugby league playing and television career in this book.

I am honoured to write this foreword. I know why I was asked of course. I never mentioned a fee! But even if he'd offered me cash I'd have turned it down flat. It's impossible to believe that years ago people said our partnership wouldn't last. It has lasted and what a thrill it has been to sit alongside Stevo for all these years. He's clocking on a bit now of course. He hung his boots up over 30 years ago. A lot of the viewers don't even know he was a rugby league star. I must say that if you look at him these days it is hard to imagine. Once upon a time all the inches he's got around his midriff were up there on his chest! Stevo is gregarious, larger than life, loud and the smiling face of Super League. He's twice more dangerous now than he was back in 1988. He's my mate and we have stuck together like glue. He's also a thoroughly decent bloke and gives up many hours to raise money for charity.

I hope Stevo doesn't tell too many truths in this book. But just in case, let me state right now that I **do not** dye my hair. Imagine if I hadn't made that phone call all those years ago. British television audiences would never have been thrilled with commentaries such as:

Eddie: 'Bobbie Goulding has decided he wants to play for Wales, Stevo in the 2000 Rugby League World Cup ...'

Stevo: 'Och aye the noo Eddie ...'

You can't make up scripts like that. Enjoy the book and here's to the future!

Eddie Hemmings
August 2007

1

WHAT AN UGLY KID

It was the worst winter for decades. Snow had trapped the town like a giant's grip, nothing moved. Cars, buses and trucks were stranded for days. Nothing could get through. The world had come to a standstill. Everything had stopped except me. I wasn't going to be denied and out I popped five weeks premature gasping and struggling for breath. All two and a half pounds of me entered the world and I was no bigger than a rat. To add extra discomfort for my mother, I was a breach baby. I came feet first. This was something she never forgot, saying, 'He came out awkward and has been that way ever since.' Add to this the fact I was born asthmatic and it's obvious my birth was a sob story. To say I battled to survive is an understatement. Six weeks in an incubation chamber did little for my looks, not to mention my hair. My father, Albert, often described the event as the reason I wasn't the prettiest baby on the block. Either way I made it, thanks to several tubes attached to every part of my tiny body.

I owe a lot to the medical world. Even today I am fascinated by the wonderful job doctors do to keep the human race ticking over. I never knew the man who eased me from my mother's womb. To be truthful neither did mum, who evidently didn't have a hard time giving birth, not surprisingly when you take into account how small I was. 'You fitted into a pint pot,' Dad would often say. No I tell a lie, he said it all the time. He also added that I had made up for it big time ever since. This was a gentle nudge that I had put on weight since that fateful day of 27th January 1947.

I could bore the reader for hours about the hardships and pain I endured to succeed in life, the slums where I was brought up, the struggle to get food, the way society had left us fighting the system to survive, the sadness and hardships we endured week in week out and the ... oh bollocks, it wasn't like that at all. Yes we didn't have the best of things but as a kid what you don't know doesn't hurt. Ignorance is a blessing in many ways, and I know both mum and dad had to struggle to survive to give me the best chance in life. I just got on with the job of enjoying what I had. Lobster, prawns and champagne were unheard of. Dripping on bread was a luxury, heaps of salt and a spread of Bovril. Wow that was good food. Fish and chips and pork pies were all part of my staple diet. It was a cholesterol bomb that would nowadays make a dietician shudder. Even to this day the area around my hometown of Dewsbury (called the Heavy Woollen District in those days), has the highest rate of heart attacks in Britain! Add to this the huge unemployment and it was obvious that the area was never going to appear in a *Thomson Holiday* brochure.

It wasn't called the Heavy Woollen District for nothing. At that time, soon after the Second World War, the mills in the area made the finest blankets and suit cloth in the world. The material would last for ever. It was fine worsted weave that was the envy of manufacturers worldwide. It still is the finest cloth, despite the global attack of cheaper manufacturing and the birth of synthetic cloth that made clothes a throw-away item. Nowadays choice is the norm. In those days we were lucky to have one suit. At least that suit could last a lifetime. Not that we wore it all that much, just for weddings, funerals and church services. And if a family had the money they could pick and choose from a tailor of note. Our family didn't have money so we did the next best thing. We selected from a catalogue (*Littlewoods* I think) and we would wait with anticipation for the box that brought the suit. It never fitted of course because mother would order a size bigger than needed, 'That will last you a good three or four years,' she would claim. This attitude was frugal verging on common sense. We knew we had to endure many months of having the bloody thing pinned up or quick stitched to make it look anything like a suit. It didn't matter of course because all the other kids were just the same. Little wonder my fascination for Charlie Chaplin still exists to this day. Now there was a man who could look like an idiot wearing anything!

All this came about because of a weird ritual called Whitsunday. This was where some religious event turned the entire neighbourhood into a fashion show. Outdo Your Neighbour was the name of the game. Children who wore suits that fitted clearly indicated they had a bit more brass than the rest of us. This wasn't hard. Nearly all families in our area had little money. This didn't matter a jot when it came to that awful bloody Sunday. After hours of 'quick stitching' we were thrown out into the streets to show off our finery. We wore a suit, shirt and even a tie! We then trotted off to all the other houses to show what we were wearing. This would then attract a few coppers into our jacket pocket. 'Oh doesn't he look nice,' was the cry followed by the rattle of coins (well not so much a rattle, more of a single clunk) after which we retired back into mother's arms to count out the booty.

'I said you looked smart,' mum would claim. 'Look at all the coins in your pocket. Oh I'm so proud.' She was proud too. And like all my mates I would then hope and pray for the sun to go down, for evening service to be over and for me to take off the suit. The suit was put away in the wardrobe (okay, cupboard) until next year, or until some relative either got married or died.

I have a brother, Derek, who is much older than me. He is certainly more attractive, and without doubt, has more brains. The eight years' difference in age was difficult because we couldn't play games with each other like most siblings do. By the time I grew up enough to realise a little of life, he had joined the RAF. Like most older brothers, he teased the hell out of me and often referred to me as the 'Ugly Kid'. We still to this day call each other 'kid' when we speak on the phone or get together and I'm proud to say he doesn't add the 'ugly' bit anymore. This is no surprise as he's far from an oil painting himself. We never saw much of each other in my tender years because he was mostly on camp or on a base overseas. We don't get much chance to cross paths these days either. He was a good influence later in life and we always have a good laugh about who's going to buy the round in! Like most Yorkshire men, we are careful with money and whilst I was tagged with being a tight bugger later in life I can't hold a candle to my loving older brother. He often tells me that mum dropped me when I was about six months old and I never recovered!

Derek was talented at art and I followed suit, as I love anything to do with art these days. I won a competition for my artistic ability when I was about six or seven which was one up on dear old brother, or so I thought. The local paper ran a competition for youngsters to paint a picture of Davey Crocket who was big at the time at the cinema. The prize was a full Crockett outfit complete with gun, boots and a silly fur hat. I was over the moon when I won and was presented with the prize in front of a full house at the Pioneer Cinema. Boy was I proud and I wore the bloody outfit day after day. In fact mum had to prise the outfit off me each night as I wanted to sleep in it! It was many years later that my adoring brother told me the truth. Mum left the picture out on the kitchen table before she found an envelope and stamp. It was at this point that Derek cast an eye over my effort and decided to add a bit extra. It was enough to convince the judges that I had a talent well above my age. I was shattered. 'Must be worth a couple of drinks at least,' he added with a laugh and we proceeded to get drunk (at my expense) and discuss how things are not always what you think! So to those hundreds of kids who also entered I say, 'Sorry!'

Mum and dad were proud people. They did all they could to help me to have a better start in life than them. Having to endure a war must have been difficult, especially for dad. Despite several attempts to join the forces, he was turned down because he was a coal miner. I'm not saying he was eager to go to the front and have his head blown off (far from it) but I know he had to endure so much aggro from people who wanted to know why a fit chap like dad wasn't doing his bit for King and Country. Telling them he worked down the pit earned scant regard from some who often claimed he was a bludger, a waster or even a coward. He tried of course to sign up. He told a few 'porkie-pies' but the draft board only had to look at the tell-tale signs of the black cuts on his face and hands where the sharp coal had made its mark. Such tattoos displayed the real story of hard graft and danger all miners endured down those god-forsaken holes. He was branded for life.

Whilst it ensured dad didn't have to go off to war, working down the pit evidently did little to enhance his sex appeal! Girls were far more impressed with a uniform than a bloke displaying the hazards of swinging a pick in the bowels of the earth. I realise now why the government needed such men. Without coal there was no power to produce the weapons needed to overcome the enemy. Still, it didn't stop many drunken army, navy and air force personnel having a good old fisticuff with dear old dad who soon realised a scar from coal compared to a scar from a bullet did little to enhance his chance of loosening a lady's knicker elastic!

My dad was a proud man. He was Labour through and through. He hated Winston Churchill and later Margaret Thatcher. He was stubborn and argumentative too and if anybody said that something was white he'd swear blind it was black. He was slim in stature and had the skinniest and whitest legs ever seen in public. Remember, poor dad would never see daylight until Sunday due to the fact he would walk five miles to the pit head in the dark, do the shift and then walk back black as soot itself in the dark again. I still remember sitting on the doorstep waiting to hear all the pit lads' boots scraping on the roadside late in the evening. You knew they were not far from home when you heard the crunch of their steel capped and soled boots. 'Dad's home soon mam,' I'd cry. This was the time to start pouring hot water into the little tin bath in front of the large fire. I guess working down the pit did have one advantage. We had plenty of coal to burn. It was a treat for me to wash my dad's back and work out the grime etched into his skin. Anyone who has heard the take off of the Hovis advert by Tony Capstick will understand this, although unlike the Tony Capstick version, dad never threw mam onto fire because all she had on the table was brown bread!

We knew dad was proud that he worked in such difficult and dangerous conditions. I remember he once boasted how low the coal seam he worked was, 'No higher than the cupboard under the sink,' which bemused me somewhat seeing it was barely three feet high. Once I took him to task so he proudly slid not just under the sink but right inside the cupboard, demanding I shut the door. I did but just at the same time, mam called for some help getting the washing up from the cellar, not realising of course that dad couldn't turn the door handle from inside. Ten minutes later we came upstairs to hear him yelling, screaming and cursing from the sink area.

'Why is your dad in the sink cupboard?' She cried, quickly opening the door and dragging poor Albert out. He looked like a folded deck chair. I'm sure I still can feel the leather belt being stropped on my bum to this day. My parents weren't cruel in any way. They were just tough enough to ensure I got the message. Besides, it was a breeze when dad meted out the punishment. Often when I'd crossed the line and did something wrong, mother was the first to clip me around the ear. She did it bloody hard at times whilst shouting, 'Wait until your father gets home from work! He'll give you what's for.' In fact I was pleased when dad did get home because he would take me behind the cellar head door, shout at me to bend over, and then proceed to smack the wall with his belt whilst shouting out loud enough to convince

mum I was getting the belt. These days of course my poor
parents would have been brought up in court through some
new law preventing smacking or some other legal protection
committee's ruling. Obviously children need protection, but
I don't think there's anything wrong with a clip around the
ear to keep them in check. Come to think of it, some of the
little blighters' antics today deserve nothing short of a
baseball bat! Let's just say mum and dad were 'firm' and I
don't think it's done me any harm at all.

My dad wasn't a big man. He was small, thin and even
wiry. But he was strong and despite his thin white legs he was
often mistaken for an Italian. This was because of his tanned
face and jet black hair. He kept this black hair without having
to dye one grey hair until his death. I still can't understand
how his face could be exposed to the sun for two minutes and
look brown as a berry! His Clarke Gable moustache didn't
actually set the ladies' pulse racing but his singing did. Wow
he could croon with the best and he loved to emulate Bing
Crosby. Even now when I hear 'We are poor little lambs who
have gone astray, Bah, Bah, Bah...' (sadly I do not hear it
often these days. Even Cliff Richard gets more airplay) I
shed a tear. When dad passed away we played it at the
funeral and there wasn't a dry eye in the place. I often think
he's looking down saying he thought Bing just didn't have the
right key on the 'Bah, Bah, Bah' bit. I miss him heaps, as I
do mum. Mum was the person who borrowed some money
to buy me some real football boots when I played my first
competitive rugby league game for Shaw Cross. Shaw Cross
is the famous boys' club on the outskirts of Dewsbury. I say
real football boots, because they were the old fashioned type
that needed a shoe last to hammer home the leather studs,
tacks and all, and of course the strap of leather that came
over the top. They may have been ancient, but to me they
were the bees' knees.

I never knew how mum and dad met, but I'm sure it
wasn't at some fancy ball or cocktail party. Either way, they
ended up tying the knot due to the fact a bump had started

to show on mum's waistline. After considering the lack of food through war rationing it was obvious that mum was in the family way! So they wed, and bonded together to give me a start in life which I could never repay or regret.

I soon realised that my mother, Alice (she changed her name to Alicia later. It sounded posh), and my dad, Albert (who my mother called Mick), should never have married. They just didn't get on with each other. My early years left me feeling like the meat in the sandwich. My parents made arguing an art form. Hardly a day would pass without some shouting match, usually over the most trivial of subjects. The shouting matches were always conducted at a high level of audio too. Boy my mum could shout and despite the slim stature of Albert he gave back even more. I don't know the psychology behind such behaviour, yet I know they somehow still had feelings for each other, despite never really showing it. Well that's what I consoled myself with. I just shut the arguments out of my mind and carried on living my life as though I couldn't hear a thing. Thankfully all this swearing and shouting used to subside when either my father went to the bowling club or the pub, or mother had to go and work her night time shift at the pub down the road.

I know how hard both my parents worked to scrape a living. Like most families just after the war, rationing still had the effect of keeping the good things in life away from everyone except the people with a bob or too. We didn't have a bank account. We had cash and when we had spent it, we scraped and borrowed from the neighbours. Mother was a proud person who knew she had to work extra to ensure we had what small pleasures were available. I think they called children where both parents worked 'latch key' children. Not that we had a key each; there was no need when it was hung by string behind the letter box. All we had to do was lift the lid, grab the string and bingo, out popped this huge key. I often wonder what the insurance companies would think about this. It didn't matter because there wasn't anything worth pinching in the house to start with.

Saville Town was a mixture of haves and have nots. At the top of Warren Street near the fountain dedicated to the wealthy Lord Saville (who I might add owned all the land and houses, you name it, he and his family held the lease), the mill owners and top brass resided. On coming further down the street, the surroundings changed somewhat. I often, with tongue in cheek, refer to my first home as being a cute, terraced house in a rustic area. In reality the terraces were slums and the only rustic things were the railings that surrounded the school playground. We lived next door to the fish and chip shop. This was a bonus when we needed fast food but a nightmare when the smell of frying dripping wafted into the house. I swear I could see the smoke coming through the walls! I loved it of course and thanks to the Gaunts who owned the chippie, I got my first taste of commercial enterprise. Such was the popularity of the place; the queues would snake past our front door. I sold them old copies of comics to help ease their waiting time. It worked too. Most people left them inside the shop after being served so I could retrieve them and never went short of product.

Sadly, real chippies are a thing of the past. They've been replaced by curry houses. This isn't surprising. Nowadays, Dewsbury is home to the largest community of Muslims and boasts the second largest Mosque in Europe. It offers the community religious learning second to none. The Mosque was built on the area we referred to as the 'Wreck'. This was due to the fact that some German bomber decided to not bother going any further towards the docks of Liverpool and dropped his load in Dewsbury instead. Many of the old stagers in the town often referred to the proud moment they scared off the Luftwaffe with their Home Guard guns blazing away into the dark night. Although this sounds romantic, it was actually impossible as the men in charge of the gun hadn't had any real ammunition for months! Either way, the Krauts dropped the lot on Saville Town, blasted the 'Wreck' and took out two houses in our street. This was a blessing in disguise. Such was the damage done to both houses that the remains were razed to the ground and never rebuilt. These gaps provided a free passage to the next street which held the toilet blocks. They saved many people the frustration of having to walk a long way to dump. Not having a toilet in the house was a pain in the arse (so to speak). Having a toilet 185 yards away which involved crossing two streets was hardly a luxury. Throw in the fact that each toilet had to service no less than four families then we hoped and prayed we avoided diarrhoea! The toilets had no electricity and were damp, cold and sometimes wet. They were sometimes wet because at least four times a year some rotten bastards used to pinch the lead piping which ran from the thunder box to the toilet pan.

I often smile when I see tender adverts on TV with a cute puppy running off with softer than cotton wool toilet paper. These days we take wiping our arse for granted. Back then we ripped the local paper into squares and hung it on the back of the toilet door on a nail. If that cute puppy had come running down our way with a toilet roll in its teeth it would have had its backside kicked all the way back into the posh area, minus the roll of course. I once told this story to a workmate at the *Daily Sydney Sun* newspaper. He looked shocked and thought for a while before suggesting I had come full circle. 'You know Stevo mate; you started wiping shit; now you're writing shit!' (Many have suggested since my switch into television that I now talk much the same, but I digress.) No doubt many have had to use the 'po' from under the bed which is a great relief at the time but not the most attractive thing to get rid of later. Carrying the damn thing those 185 yards was bad enough, but passing 15 houses in the process was a tough assignment. Naturally one sneaked out after dark, which was fine until one reached the toilet block to find one of the other families in there. Standing around like a spare part with a piss pot in one's hand isn't the best way to spend an evening.

If we didn't laugh we would have gone mad. Frankly most of us should have been dragged screaming to the nearest nuthouse, but we did our best. Talking of doing our best, my grandfather from my mother's side was amazing. He could lay a 'seven pounder' at the drop of the hat. Mum said he had bowel problems. Boy, you could say that again.

Whilst we were quite content with a floral piss pot, I always knew when granddad was coming to stay; mother would get out the old rust bucket with a lid on top. 'Oh no, not again mam,' I'd wail.

'Stop being cheeky and get my dad's room ready,' she'd reply. His room meant I had to scramble up into the attic onto a fold away camp bed used in the army. On top of that I was expected to remove and dispose of the old rust bucket. It was only later in life that I realised what can happen to a person's guts when they take on board 15 pints or more of Tetley's best bitter. This was a feat that granddad could do standing on one leg.

Once in a snow storm, I refused to carry granddad's 'parcel' as he fondly called it. I was going to stand my ground until mum suggested it would be better to have it outside rather than fermenting at the top of the bedroom stairs. 'Be a good lad, love,' she said. I grabbed the damn thing in such a rage that I slipped and spilled the bloody lot down the stairs. This earned me not just the task of cleaning up but also a crack on the arse as a bonus.

Granddad only came when his second wife Lizzie had thrown him out of their house. This was a regular occurrence. He was a huge man who was stabbed by a bayonet in the First World War and loved showing the huge scar to me. He would frighten the shit out of me by telling me about what he did to the other bloke, 'The Gerry squealed like a pig, Mikeeel,' (that's how my name sounded in his Irish brogue).

At well over six foot granddad was a feared man about town. He took bets at the town's pubs, he loved a wager and I never knew if he ever did anything more than go from one pub to the other in Dewsbury every day. He once showed me a £5 note which looked like a table cloth, white and crisp; I'd never seen anything like it. 'One day you'll have a few of these and then you can say you've made it laddie.' He also taught me the truth about making a deal, 'once the handshake's given, you have to stand by your word,' he told me.

Once I came home from school playing a squeeze box which was a long way off from being in tune, and after many minutes of listening to this awful sound granddad offered to buy it for half a crown. This was a fortune at the time. I grabbed the offer gleefully thinking he would just throw it in the cupboard when he was eventually allowed back into Aunt Lizzie's place. He pressed the large coin into the palm of my hand and declared quite clearly that he now owned the squeeze box. I smiled and said, 'Yes.' He then threw the squeeze box straight onto the fire! I cried for hours.

Even though it was nice to get back into my own bedroom, I missed granddad when he left. He was a character, that's for sure. His tales kept me spellbound for hours. He told me that Aunt Lizzie once got so fed up of him not coming home for Sunday dinner and staying in the Black Bull pub instead, that she decided to take his dinner down to the pub to show him up in front of his mates. She walked straight into the tap room and plonked the plate on the bar announcing, 'You spend all your time here, you'd better eat here.'

She started to walk out only for granddad to tell her, 'Lizzie, you've forgotten my mates' dinners. Bring the rest of the joint back with four plates, knives and forks!' I knew it was true because he came to stay at our place that same night.

Dad never liked him staying with us because there was another mouth to feed. My dad was from the old school. He worked hard, earned the wage packet, gave mum her house keeping and kept the rest. There was no sharing the responsibility. He had his money, mum had her money. In fact I don't think dad had a worry in the world. Mum worried enough for everyone, yet seemed to thrive on overcoming problems. In contrast to my dad, my mum was a big woman. She was smart and attracted more than the odd wolf whistle throughout her lifetime. She was strong both mentally and physically. She had a will to work that shamed many men. Her job was a cloth sorter, akin to a wool sorter only with rags. I'm not too proud to admit many a good pullover or pair of pants came out of that warehouse for me.

My mum went to school in Crackenedge Lane and was in the same class as a bloke called Eddie Waring. In fact they admitted they had a crush on each other at the tender age of 12. She would often say later in life how well Eddie had done on TV and that she was proud to have known him. Ironically, many years later when I went into the same line of business, mum kept saying that I should get a real job. How on earth could I make a living when I only worked at most six hours a week? 'How do you work that out?' I asked.

'Simple, it's in the TV guide. You and that bloke Eddie are on Friday night and Sunday night for a couple of hours, and an hour on Wednesday. Me and your dad had to work at least 40 hours to survive!' Bless her.

Both my parents were good to me and allowed me to find my feet early in life. This was mainly through them working so long that I had plenty of time to myself. The results of which are apparent even today. I could cook a dinner by the age of 10. I still enjoy cooking to this day. I enjoy time on my own and don't think anything at trotting off overseas solo. This latitude allowed me to take risks, stretch out, see the world and not fear the unknown. Also because my parents argued so much and wouldn't speak to each other for such long periods, I try to get any problems sorted out quickly. Although I have a temper and explode at times I do try to sort any problems quickly. Am I abrupt? I think I am at times. I shoot from the hip, which doesn't go down well in some circles but if people don't like me then it's their problem not mine.

Like most children, I hated school. I never wanted to be a scientist and realised at an early age I would get my wish. Only art, geography and sport appealed to me and to be fair, I threw everything I could into all three subjects. Sport was important to my survival at school and it was the only thing that kept me going. Victoria Secondary Modern was hardly a temple of learning. It was rough, tough and uncompromising. Pupils were respected more for their physical skills and presence than their academic skills and so as a 'first former' we received the full gambit of threats and bullying. There was also the odd occasion when the older boys took great delight in hanging younger boys upside down over a 30 foot wall or pushing their heads down the toilet and flushing it!

My mother didn't help me either as she sent me off for my first day at the big school in of all things, a uniform. This was like a red rag to a bull! I pleaded with her to see sense but it fell on deaf ears. 'My son goes into that building smart as a button.' Sadly I didn't come out looking that way after the first day. My blazer was ripped, so was my shirt and the tie had transformed from a Windsor knot into a winkle knot. It had been pulled so tight that even she got frustrated and threw it in the bin. To say my mum went ballistic is an understatement. She vowed the boys who had done this would pay the price. I think she would have killed them at the time if she had got hold of them. It was an expensive lesson for both of us because I know mum worked extra shifts at the pub to earn the money for her little angel to wear the official school uniform. It was a relieved boy who walked into the playground on the second day of school wearing jeans!

Why people call them 'playgrounds' is beyond me. Playgrounds are more like battle grounds. I couldn't believe the amount of aggression on show in our playground. It was frightening. I had no option other than to stand up for Saville Town as opposed to other areas of Dewsbury. I stuck with my gang and everyone else did the same. If anyone from another part of town upset a mate, it was one for all, all for one. Thankfully the teachers were aware of all this and tried to keep control. They did to some extent by putting pupils into four house units according to surnames. Whilst at Victoria, pupils would fight for their house at sport yet as soon as the whistle blew to end school, everyone went back to their gangs. It was war again after school hours. I soon picked up the protocol for meetings between the gangs. We used to stand across the street from each other hurling abuse, and then the gang leader (the biggest, tallest and ugliest boy in most cases) would negotiate with the opposing gang boss to nominate somebody from their own gang to fight! Not surprisingly they would pick out the smallest, weakest looking bloke from the opposition. They didn't want to loose as pride was at stake. Because I was far from large in those days, I was selected quite often. I'd go into the middle of the gangs to fight until first blood was drawn. Then it was all over. Usually it was my blood that was all over me. Everyone would then cry, 'Fair fight!' and off we went, just like that!

It soon dawned on me that those gang leaders were never at the front when it got physical. I can't remember any of the leaders raising a fist in one of the battles, never mind spilling blood for the cause. It quickly became apparent that it was all bravado, a group thing, where numbers equated to strength. Get the leaders alone and they soon turned into friends. I had plenty of bashings in the early days, yet never backed down. I gave my best in any fight. Not that I won any fights but my efforts somehow got across the message that I could handle myself. Add the fact that most of these so-called toughies never wanted to play sport, not even cricket and especially not rugby league meant they didn't rate in my books. It takes 80 minutes on a playing field to find out what makes a man tick. Out there there's nowhere to hide.

My first introduction to rugby came at a tender age. All the kids in our area played rugby in the streets, or on the bombed out rec which had a dust bowl look about it but it could have been Wembley as far as we were concerned. Our biggest problem was getting a ball. More often than not we played with a rolled up bundle of rags (this is where mum's day job came into play) and played for hours on end with games often having score lines like 128–122. We just couldn't get enough of rugby league. I know that one school holiday we played four days straight: from 8.00 am; paused for lunch; continued on until tea time; and had to be dragged away by our parents otherwise we would have played until midnight. I think I was on the losing side in the end but with a score line of 815–830, we gave our opponents a run for their money.

Every now and then someone got their hands on a scruffy ball with a busted bladder which made passing a little easier but kicking a farce. One weekend a new kid on the block boasted that his father had a brand new ball! We didn't believe him because nobody in our neck of the woods could afford one. He shocked us one day by producing a cracker of a ball. It was real leather and looked stronger than the Lone Ranger's saddle bags. It also had writing all over it which we thought was weird. Still it was a huge bonus so we played all day and kicked (a rarity) seven bells of you-know-what out of it.

Sadly, we didn't see the young kid again for several weeks due to the fact he'd copped a good hiding from his father and wasn't allowed out. It turned out it was a special ball all right. The writing on the ball turned out to be signatures from a touring Australian Kangaroo team. It was worth a fortune in those days so what it could fetch on eBay today is anyone's guess. We comforted him somewhat by saying at least some of the great Australians had had the privilege of playing on our street.

All my mates couldn't wait for the end of school as each weekday, without fail, we passed, kicked and tackled our hearts out. Like most kids we had our own star players. Old school friends I still see today like Philip Robson would be Eric Ashton, Alan Gissing was Derek Turner, Tony Firth was Jeff Stevenson and Richard Cave was Tom Van Vollenhoven. All were world class internationals. But my hero in those formative years was a half-back at Dewsbury called Johnny Bullock who had a habit of patting his thigh to indicate to his players which way the play would be going. I did just the same, often shouting out, 'Come on Johnny!' during our extended matches.

My aunts from my dad's side took me to see Dewsbury for the first time. All four of them: Dora, Ivy, Doris and Margaret were fanatics of the club and never missed a game home or away. In fact Doris and Margaret go to each Dewsbury game even to this day. From that first visit, I was hooked. Like all the youngsters, I dreamt that one day I would play for the club.

The players at the time didn't enjoy many wins and I often laugh at the way I would be so downhearted when they lost. It took me years to realise the importance of mental toughness and the advantage of saying little but doing plenty. Mantras such as 'The harder I work the luckier I get,' spring to mind. The thing is, most of the time it works and to be successful in life it's impossible to cut corners.

Nearly every kid in our district went to the same school. We all wanted to be the tough guy, James Dean. We wanted to dress like Elvis Presley and later the Beatles. I can't say I looked snazzy in my Teddy boy outfit. I wore tight pants with a single button link jacket akin to a frock coat. I actually used to inform the tailor how long the coat bottom should drop to. Usually thumb's length, or for the real daring, the finger. My first jacket came from Burton's the Tailors and was bright green with black velvet lapels, Christ we looked like plonkers, but fashion is all that counts and to pull a bird we had to look the part. I did look the part – a spare part that is!

We'd all meet at the bench midway down Warren Street, talk bullshit and send the tallest and oldest looking kid to the off-licence to buy brown ale because at 14 and 15 years of age it was dangerous to try the pubs. This was not because we looked too young. Far from it, it's just that nearly all our parents would be in there anyway. So, street drinking it was until the age of 16. This was a magic age where even landlords and parents would turn a blind eye to sneaking into the tap room out of sight. The community classed it as a safeguard as they knew where we were. It wasn't bad logic really. The Saturday night dance was all the rage, big time Charlie. Boy we dressed to kill. We slicked back our hair and created the largest quiff we could. The bigger the quiff we had the better because the girls loved them. This was a fact I never understood. I know many girls suspect the size of boys' feet relate to the size of their penis, so maybe they were thinking on the same lines about quiffs. Getting that quiff was no easy task. We needed Brylcreem or California Poppy Oil. This was expensive so most of us elected for the carbolic soap option where we would froth up a lather and then smear it all over our heads. It used to go rock hard and would have been deemed too lethal to take on board an aircraft these days. Boy it was sharp. Many a girl would be escorted home from the dancehall by a smooth, smart, cool guy only for his dreams of quick grope to disappear when the rain started to fall. 'Why is your hair going frothy?' was hardly the green light for foreplay.

I was no oil painting. I had to use every ploy available to pull the girls and when I told my mother this, she once again came up trumps. She summoned me to sit with her, look into the vanity mirror and tell her what I saw. 'Me and you,' I replied.

'And don't you think your mother's attractive?'

'Of course,' was my reply.

'Right, what you need is dancing lessons son!'

It took me many years to realise what she was saying but my dancing lessons turned my life around. Each night for months we would draw the curtains of the living room (we called it the living room because that was the only room we had) and I would stand on mother's feet and slowly glide through the steps one by one, day in day out, until I could waltz, foxtrot, quick step and boogie with the best of them.

Man I had found rhythm!

In those three or four months of practice not once did I stop standing with the lads at the edge of the dance floor, admiring the birds like vultures awaiting a feed.

In those days two girls would dance all night with each other awaiting the approach from the dumbos on the sidelines, only to tell them to bugger off.

Getting rejected after walking the length of the dance floor gave our mates great delight. We were all in the same position until that fateful day when I stormed into the fray, split up two girls and started bopping and jiving with the pair as though I'd done it all my life. The girls were impressed and word soon got around that Mr Stephenson was open for appointments, so much so that I often paired up with a special fast jiver to enter the dancing contests. We won a few contests as well, and enjoyed the prize of 10 bob on more than just the odd occasion.

I still love dancing to this day and it did wonders for my agility on the field of play, not to mention other things.

Sadly, all this flitting around the dance halls wasn't doing my mind any good. I hooked into the wrong crowd. My enthusiasm for sport waned and I got into trouble with the law. I thought I was a big shot and was involved in a few fights. Eventually one guy called the police and I found myself in court. Thankfully the fines and detentions brought me back to earth. The guidance of my parents helped steer me the right way.

That right way was a youth club I joined. It was run by an ex-copper who introduced me to the boxing ring on the first night I attended. Three knock downs later (me not him) and I was back on track. I was sore and bruised, but back on my way in the right direction.

On leaving school at 16, I, like so many, found it hard to find work. Once again mum helped and begged a favour from a friend to give me a start in a sheet metal factory. It sounded like a macho kind of job so I jumped at the chance. It was a case of hello world, here I come.

2

CORSETS, DRAPES AND SCRUMS

So off I went into the wide world of employment complete with new boiler suit two sizes too big. I loathed work. From the very first moment I walked into the place I knew it wasn't for me. This was confirmed when all I did for the first three days was go to the butchers for pies and make tea for the morning and afternoon break. They paid me £4-10 shillings a week. I felt I needed to work at something more taxing than being a bloody tea boy. Apart from sweeping up drill waste, fetching lengths of steel and having my steel capped boots welded to the work bench, things didn't improve. I resigned. I told my mum's mate, who was far from friendly, to stick the job where the sun don't shine.

It was great. Five days' pay meant I earned just under £3 after tax. I found myself staring at the dole office. It was not the best start to my working life. Mother went crackers and threatened to kick me out of house and home. She threatened to keep my first ever wage, which traditionally the wage earner kept. The doom and gloom continued as it took me nearly four months to find another job. I went to interview after bloody interview. I trailed all over Yorkshire only to be told my credentials weren't up to scratch. It suddenly dawned on me that my education, or lack of it, **was** a key factor in getting on in life. After my problems with the law, the last thing I needed to do was mope about the streets with nothing to do except take the 'easy' option! Thankfully any ideas in that direction went west when I thought back to the stupid things I'd got involved with. I told myself how lucky I was that I had only got fines and detention. I swallowed my pride and convinced myself I would take the next job irrespective of what it was.

To say my new job was different was an understatement. I became an assistant on the drapery counter at an old fashioned store called George Wilkinsons. The building was at least 300 years old and the inside looked even older. It was like turning back time. There was dark brown paint, dingy lighting, old fashioned counters that today would have made the TV show *Are You Being Served* seem modern. I wanted lots more out of life than work in a shop, but at least at Wilkinsons I didn't have to make tea. I also got to mix with the general public. Most of the clients were rather posh. The store catered for the upper class in Dewsbury, which amounted to about 1 per cent of the population in our area. Unfortunately the customers, posh or not, had a tendency to look at the shop workers as though they'd just farted in their general direction. Too often the customers were rude, arrogant and demanding. But despite the shop workers not having a lot of brass, we at least prided ourselves on being friendly and definitely not snooty. The trouble was, instead of packing the job in, I started to enjoy it. I took the piss big time, 'Oh Mrs Roger-Smyth I think you'll need an extra yard for the bay window curtains,' when they really didn't need it anyway. 'And don't forget the Rufflette tape, only the best for that sort of fabric, don't want to be walking into the market and buying that cheap stuff, do we now?'

The three-story building that Wilkinsons occupied was listed. The inside should have been condemned. Mr George Wilkinson himself sat in the centre perched high above the counters. He looked 90 at least. Connected to the cash centre were wires where wire mesh cages shot from counters. Money and bills were sent up and a receipt and change were sent back. It was like a Keystone Cops caper, only slower.

I'm sure bus tours turned up just to witness this ancient ritual which took ages, although my section boss (Curtains, Drapes and Furnishings) Mr Cave said it added a touch of class to the establishment. Still the weeks went by and I got used to talking in a nice way, rather than in broad Yorkshire, 'Yes ma'am, no ma'am, three bloody bags full ma'am.' I settled in. It was fun, especially as the 'Foundation' section was opposite our counter, complete with bras, corsets and the lot! Mr Cave and I had great fun guessing whether a lady was 36B or 38D or if she would need extra bones in her tie up corset.

Of course if we weren't busy we had to help out, running downstairs to blow dust off an old 46DD bra box or whatever. Even to this day I can spot a 36 or a 38 cleavage from 50 yards away. So if you do catch me having a glance at a lady's breast, I can assure you it's all in the act of improving my knowledge of the female uplift, nothing else!

The job had its moments, though. Not all the ladies in Dewsbury needed a 46DD bra or a support system. Some were quite attractive. Unfortunately not many of the young, good lookers were desperate to purchase a Spirella corset; Marks and Spencer had cornered the young market in underwear. I have witnessed knickers so big that Bridgette Jones could fit in them twice, no problem! It was an eye-opener, especially the stock taking period. Poor old me had to stay back after work with one of the girls from the underwear department. It was tiring work, we didn't finish until gone midnight at times and I didn't even have to guess her bra size. She left me plenty of time to read the tag. Oh and before you ask, she also purchased her knickers from Marks and Spencer.

The only setback to this employment caper was the fact I worked Saturdays and couldn't play or watch rugby league. As you can imagine, I took plenty of stick from my mates who ribbed me constantly about it. Sometimes they let a nice girl I was trying to chat up know I worked in a bra and corsets store. It doesn't do a lot for a young boy's credibility, believe me. The urge to play rugby again was forcing my hand and even though I'd played a couple of mid week friendlies with my mates, I longed for the excitement of playing competitive rugby league. Thanks to one of my buddies, Alan Gissing, I took up the game again. Alan dragged me up to Shaw Cross Boys Club on the outskirts of town. Shaw Cross is a famous club which over the past 50 years has turned out well over 300 professional players including well over 50 full internationals like Mick Sullivan, Derek Turner, Tony Halmshaw and David Ward.

Alan informed me that his Rovers' team was short on numbers and needed a full-back, winger and a hooker. 'But I can only play scrum-half,' I said.

'I know, but our captain's number seven and he's the best player we've got.' I followed his advice when the coach, David Bradshaw, asked me what position I played.

'Played a few games at full-back, winger and hooker.' I rattled off.

'Great,' was the reply, 'you're in for Saturday's game.' This was despite the fact I hadn't walked a step on the training ground.

The first thing Bradshaw did was kick up a high ball and requested I catch it. I didn't get near the thing. Then he raced me over 50 yards and beat me. Then he smiled and said, 'You're a hooker aren't you?'

Before I could answer, Gissing said, 'Yes he is,' and so my career began a lie.

The truth was soon to be exposed but I felt proud enough to tell my parents I was picked in the team to go to Hunslet Parkside to play their juniors.

'Well done,' said dad, 'they're one of the top teams.'

Mum, bless her, went out and bought me some football boots. They were real old fashioned boots. They had leather so tough I spent two days smearing dubbing into them to even allow my feet to get near them. Dad belted in the studs and I was off and running. Well I wasn't doing so much running as standing around behind the goal posts watching

Hunslet Juniors trying for the conversion.

32–0 wasn't the best score, especially as we had another half to play. Bradshaw wasn't best pleased and with a scrum count of 18–0 against us, I expected a real bollocking! But he didn't loose his rag. He just kept calm and suggested I'd never been near a scrum in my life never mind being a hooker. Then he patted me on the back saying, 'Don't worry, things can't get much worse.' He was right. I won one scrum. This was a 100 per cent increase on the first half. What more could one ask for? The final score was only 52–5 so at least we scored.

The coach could see the disappointment on my face. Before I went to the washbasin to clean up, he shouted out that I was first man picked for next week. I can't even start to describe what that meant to me. He showed faith and understanding. If it wasn't for 'Brad' I wouldn't be here today writing all this. As they say in the USA: 'He's the Man!'

The team slowly improved and started to win games. We even gave the best teams a run for their money. Yet we just couldn't seem to win a trophy. As hard as we tried, we came so close yet never brought home the bacon. We even lost in the Heavy Woollen District Final against St John Fisher. But then the great day arrived and we finally won the Heavy Woollen District Cup. It wasn't possible to meet a happier bunch in the world. We celebrated big time in my local pub, the Scarborough Hotel, despite all of us being just 17. Not that we cared, neither did the landlord. His till was ticking over nicely, thank you.

For the team, losing so many finals made this win even better. I go along with the old adage that to enjoy success a team has to learn how to handle defeat. It was after one of those losing finals I vowed to break the mould. One of the opposition came over and sneered whilst I was looking at my runners up medal, 'Not worth a cream cracker. This is what it's all about,' he yelled as he trotted off displaying his winners' medal to all and sundry. He was right but not for the reasons he thought. Of course medals are part of competitions. They are a keepsake a sportsman should be proud of. After that day I knew there was only one reward for all the effort I'd put in and that was the satisfaction I gave myself. It was the knowledge I'd achieved my target. That's what I call being a winner. I didn't need to look at my trophy cabinet to prove I'd done well. That's the major reason I enjoy golf so much these days because it's a battle within myself, irrespective of who I play or whatever difference in the handicap.

A week after winning the trophy we soon came down to earth when we were beaten in the Leeds and district final at Kirkstall Road by Market Boys Club. We were beaten by the odd point and we all felt deflated. This was mainly due to the fact the referee gave some dubious decisions against us. Yet within minutes of getting on the coach to go back home we forgot about it and started looking forward to next season.

The Rovers' team attracted plenty of attention from the professional clubs. Leeds chased Peter Fozzard, Halifax chased Darryl Woolin and Featherstone chased Stuart Hall. The local clubs (Dewsbury and Batley) tapped up all the rest of the team. We knew we were making some impact. So much that Albert Fearnley the Bradford coach took me to one side and informed me they wanted to sign me at the end of my final season in Junior League. I was over the moon; Bradford Northern (along with Leeds) was the big club. I was going to the big time – or so I thought!

Halfway into that last season, Fearnley let it be known they felt I wasn't big enough to endure the rigours of top class league and suggested I accept any other offers going. This was a polite way of saying I wasn't good enough! But it made me more determined to prove them wrong, and I think I did. I became a good friend of Albert in later years through my involvement in the Rugby Football League Coaching School. We would often laugh and tease each other over the incident, especially when eight years later; Bradford offered to buy me from Dewsbury at a huge transfer fee. My club politely declined.

Those junior years at Shaw Cross sorted out my life. There were no silly antics anymore, no gangs, no rough stuff, no fighting and no stealing. I remember bumping into a guy that I thought I knew from many years ago. His face was so familiar. 'Don't I know you?' I asked.

His reply stunned me, 'You should. I'm the police officer that you handed down the roll of lead to from the Baptist church roof when you were a young lad.'

I remembered then all right. I was thankful he was the type of copper who realised the roll was just a small piece of flashing. He gave me a kick up the backside and told me to bugger off back home. Needless to say our chance meeting 20 years later forced us into getting blind drunk that night. I owed him big time.

I can't believe how some of today's youth won't join a youth organisation; they don't know what they're missing. Support and guidance are key factors in life; reject them at your peril. I owe a great deal of my success to the warmth and friendship of the Shaw Cross club. The stalwart behind the club is Dougie Hird, one of life's gentlemen who has given over 50 years service to the game. He still trots down to the new sports club everyday. He was awarded a gong from the UK Sports Council many years ago. In my opinion, this man deserves at the very least an OBE for his efforts. In all the time I've known Dougie, I've never seen him flustered. His calmness went a long way towards making Shaw Cross the great club it is today. At least one thing he did get from the government was a grant to ensure a new club house could be built. Although the introduction of the bar license forced them to drop the 'Boys' from its name. It was a proud moment for Mr Hird when he laid the foundation stone. It was an even bigger moment for me when they requested I officially open the club house 12 months later. I try to get back from time to time. Dougie and other long serving members of the club such as Alan

Lancaster and John Mathewman always make me welcome.

I loved those years. It wasn't just the Shaw Cross Club either, I was fortunate to be selected at Inter League and County level. The Heavy Woollen District side had some great success at a time when ITV stepped in and did live television games on a Sunday afternoon. For those who can remember so far back, the likes of Roger Millward, Bernard Watson, John Maloney and Alan Watts displayed their skills under the watchful eyes of commentators Bill Fallowfield, and Keith Macklin. They were great days and fun times and even better, we were on the telly.

Those were proud moments for my parents. Mum only ever watched me play twice in my career. The first time was my first game at Hunslet which she never told me about until many years later. She hid behind some bushes to make sure I didn't see her. The second time I wish I hadn't seen her either! It was during an inter-league competition at Thornhill Park where Heavy Woollen District were playing Hull District and like most games against the boys from the Humber, it was quite tasty with low flying aircraft all over the shop. Midway through the first half I was just locking into a scrum when the entire crowd started yelling and screaming. I stood up and looked as my mother raced across the field and ordered me off!

'Michael, I've been watching long enough, and they've put you in the middle of this thing every time, let some other bugger have a go.'

Embarrassing wasn't the word as the referee escorted her off whilst dad slid away to the nearest pub. You can imagine the looks the Hull forwards gave me and the abuse and flying knuckles that followed. I often wake up with nightmares of those guys saying things like, 'Can't hurt little Mummy's boy can we?' or words to that effect. Hull people are so understanding.

It's not easy to ban your own mother from games, but father threatened to leave home if she ever did it again. This made me more nervous as she probably would have helped him pack!

My mum saw the light. Even when she took over the pools office at Dewsbury RLFC, she would count the money, knocking back the odd gin and tonic whilst her son was being belted out on the field of play. She even refused to see me play at Odsal when I skippered my home-town club to Championship glory. But I understood she just didn't want her poor baby to loose his good looks!

Eventually the day came when I weighed up my options of which professional club to join. For me it was easy, for after nibbles from several clubs, only one offered me money. Dewsbury offered me £200 to be exact. They offered £50 when I signed, £50 when I turned up for my first training session, £50 when I played my first game and £50 when the season finished. It wasn't much but at least my home town club wanted me and I was no longer an amateur. To be honest, when Dewsbury came to sign players from our team, my name wasn't on the list. Thankfully, Dougie Hird informed them he was sure I was one player who would make the grade. In my books, that man deserves a knighthood!

Since rugby league's breakaway from union in 1895, our game has endured so much hypocrisy and abuse. Those 'professionals' no longer seemed to fit into the sporting society. It was as though we had some kind of disease. During my school days and youth, I also played water polo for my town and should have played for my county. Yet that signature on the RFL contract not only prevented me from playing amateur rugby league, it also banned me from any other sport too! How daft is that? All that training and comradeship was just thrown out the window. It was as though I had been caught with my hand up the vicar's wife's dress at Sunday sermon. I enjoyed the polo crowd at Dewsbury baths. The baths of course became famous when our own Eileen Fenton became the first woman to swim the

English Channel. Her huge painting adorned the entrance to the baths and for a young kid she looked divine, like a real heroine. I had the pleasure of meeting her a few years ago when Dewsbury gave the House of Commons Speaker, Betty Boothroyd, the freedom of the town. She looked as fit as she did on that painting. I often wonder when they built new swimming facilities if they ever gave her that huge portrait. I hope so.

I mention the fact I should have played for Yorkshire at water polo. I was selected and was supposed to be picked up at 6.30 pm by some Yorkshire official in front of the Town Hall steps. It was a bright, sunny Wednesday evening and they were supposed to take me to the venue in Sheffield. I arrived at 6.00 pm sharp, and waited until 7.30 pm before I realised they just weren't coming. That hurt, even after they tried to say they waited 30 minutes for me. I knew they didn't. I still fume over the deception; I say that because I was the only player who was selected from a secondary modern school. All the other players were made up of grammar school or technical college students. Lucky for the team, one of the supporters had taken their son along, just to watch, of course. He was 'fortunate' to be on hand to take my place.

Despite the snobbish attitude within swimming, we were a great bunch. Because the baths were directly opposite my school it was easy to attend training. Guys like Malcolm Marriott and Roy Gray helped me no end, but it was Mr Grimes who ruled the roost. This guy was hindered by a club foot, yet taught thousands of kids over the years including Eileen Fenton, and even my mother!

Mr Grimes was always called 'Mister'. I don't think anyone knew his first name. What respect I had for him. I've seen him turn screaming lunatic kids who were clinging to the changing room door for dear life into quiet well behaved little darlings within minutes. He'd have them jumping into the pool and grabbing the end of his survival pole not long after. Roy Gray's wife, Roberta, followed in the footsteps of the great man and learnt quickly. One look from her was enough to send grown men fully clothed into the water without a murmur.

Mr Grimes was a wonderful bloke. He retired from regular work years ago yet still offered his services to youngsters who couldn't swim. Another example of stupidity within sporting bodies was the fact he couldn't charge for his coaching and guidance otherwise he would have been struck off the swimming association board. He never asked for money either, yet if someone put the odd quid on top of the towel in the first cubicle then that was their business!

Oh the memory of hot steaming cups of Bovril before the swim off, and the pints of beer afterwards with the women's section who swam their competition on the same night. It was not surprising that I became a breast stroke specialist. It was time to move on.

3

FIRST SCRUM BELT 'EM

With a £50 cheque in my pocket and a few extra in the savings bank, it was time to go off on my travels yet again. From my early teenage years, each summer in the off season I would pack my rucksack, tie on my sleeping bag, roll up my tent and set off into the unknown.

Travel fascinates me. Even today I yearn to see different places and countries at every opportunity. Going overseas has become second nature. I rattled up most of Europe over a period of four to five years.

Hitchhiking can be a dangerous mode of travel, especially for youngsters. In those days we had to be careful, so wherever possible, I would always travel with a mate. There was one incident when Jimmy Carruthers and I hitched a lift from Frankfurt to Basel. The driver (a real pervert) got his 'old feller' out. Fortunately I sat in the back but my mate, Jimmy nearly climbed out of the window from the front seat! Jim vowed he would never sit in the front again. To be fair I sat shotgun for the next few lifts until he calmed down.

Sadly my first venture across the water was under pretty awful circumstances. My brother, Derek, had just got married. He'd taken his new bride back to Germany where he was stationed in the RAF. After only a few weeks they were involved in a horrific car crash which killed the driver, his wife and my brother's new bride Jean. My brother was shattered and felt guilty at the fact he survived. The doctors said it would be some time before he got back to normal.

Several months passed and he showed no sign of improvement so the doctors decided that bringing his younger brother to Germany could help.

I boarded a boat from Harwich to the Hook of Holland at the tender age of 13 by special permission of the RAF. I then took a train from the docks to Beilefeld. From there, my brother picked me up and took me back to the station at Gutterslaugh. I lived on camp and mixed with the servicemen for over four weeks. I went out on the rampage into town on a regular basis and was probably pissed up half the time. It certainly seemed to work as my brother brightened up. He and I became much closer. When I was in my early years he'd already gone to join the RAF so I usually only saw him briefly when he was on leave. That first trip gave me the confidence to travel again. The following year I was supposed to go to Scarborough for a long weekend. Instead I ended up being deported out of Paris and dumped back on a ferry to Dover. This did little to convince my mother she could trust me. Dad understood and calmed the waters, which was surprising seeing as though London was the furthest he'd been (he never missed a Wembley for years).

It was amazing to see mum cry each time I set off on another hitchhiking trip. My dad read the paper without showing any emotion at all. It baffled me. Each time I was about to leave the door, my mum said to my dad 'Michael's on his way again.'

Dad lowered the paper and said, 'Ah well, think on.' Christ knows what he meant, but I took it to relate to 'taking care'.

Oddly, each trip I took I encouraged a different mate to join me. This included a smashing bloke called 'Sully' who was half Indian and half Jamaican. He forever spoke about how he one day would travel the world just like his dad. I gave him the chance. We both saved up like mad and set off with no idea where we were going. Sully was a smart looking guy; he dressed to kill and thought every girl in the world fancied him. He lived in a different world than most and we weren't far into our trip before I realised that he hadn't grasped the intensity of what 'rough travelling' was all about. He turned up for a farewell drink with the gang in high heeled Spanish boots!

'What the bloody hell are those?' I enquired.

'Boots man, real cool boots ... you said I needed boots so I got the best, the chicks will go wild.'

The chicks may have gone wild. I certainly did when after walking just half a mile those silly Cuban heels dropped off! We did make it to Bruges before a combination of home sickness and lack of money (I found out later he only had £6 on him) brought our journey to a halt. He went back home and I went on to Italy, solo, avoiding perverts all the way.

My last trip before playing professional rugby league was going to be a good one. I travelled with Jeffrey Halmshaw. He was a close mate and we enjoyed each other's company on a trip through 11 countries, going as far south as Turkey. We had a ball, worked when we could, gave blood when they paid, and somehow got used to drinking a Greek wine called Domestica. It tasted more like Domestos. We also drank Ouzo spirit which, surprisingly, was cheaper per litre than a bottle of Coca Cola. No wonder the Greeks drink it with water. We both enjoyed art, so Rome, Paris and Istanbul provided us with much pleasure but the highlight was Michelangelo's David in the Accademia Gallery in Florence. It's the most beautiful thing I've ever seen although Jeff was more taken with the girl on the desk. To be fair, the girl had great structure, nice curves and yet I suspect she had the odd blemish hidden away. This is something you can't say about David.

We got some work in Florence due to the fact the Italian government had appealed for helpers. This was after the floods several weeks before had nearly ruined some great works of art. We loaded crates onto trucks for days. All the crates were going for restoration, so who knows maybe I have handled some of the masterpieces of the art world. We were billeted in an old prison hospital where row upon row of straw beds were lined up against each wall and where on the first night Jeff stopped me from belting some Swedish bloke who started pushing me in the back as I slept. Thankfully he wasn't trying to fondle my arse but with near perfect English explained that he just wanted to show me how I should prepare a straw mattress before laying on it. His hands quickly attacked the straw, hollowed out a place for my hip and shoulder and then he bade me good night. We all slept sweetly ever after!

We were never paid much for the work, apart from free accommodation, food and, yes, drink. We got all the vino we could handle. But don't ever think when tasting the next Italian wine that they only send the rubbish overseas. Be assured that on this occasion they kept it back for us during those exciting times. They were also keen to stop people from smoking, I'm sure it wasn't just for health reasons either because I swear blind anyone lighting up after a few glasses of that stuff would blow the entire city to bits.

After nearly three months on the road I came back to England to prepare for my first ever professional training session. It was 1966 and the great Mick Sullivan was first team player/coach. He was a man I admired from an early age. He still holds the record for the most Great Britain appearances with 46 caps. I didn't expect anything outrageous nor did I feel I couldn't keep up with the pace. I trained every day. This was unusual in those days, but I knew that what I lacked in basic skills I made up for in eagerness and the will to win. But what transpired that first night was a shock to say the least. We were told in a letter that all training gear would be given out. This included boots, running shoes, shorts and training shirts. I arrived expecting to meet all the squad. Not on your life. All the new guys were shunted into the away dressing room where a pile of 'rags' (that's the only way I could describe it) were strewn over the rubbing bench with about 20 so-called professional footballers scrambling for gear as though their life depended upon it.

When the scrum broke up I was left with an old jockstrap that looked as though it had never seen a wash tub in its life. It was grey with elastic that had given up years ago. I'd also managed to grab a shirt and shorts that matched the dull grey colour of the jockstrap. The only things that showed any hope of colour were the socks and they had holes in them. Welcome to the world of professionalism!

I was baffled by the limp jockstrap which wouldn't have supported a ping pong ball never mind either of mine!

'Tie a knot in the elastic,' was the cry, so I did. I tied a total of 12 of them. Yet the bloody thing still looked like a mangled grey squid.

'What do the first team get then?' I enquired. 'Washed,' came back the reply.

For those who have never had to consider the science of a weak elasticated jockstrap, rest assured it's uncomfortable. It also looked stupid. It looked as though there were two carbuncles stuck on my arse when I ran around the training paddock. To say I was disappointed was an understatement. Even Shaw Cross had been better than all this. I completed the training routine in a daze.

I had signed along with three of my Shaw Cross team mates, Max Fletcher, Keith Boocock and Bob Nicholson. Things weren't that bad because we stuck together, but at that first night we soon found out our 'enemy'. This was the guy who we would be fighting for that place in the second string.

Max Fletcher never needed a boost in the confidence stakes and showed the same aggression he'd become famous for at junior level, even at training. He made it quite clear he was going to be the new star on the block and swaggered around like he'd been a pro all his life. Things went well for him until he collided with a couple of the old stagers during a final game of touch and pass. Within seconds poor Max was flattened with a sweet upper cut that Mike Tyson would have been proud of. Welcome to the big time!

To be fair to Fletcher he was the first of the four of us to make it into the top team and gave good service whilst up there. Sadly he had to drop from the scene through injury. At least he showed us the way in that first season.

One of my first games was at Featherstone where a red hot reserve side included the most frightening front row I have ever seen. They had in their ranks Eric Fawley (a prop who sadly had a conveyor belt chain snap around his head and survived), Les Tonks (a huge man who would have been an ideal understudy for Shrek) and Vince Farrar (a hooker who was cross-eyed). Formidable is the word I would use to describe them. Fawley was well past his best but still had that devil in his eye. Tonks and Farrar went on to become great stalwarts for the Post Office Road club. I remember one referee calling Farrar out from the scrum after a bit of fisticuffs and warned him for not looking at him whilst he was talking to him. To which he replied, 'I am!' Most of his team mates joked about him saying that when he cried, the tears rolled down his back!

It was a hard baptism that first season but it did have its highlights. One was being the first of a few players to play a professional game on a Sunday. The game was against Doncaster Reserves at Tatters Field. Dwindling gates had forced the RFL to trial games on the Sabbath to test the market. Dewsbury was the first team to try this. Ironically the next season we blazed the trail when I played for the first team on a Sunday to make history yet again. So I had been part of two records within 12 months and was also selected into the top side. Could it get any better? Not much.

To be fair to Dewsbury, the club president Brearley Bailey promised me I would get a chance to play as many games for the reserves as possible. I shared the hooking role with Brian Smith and Roy Firth. Sometimes I played for 60 minutes, other times I played for only half a game but I was learning and didn't lose hope. If there is one thing a coach must do, it is to ensure they give all the registered players at any club a good chance. It's important not to give them just a couple of games before throwing them on to the scrap heap. Hope springs eternal! We three hookers knew that Peter Mullins, the regular first team rake, was going to be hard to overthrow. He was quickly becoming the new star at number 9. He took over from Alan Lockwood, the hooker who helped me in my junior days. Peter also played for Great Britain A-team and attracted attention from several big clubs

In my second season, Dewsbury couldn't turn down a huge offer from Bradford Northern for Peter. This meant the first team birth was wide open. Mullins signed for Bradford in a huge blaze of press glory. He was photographed with the Bradford coach, Albert Fearnley, arm around his new signing, smiling for the papers. It did cross my mind that Albert had signed the wrong bloke, yet at least he had done me the next best thing by giving me a chance to break into the big time. Roy Firth had more experience than me, and to be fair, I wasn't upset or surprised that Roy got the nod for he was a good, solid player who at least could strike for the ball better than I could. Possession was vital for success in our game. Full credit also goes to Brian Smith who although well past his best, offered not to stand in my way. He supported me by telling the club I should be given more game time and not share matches any more. It was a great gesture and one I've never forgotten.

Dewsbury was again the surprise package in the Challenge Cup. Despite getting beaten by St Helens at Swinton in the semi final the previous year, the red, amber and blacks were proving to be no pushover yet again. We drew Widnes in the quarter final at home.

Poor Roy Firth hit a bad spot and just wasn't firing. The week before the quarter final clash they decided to throw me in at the deep end. It was my first top game. I was excited but frightened to death and I just hoped I didn't let anyone down. The coach set off for Liverpool City's Knotty Ash stadium. No more knotted jocks straps; clean, smart training gear and polished boots for me from here on in. This was going to be different. It was, especially when the bus stopped half way down the East Lancs road and pulled into a café car park. Boy, this was the big time. We didn't even cross their doorstep, just opened up the luggage compartment and there, in all its glory, was a bloody tea urn and a box of sandwiches!

Tom Clarke was the secretary of Dewsbury for years. He looked and acted like Scrooge. This was to be my first encounter with a guy who only smiled after arguing for ages to get expenses down to at least 50 per cent less. Tom was a one-off, and on my first trip I was hoping I wouldn't be the same, a one-off.

I can't remember much about the game apart from me scoring a freak try where the ball bounced off the back of prop Trevor Walker and I dived under the posts to win the game. The other memory I have was getting changed in the worst dressing room imaginable. Nails were battered into the walls for clothes to hang on. There was dog shit on the floor, mould growing in one corner and that unmistakeable aroma from a toilet that obviously hadn't been flushed since the last home game. And when George, the kit man, started handing out pieces of plastic sheeting I was bemused. I didn't know what was going on. 'Don't worry lad, just put this over your clothes, it will stop them getting wet when the kids piss down the cracks in the stand above just before full time.'

I got changed early because it took a long time for me to strap my shins. It always did and I often looked like an Egyptian mummy. I awaited the game plan, the advice, the encouragement and guidance, and when captain Alvin Newall came over to speak to me he just said, 'Alright kid, you'll be fine. First scrum, belt 'em, make it hurt.'

'Belt who?' I thought. Prop Trevor Walker was quick to put my mind at rest by informing me I could take my pick from anyone in the front row!

Great. All those days and nights I spent training and striving to get to this moment and the only advice I got was to belt someone. But a win is a win and I did okay. A winning bonus of £8.00 ensured the atmosphere coming back to Yorkshire was great. I even had enough sense to turn down the chance to play 'Chase the Ace' with the regulars. Nobody was going to take the bonus away from me. I was even reluctant to take up the offer to go and 'do the town' when we got back to Dewsbury, but I did. I knew it was important to be part of the team. Trevor Walker took me under his wing, saying, 'Stick with me son, I'll show you the ropes.' He did too, all night; I never once put my hand in my pocket to buy a drink! Trevor was amazing, he was an icon in the town and I loved the limelight even if most of the time I was in his shadow.

The dream continued when they opted to throw me in for the quarter final against odds-on-favourites, Widnes. They arrived at Crown Flatt in cocky fashion, swaggered off the coach and looked like a team that just had to turn up and book their semi final berth. But they hadn't taken into account the nature of the Dewsbury ground which from one corner diagonally to the other, dropped an amazing 11 feet! The old timers referred to it as the 'Nine Hole', I don't know why, but our captain, Alvin Newall, knew how to get the best out of it. He just kicked, kicked and kicked again. The poor heavy Widnes forwards found themselves turning around and around. Newall also dropped three goals in the first five minutes and we hung on for an amazing victory. The fans went wild but I knew I wasn't a certain inclusion in the next game, never mind the semi in three weeks' time against

Barrow. I'd been hammered in the scrums by former Great Britain international, the old stager Bob Dagnall who cleaned the floor with me to the tune of 16–5. Remember, possession is vital, and although we had won with not much ball, everyone knew, myself included, that to have any chance to get to Wembley, a team had to win at least 50 per cent of the scrums. At least I wasn't a one game wonder. I was a two game failure!

Sadly, like the season before when the great Mick Sullivan nearly shocked the mighty Saints, we lost another semi final, again at Station Road Swinton. It was an awful feeling and I wasn't even playing. Little did I know the same fate would befall me eight years later. But determination was my key and I did get back into the top side later on that year. The team started to reap the benefit of giving the youngsters a run. Jeff Greyshon, Nigel Stephenson, the Bates brothers Alan and John, Harry Beverley, Joe Whittington and John Clarke were just a few players given their chance by President Brearley Bailey. After years of buying cast offs from other clubs, Brearley Bailey convinced the committee that junior development from the Dewsbury area was the way to success. Sadly the great man passed away before we made it to the top but we all knew he was the one that started it all.

One good signing at the time was John Davis from Leeds. He was the former Welsh Union international who found it hard to force his way into the Headingley setup. Instead he opted for regular first team action with us. Not only was he a revelation for the side, he alongside John Bates and Jeff Grayshon formed a formidable hard and fast running back three. His spark lifted us all. We were absolutely desolate when tragedy struck as we played against Batley in a local derby. He dropped dead on the field of play. John made one of his trademark long range breaks and raced towards the full-back with me in support. A great, low tackle brought John down and I shouted for him to play the ball quickly. He struggled to get up onto one knee, looked at me and I saw his eyes roll before he dropped dead at my feet.

I was devastated. I knew it was bad and quickly called for the club doctor but after 20 minutes' attention, the doctor took poor John from the playing area on a stretcher. When play resumed for the last five minutes before half time, I just walked around in a daze. As soon as the referee blew for the break, I rushed into the dressing room to find that John was already on his way to hospital. One look at the doctor and the physio confirmed that there was no hope.

I think all the Dewsbury team realised that John was dead and we wanted the game to be abandoned. The officials were only told that John was on his way to hospital, nothing more, nothing less, so they allowed the second half to restart. The crowd didn't know the real story and we were 'encouraged' to play the second 40 minutes.

I guess I must have been in shock as I don't recall that second half. I've no idea who scored or what the result was. And then to add further insult, some moron took advantage of the confusion inside the dressing room. He slipped in at the same time as the medics and stole everything from our clothes – money, watches, rings you name it. If ever someone should rot in hell it's that thief!

John Davis was only 31. He was a great guy, a super fit PE teacher, yet he never knew he had a heart defect. On one side of his heart he had 10 or so layers of skin and on the other side he had just one. His heart exploded that fateful day. It shook everyone connected with the club and at first we all wanted to stop playing. It took plenty of counselling for us all to change our minds, especially me as I had been selected to play for Great Britain U23 against France just three days later. It was my biggest honour. I dedicated it to John and wore the black arm band of respect during the match.

We won the game against France and whilst all the side went out to celebrate that night I just slipped off home alone with my thoughts.

Ironically, the incident brought more awareness towards players having a full medical before being allowed to play for a professional club. The RFL made it a rule that all players must be tested. I like to think that John Davis was instrumental in saving many future players from the same fate.

4

SHIT BUSTERS

Despite this tragedy, the team got back on their feet again. A new feeling of comradeship entered the club. There was little doubt that President Brearley Bailey knew deep down that a youth team would start to combine and produce some good results eventually. But instead of the side grabbing the odd victory over some of the lesser known clubs, we started to give the big boys a run for their money. Suddenly we started to win more games than we lost, something that hadn't happened for quite some time. The old timers suggested the club was on the verge of repeating the good old days when the likes of Joe Lyman led them to Wembley for that first final in 1929. It was also reminiscent of the glory days when Eddie Waring managed the club during the Second World War.

Obviously my father was a good yardstick as he had followed the club with his sisters during those trying war years. He often regaled us with stories of the great Vic Hey, the famous Australian who was regarded as the toughest and most robust stand-off the game has ever seen. Hey had the knack of sidestepping off both feet. When the opposition became wary of his antics, he had the build to just run over the top of them. These were three options that would have confused any would-be tackler. Years later I had the pleasure of meeting up with Vic in Australia. He often spoke about the good times he had with both Dewsbury and Leeds. He also had the foresight to understand where rugby league should be going in the future. He even wrote a book called *The Man's Game* which described in great detail what the game needed to do to expand. The tips and inside knowledge set out in the book are fascinating. If you ever get your hands on this item, snap it up quickly. It's a fantastic and searching read.

There was a buzz about the town. In the past, rugby players were just another face in the crowd. Suddenly people started to talk league and would stop us in the street and chat away about the club and the game in general. Most of our team of course were from the area and the fans could relate to that.

I also settled down into a regular job after spending a happy time painting council houses throughout the district. This had been fun but there was an uncertainty about the work because some days I arrived and found out I was being laid off after that shift. I also learned the fast way to protect my tools and body at times seeing as plenty of contractors had no qualms about who they employed. The cross section was often a wide spectrum of the human race. Contractors gave drop-outs and blokes who had just come out of jail a brush and a can of paint. For some it was 'make a quick quid time' where some of the blokes would not even bother painting the bottom sections of windows because the inspectors never bothered to climb a ladder and check. This wasn't painting by numbers so much as painting by sections. We were paid for each section we finished. These days they refer to operators like that as cowboys. We just called them thieves. We couldn't leave anything lying around including the brushes we used to apply the paint with! The dodgy blokes worked on the principal that if you couldn't find your brushes they had first chance to get the plumb jobs on the ground floor. The ground floor jobs were a lot easier than carting a ladder about all day.

The boss was a huge man called Malcolm Marriott. He had big shoulders and a jutting chin that more than matched

Kirk Douglas for it stuck out a mile. Malcolm was a character from the old school. Handling this group of blokes was not an easy job, but he had a knack of keeping things under control. It wasn't often that things became excited and when it did he could handle himself.

I met Malcolm through playing water polo for Dewsbury and we became good mates. I have to thank him for many things including helping me to get through a tough period in my early life. On one occasion I think he saved my life. I was playing against Huddersfield Water Polo team, marking a huge chap who was a county player with a reputation for playing it hard under the water. Those who think Water Polo is a sissy sport, think again because often what goes on out of sight of the officials is lethal. This particular evening I was more than struggling to mark this beast. He had already split my lip and decided to push himself off my body and get a lift out of the water by planting his foot in my groin region. If that wasn't painful enough, his bloody foot got caught in my trunks and I was forced down deep into the depths and left struggling for air. Thankfully Malcolm swam under and pulled me apart from this hairy monster just in time. It was a scary moment that left me wondering if I should rub my crown jewels or count them.

The fact that we got paid at the end of each day should give an idea of the type of blokes I worked with. On more than one occasion, the police arrived midway through the day and bundled one of their suspects into the police van. It was quite interesting to see the poor bloke arguing with the coppers to let him get his day's wages before he was whisked away. Malcolm would dip into his pocket, pay him up on the spot and wish him best of luck before telling him he had a job when his 'holidays' were over.

Drinking made up part of the day and lunch was nearly always a liquid one. This wasn't good for an up and coming athlete like me. The times I had to endure barbs from the lads because I stuck to soft drinks, or at best had a shandy.

When it was pub time it was dart time. I couldn't throw an arrow for my life when I first started on the sites. I soon learnt. I had to learn otherwise my day's pay would go out the window with a cry of, 'Double eight and top to finish.' They were fun times but hard when I wasn't winning, although I concentrated fully, not just because money was at stake but Malcolm didn't like to leave the pub a loser. If anyone just happened to beat him in a couple of games, he would challenge them for double or nothing. This would often see our lunch hour turn into a lunch two hours and often three hours. After he had a few drinks his throwing got worse and because I was sober, my throwing got better. But it sure was a lot warmer in the pub earning a shilling than out in the cold.

Fridays were something else. We would all get to work early and finish early. We would then have a pub sports' day which included not just darts but a round robin of dominos, cards and a weird game of cricket on the pub carpet where a bottle of turpentine was the wicket, a paint scraper was the bat, and the ball was a small black thing that I later found out to be a squash ball. Don Bradman eat your heart out. Four points were scored by hitting the wall and a maximum of six points were achieved by sending the ball over the bar! Not that the landlord objected because these guys could drink for Britain and attempted on many occasions to set national and world records for downing ale.

It wasn't the right environment to succeed as a sportsperson but I held my nerve on most occasions and picked up a lot more money than headaches from hangovers. Once a young kid from Hull threw about 15 pints down his throat and challenged me to run from Wakefield back to Dewsbury. It was the easiest bet I've ever picked up on. Sadly he turned down the chance the following Friday to get his own back.

It was a great laugh but I needed a bit more stability so I could concentrate on regular work and combine it with my training schedule. My opportunity came about, yet again, by sheer luck from a conversation in a pub with a mate who had decided to leave town and seek his fortune in London. He suggested I take his job. 'Great, why not?' I replied. I took the job but I have to admit that I told a porkie pie to secure the position. I said I had experience at painting and decorating. I went from slapping the green or blue council paint on gutters to hanging wallpaper in a country mansion in the Yorkshire Dales. This was at the courtesy of one Joseph Shepley and Company, decorators to the finest!

Don't ask me how I did it, but I did. I learned quickly and enjoyed the job for several months before I had to switch trades. This was because of the lead in the paint which started to give me a bad rash and affected my asthma. It was starting to play havoc with my training too. The obvious thing was to switch me into the plumbing department. Wow, two trades in a year. I never once knew what both trades were all about.

I must have been lucky for I just muddled my way through it, used common sense and kept asking and learning. I must give credit to meeting up with the one and only Edward Summers who had spent years learning the trade. I latched onto his side like a limpet mine. Whatever job came up he would ask for me to help him and I would be there like a shot. We looked the part, both toddling off down the streets of town with plumbers' bass (an odd canvas bag that plumbers swore by) over our shoulders. Neither of us could drive so the company gave all the town work to us as well as the shit jobs too. As a painter I could sort of get away with telling the girls what I did for a living. When I was a plumber, I couldn't. I was the shit-man. Or should I say we were the S-men. We didn't mind either and felt rather proud walking around with the drain rods tucked under our arms. It was not the nicest smelling part of plumbing but it was interesting to say the least.

Dewsbury has a wonderful market which opens on

Wednesdays and Saturdays when thousands of shoppers look for a bargain. It also proved inviting to the pick pockets who enjoyed the closeness of such huge crowds pushing and shoving each other. It was a dream for them and a busy time for Edward and me. This was because as each wallet or purse jumped from one bag into another, they would do a switch. This meant taking the money out of the wallet or purse and dumping the evidence down the toilet. The result of this was a blocked loo. We used to get regular rescue call-outs to cafés and restaurants to unblock their drains. I laugh when I see the film *Ghostbusters*. It could have been adapted to Eddie and me riding off into the sun with drain rods and plungers akimbo to the strains of '*Who ya gonna call? Shit Busters!*'

Eddie was unbelievable when it came to his beard. It grew so fast, he could shave at seven in the morning and have a five o' clock shadow half an hour later. He looked ill and grey all the time. The greyness coupled with his Miami shadow and jet black hair made him look like he was on his last legs. He drank like a fish and smoked non-stop. He hardly ever ate anything in large quantities and was thin enough to induce passers by to throw a few coins to help him buy a cup of tea. He oozed the need for sympathy. We both knew what advantage such looks could bring two smart, about town shit-clearers. This was the ability to con free drinks. Before any drain job, we would act out the 'falling stooge' trick. This was where Eddie, at a given wink, would faint. Just like that. Bang. He hit the deck like he'd been hit by Sonny Liston. Olivier, Burton, O'Toole or Brando would have cheered at such acting. It was a superb piece of theatre that often went too far. I had to try hard to convince people witnessing the incident that he didn't need an ambulance and that I knew how to revive him. The best way to do this was with a drink of course. It was amazing how people would come out of their houses and help us inside. It didn't matter which house it was (but the larger the house the more chance of scrounging chocolate biscuits). How we kept our faces straight is a wonder but, Eddie was a pro. He even threw in the odd moan when he'd heard the magic words, 'Do you think a cup of tea may help?'

Whilst the kettle was boiling away, Eddie came round a bit. I then hit them with the, 'You wouldn't have a drop of Brandy would you? Maybe that might just help.' Nine times out of 10 it worked, though the hardest bit was getting a sip of brandy myself before Edward slugged the bloody lot. I mean let's face it, I'd had a shock. The thought of seeing my mate nearly die was hard to take. My nerves needed steadying too.

There was only one time we nearly got caught out. This was when the normal method of convincing people not to call for the ambulance failed. Someone made the call and the ambulance arrived before we could get Eddie indoors. 'Shit,' I whispered to Eddie, 'Start getting better pretty quickly.' But we shouldn't have worried because the ambulance men took one look at him and carted us both off to hospital. Once at hospital, they sent down Eddie to A and E for tests whilst I had to fill out the forms. Ten minutes later we were out of there like a flash leaving the nurse wondering where Mr M. Mouse and his mate had gone.

This was light relief in a job that had some horrific moments. For example clearing a still born baby was not unusual. Don't you ever think that men's toilets are worse than women's toilets. Far from it. Some of those 'ladies' must have passages halfway up their backs. Why do people still continue to use the pan when it's nearly full and has no chance of being flushed away? I know. It used to confuse us too!

One of the perks of our encounters with the sewers and drains of Yorkshire was the time given to clean up afterwards. This was all done in work's time of course. And rightly so, as we did the worst job going. We used to go to the local baths to swim away our problems. We loved it. There were warm showers and a nice little swim afterwards, followed by a quick half of ale before clocking off. It was a tough life but someone had to do it.

Not only were we the best pairing to clean any drain in town, it brought us close to all the pub landlords and café and restaurant owners. We never went short of a drink or a meal because they knew how important we were. Not many people take too kindly to eating or drinking in an establishment that has the wonderful aroma of shit seeping into the public domain. One other thing it did was to ensure I never got too big headed either. Being spotted by league fans was one thing, stinking of the local drains was another. So whilst many Dewsbury supporters waved and wished me luck for the weekend's game, not many ventured close enough to get a whiff.

At the club, my performance on the pitch caught the eye of the Yorkshire selectors. I wasn't the only player at the club to catch their eye. John and Alan Bates, Jeff Greyshon and Nigel Stephenson were all pushing to gain their first cap, another indication that my home team were performing at the top level. It was on my first trip with the county side to Cumberland that I found out how far behind Dewsbury was in the grand scheme of things. I knew we were just a small town club with average gates of just 2,000 to 3,000. The size of the club held back any ideas of being paid big money like players at the top clubs at the time such as Leeds, St Helens, Wigan, Bradford and Salford. Salford had shocked the rugby union and rugby league world by snaring Welsh star David Watkins for huge money. It was rumoured he pocketed £8,000. A fortune in those days.

Talking to the other county players soon made me realise how far behind the eight ball I was. I was stunned. Most of these guys were earning five times the amount we earned at Dewsbury! We stopped off at Keswick for lunch and a rest before going on to Whitehaven and even the top players at

Leeds (wingers Alan Smith and John Atkinson) were buzzing with excitement at the amount on offer at Salford.

We won against Cumberland and on the way back we stayed overnight at Keswick in a grand hotel with a posh bar that stunned the wallet. We were all overjoyed when the county officials slapped a wad of pound notes onto the bar. 'Drinks are on us!' shouted Jack Meyerscough, the Leeds chairman.

We had a ball. So too did David Jeans, the big prop from Wakefield Trinity who showed me another huge roll of notes. 'Where did you get that sort of money?' I enquired. 'That lot will choke a donkey,' I added.

'Never mind,' was the reply, 'I've just signed for Leeds.' It was as simple as that. The transfer was done in the bar and Mr Jeans was a lot wealthier than when he set off that morning. Obviously nobody knew where the money came from. It just happened to fall into his pocket. Such were the dealings in those days.

Leeds has always been a top payer. The club has snared most of the great players born in Yorkshire. At this time, Salford were challenging them. Their chairman, Brian Snape, had turned our sport upside down. He created a dynasty at The Willows ground by building a nightclub, several bars and booking top artists to perform in their huge auditorium. The team also played all their home games under floodlight on Friday nights and the fans loved it. This was the place to be seen. The in-crowd flocked there. Even footballers including George Best could be seen floating about the club. Brian Snape gave the fans what they wanted. His club offered entertainment where fans saw the match and then could enjoy a drink in luxury. After this they could sit down for a top class meal and be entertained by top acts from all around the world. He was a man well ahead of the times. Sadly his vision wasn't taken up by other clubs. I cringe to think that we never embraced as a game the concept he offered in the 1960s and 1970s. We all knew he'd copied the idea from Australian clubs like St George and Balmain, but who cared? The supporters and players loved it.

Every player looked forward to playing at The Willows because it gave them the full weekend off. At many a scrum, the question was raised about which top act was performing that night, followed by the odd fisticuffs at times. But minds often strayed from game plans to female plans for the ground attracted shed loads of women. They were on the look out for a Mr Best or Mr Dennis Law to cross their paths. It didn't stop us players from mixing in with the scene and testing our arm. Snape and the players at the club made no secret that he was prepared to pay top shilling for the best players. I was over the moon one Friday night when he approached me after the game and suggested anytime I wanted to leave Dewsbury he would be interested in having a 'little chat'. Salford paid their players great money and naturally I wanted the same.

Today of course players get a yearly contract and play and train full time. Boy I would have loved to have done that and not worried about earning a crust. Back then all so-called professional players had jobs, mostly on building sites. The odd one or two players did office work but to my knowledge, not one player just lived off playing money. One particular guy I knew who worked on the building sites would make a bit on the side by gambling with others about who had the largest cock! His trick was to challenge anyone on site for a payday showdown. This was not entirely a case of put your money where your mouth is, more a case of drop your old feller out and the winner takes the cash.

I must say I did make a few bob on his prowess. His other party trick was to wrap it round itself and display what can only be described as a huge 'vol-au-vent'. I kid you not. But like most things in life there's always someone bigger and better. Sadly I was there to witness it and lost a third of my weekly wage when an Irish labourer took him on. He'd been boasting about the size of his penis all week, so a showdown took place with side bets being placed right, left and centre. I went for broke, confident that no other human being could match what I referred to as a freak of nature. It was like a bull fight with guys screaming for their man to do the business. First our man proudly dropped his cock onto the towel. There was a gasp as this 'thing' unfolded before our eyes. Deformed was the only way I could describe it. But when the Irish bloke 'flashed', it just appeared to keep on unfolding like a snake. Amazingly, it beat our bloke's length by at least two inches! With hands raised the winner proudly accepted the cheers from his backers as though he'd scored the winning goal at Wembley. They were, to say the least, excited. And so was our mate who picked up a house brick and slammed it down hard onto his opposition's pride and joy!

What followed was chaos as two huge guys, both with cocks swinging in the wind (one bloodied and swelling by the second), attacked each other in a rage. It took us 10 minutes or more to stop the fight. We all paid our dues and went to the nearest pub to drink our sorrows. We had the thought ringing in our ears that there's no such thing as a certainty in gambling.

Needless to say, without getting too personal, I also knew that 'flashing' my old feller wasn't going to earn me a good living. With the greatest respect to Eddie and the drain rods, that mode of employment wasn't going to make me rich either.

By this time the company had been bought out by Beaumont and Blackburn's, the area's largest Electrical Contractors. We all went with the takeover to our new premises. The owner, David Blackburn, was a great follower of the local team and allowed me a few easy days before the game and of course, the Monday morning following the game was recuperation time. He was a great boss and I owe much to his belief that a young league player needed understanding about time off for training. This was especially vital for county training and international get-togethers although he must have been somewhat confused at times when I asked to take things easy on a Wednesday or Thursday.

Bumps and bruises from the pitch can take time to get over, so he always handed the easy jobs close to town to me, and of course, Eddie 'Carborundum' Summers. David was great, even though he must have known our antics down the drains weren't going to make him a profit. I still wonder to this day if he ever claimed back tax for both Eddie and I being a liability. They called us 'The Drain Rod Kids' but we spent most of the day chatting with the fans about the weekend's game.

Having secured a regular position in the team, I now started thinking about winning honours and even silverware. Then tragedy hit me. I suffered a bad ankle injury that just wouldn't heal and I was sidelined for two months. In desperation, the club sent me to Blackpool Football Club to a specialist physio who was reputed to be the best in the business for Achilles problems. I worked with the soccer club for a fortnight alongside my own club physio Jim Greenhall and spent hours walking, trotting and eventually running on the wide open beach in front of the famous tower. It was slow work but it sorted the problem out and I returned home fully fit.

It was a lot of fun being in a hotel for a fortnight right by the Pleasure Beach and Jim and I had the odd night out, not over the top of course seeing as I had to turn up for treatment early each morning but we didn't get bored. Far from it as staying in the same hotel was Frank Carson. He was the top star performing at the North Pier each night. Carson is as funny in real life as on stage. He never stopped telling jokes and despite him coming off stage an hour earlier, he would head straight for the hotel bar then give another live performance for the guests! Not once did he stop for breath. He was amazing, his Irish brogue and loud laughter ensured all who were there would be splitting their sides. It was doing the world of good for both my body and mind and by the time I boarded the train back to Dewsbury, boy was I raring to go.

During that stay both Jim and I went to see a fortune teller, in fact we saw two. The first was on the Central Pier. She was expensive and never told us anything of note. Plenty of drama and lots of rubbish about signs and cards. We both agreed she was a fake and laughed at the fact that we had forked out £3 for a waste of time. Further on the promenade we saw a hole in the wall with a little old lady looking deeply at a woman's palm, so we laughed at each other and pronounced we could have had our fortunes told for two bob. Sure enough the sign confirmed it, two shillings for a palm reading. Not only that she could write it all for you to take away.

'Come on,' said Jim, 'let's do it'.

Twenty minutes later we were left bemused by her proclamation that we were both going to live on the other side of the world and that we were going to be successful in our trades! We laughed again, then threw away the pieces of paper and retired to have a pint.

'It's all a load of crap.' I cried and Jim nodded back.

One thing that wasn't crap anymore was my ankle, I was eager to return to the playing field.

In the 1968–1969 season I started training every day. I wanted to get better each week. Most of our team started to feel the same way. It was a happy camp and we even convinced the club to give us our own section for the wives and girlfriends before and after the games. This worked a treat. Players' wives and girlfriends hold an important part of a player's mind set and it doesn't matter how good a player is or how fit they feel, if there are problems on the domestic scene they lose that edge. No amount of urging and support can lift a player if something's not right at home. A blazing row the Friday before or the morning of a match is hardly good preparation. A player who is unsettled at home may arrive at the ground on match day wanting to take the world on. This is good in one sense but bad in another. Whilst the aggression is alright, it can waste energy and use up too much adrenalin which leaves the player low on fuel late in the game.

I had just got married myself at this time, to Patricia, the daughter of a local councillor, Roland Tolson, who would soon join the board of the Dewsbury RL club. It settled me down and the added responsibility of starting a family excited me, as did the challenge for success.

As in most sports, it's easy to pick out the wives and girlfriends at a match because most of them do just that – match! If one gets a fur coat, within weeks the others have one, and so on. We all laughed about such things and generally avoided friction because we were all together. We all got the same wage packet and nobody got money under the table. This wasn't surprising as our secretary, Tom Clarke, was the shrewdest man with a shilling in the world. Tom was a one off. He could peel an orange with one hand in his pocket and make a player feel like a great train robber if they asked for expenses for a bus fare to training. He was a true Yorkshire man and I'm sure he invented superglue well before it hit the high streets because nothing could force him to part with money.

Rumours circulated about payments under the table. We all felt honest enough to accept the club's and players' assurances that we were all on the same winning bonus. When a team hits the limelight in any sport, people get jealous and spread nonsense in the hope they can catch someone out. Many felt that because I was the first to be selected for Great Britain, I was being given a bonus on top. It wasn't true. I did get a payment for becoming an international but that was in everyone's contracts at the club. Naturally being given the chance to play for my country and mixing with other top players started me thinking about moving to a bigger club. But I was happy, and despite knowing I was miles behind in the winning money stakes, I wasn't going to rush to the committee room and demand a transfer. Anyway, we had to get to finals and win something to prove to the world we were a good side.

To bring a bit of razzmatazz to the game, we even started to use cheerleaders like most of the top clubs. We tried using a bunch of girls to give us a lift when we ran onto the field and drum up some vocal support for the players. Lift was the operative word, because most of them could have played in our front row!

The early experiments with cheerleaders were far from a success. Agility was not their forte. Neither was their coordination and rhythm. Finally we found a lovely group of cheerleaders who danced well and lifted our spirits as we trotted out each week. Unfortunately a couple of the young, single blokes were lifting more than their spirits and it became clear to all that having cheerleaders practice their routine on the same nights that we trained wasn't a smart move. Two cheerleaders left suddenly mid way through the season after showing a remarkable increase in weight! Not surprisingly after pressure from certain girlfriends (and a couple of suspicious wives) the club disbanded them.

The demise of our cheerleaders probably wasn't a bad thing in the end. At Odsal stadium one bitterly cold day, the cheerleaders had sheltered under the dug outs. When our coach requested one of our subs to get ready to enter the fray, he had to settle down somewhat before standing up. This was because one of the girls had slipped her hand inside his tracksuit! I suppose it could be said that such things helped team morale, but that was one muscle the coach didn't want flexing.

Another thing that wasn't flexing was my back. I had been having troubles for years and just put it down to wear and tear through playing in the scrums. Little did I know I had been born with a slight sideways bend in my spine. It all came about from having an X-ray for a broken rib, which turned out to be a cartilage problem but the doctors had spotted two unusual aspects about my body. One was the size of my heart and the other was the spine defect. No problems for the heart they said, although it would eventually give me problems later in life, but the spine was another thing. A meeting with a specialist soon showed my spine was at risk and I was advised to retire and never pack down in a scrum again!

Oh great, I thought, just on the verge of making a name in the game and this bloke tells me it's all over. I was so upset it rocked me. I requested another opinion and this time the spine specialist explained my problem and how a bad knock could leave me in a wheelchair. He also added that the problem was if I was tackled head on and was forced backwards at the same time as someone was holding my legs, then it could be dangerous. Thankfully, instead of squashing my dreams of making the big time, he added that it would be possible to wear a support which would strengthen the base of the spine.

'You mean wear some type of corset?'

'Yes,' he replied. I could have kissed him on the spot.

I was soon working out the details of what was needed to help my spine. I tried many designs and after five or six different trials, I finally found the right style and the amount of metal frame needed to do the job. It didn't look pretty and was uncomfortable to wear but it gave me hope. I was left with wearing it each game until I retired nearly ten years later.

My first attempt was at Barrow on a cold Friday night with the corset supported by three aluminium straps at the back. It lasted just past the third scrum when the effort and weight pushing bent the bloody straps so much they dug into my ribs, trouble was they didn't bend out again, they just seized rigid. I went down gasping for breath and the doctor was quick to lift up my jumper and bend the bloody thing back into shape again. Unfortunately this alteration of the corset was done in full view of the opposing front row who took great delight in watching a nice pink corset being rearranged by the club medic.

'Christ, he's wearing a corset,' was one of the few barbs thrown at me that night and they never let me forget it either as each tackle was accompanied by 'Grab his corset sweetie,' or words to that effect!

I finally finished with a corset with a padded steel chunk, about six inches by three inches that worked a treat. It didn't stop the pain and discomfort but it gave me the chance to keep on playing and whilst I now struggle to get out of bed each morning, I honestly think it was worth it. It's only pain.

As the team grew stronger each week, we started to realise the opportunity to challenge for trophies wasn't just a pipe dream. The Yorkshire Cup kicked off the new season and we were keen to stamp our name on a trophy that was well within our reach. This was providing that we had a good cup draw. We did. We drew York at home. Sadly an argument between the players and the committee ensued. The club didn't think we deserved a wage rise for the new season, despite the increase in crowds due to our style of play. Our game was exciting to watch. The older players like Kevin Osborne and Brian Firth, spokesmen on behalf of the team, thought we deserved an extra £2 on the winning bonus and £1 on losing money. The club dug their heels in and so did we. As a result, we refused to play, forfeiting the game and losing any hope for trophy glory.

It's amazing now to talk about such minor amounts of

money preventing a game going on but the older players knew our crowds had increased substantially whilst our pay hadn't. All smaller clubs were the same and treated their players poorly. Thanks to the guidance from Kevin Osborne, we stuck to our guns and went on strike.

The press was unkind to us and for the first time I felt the wrath of the written word. The older players played it all down and told us not to worry. They related plenty of stories about days of old where players and committee had clashed. There was one tale where the chairman stood up in the stands late into the match and held up five fingers to his captain. The captain understood this to indicate a £5 bonus if they won. There were a few hard rushes by the forwards followed by the drop goal that sealed the game. This left the team in high spirits as they went back into the changing rooms. Once there, the captain called upon the chairman to produce the cash. 'No, I was just letting you know there was five minutes left on the clock,' came the reply. At which point the skipper attacked the boss and broke his nose. The skipper never played for the club again and the players were never paid extra.

Our team nearly ended up with the same result. Fortunately, the club backed down and gave us the extra bonus for the rest of the season. It wasn't a bad year, but again we didn't challenge for the top silverware. It was all so frustrating. Despite being selected for Yorkshire again along with Nigel Stephenson, Dick Lowe, and Jeff Grayshon, the urge for top flight success still burned deep inside.

I was playing well yet again and the press often suggested I was close to Great Britain selection. Unfortunately, I had the likes of Peter 'Flash' Flanagan, Colin Clarke, Tony Karalius and Tony Fisher to contend with. This left me with a difficult task of impressing the selectors. It wasn't easy to impress when playing for a fringe club rather than one of the big boys. The fact that Yorkshire had selected me a few times in front of Great Britain hooker Flash Flanagan gave me hope. The one thing that was in my favour was my ability to read the game off the ball; I also had a bit of pace. Since the introduction of the four tackle rule (soon extended to six), the days of huge, tough, heavyweight hookers were a thing of the past. There is little doubt that the RFL's change after seeing the advantages when Australia adopted the idea changed my playing career. At just 12½ stone, I was hardly a brute who would have frightened a dog out of the butcher's shop. All of a sudden speed was important. Suddenly it was the end of overweight hookers who just walked from scrum to scrum. Now number nines had plenty to do from dummy half and in effect were an extra scrum-half. This was the position I played at school.

Ever since my aunties, Margaret, Dora, Ivy and Doris, dragged me to watch Dewsbury from the age of seven or eight, I was amazed by the play of Hull's rake Tommy Harris. He won the man of the match Lance Todd Trophy at Wembley whilst playing on the losing side. Tommy was my hero and I shaped my style on this guy. He was a great runner from dummy half and changed the entire playing style for that position. Because I came on the scene at the same time as the limited tackle rule, many people often say I was one of the trailblazers in changing the style of play of the number nine. No way, Mr Harris was running around the field of play well before I was out of short pants!

A few years ago, I had the pleasure to meet up with the man. He looked fit as a fiddle. It was a highlight of my life. He was a true gentleman. Sadly both Harris and Flanagan (another great character of our game) have departed for the playing fields in heaven. Both men were fantastic hookers in open play and they had a huge influence on my game.

With such a huge rule change about limited tackles, it wasn't surprising I came more and more into the limelight. Yes I struggled to win my share of the ball at the scrum (a factor that I carried through my entire playing career) but it wasn't as important anymore. I believed I could achieve my dream of wearing the red, white and blue of Great Britain. Yet another rule change elevated me to top status. This was the change of allowing substitutes to be used off the bench.

Coaches soon realised they needed speedy utility players. The selectors felt I was fast enough to create problems if given the chance off the bench. I became the first hooker to be chosen to substitute for Great Britain. My dream was there for the taking and whilst I didn't want anyone to get injured, I was left wondering and hoping when that chance would come. Little did I realise it would be sooner than expected.

5

YOU CAN'T KEEP
YOUR SHIRT!

Finally, the day came when I found out I was to play for Great Britain. I shook like a leaf when I read the papers and saw my name in print. I stared for ages hoping that they hadn't made a mistake or that I wasn't dreaming and that my name wouldn't disappear off the page at any moment. The club confirmed my selection that same night. Two days later I trained alongside the stars of the game preparing for the second test against the 1971 touring New Zealanders. The New Zealanders had surprised everyone (other than themselves) and won the first test. The selectors wanted to make changes and I was one of them.

At long last the selectors gave me a chance. It went in some small way towards erasing the awful experience I encountered after playing for Yorkshire against Lancashire at Leigh the previous year. Once again we had wrapped up the county championship with a resounding win. I played what I thought was my best game in a representative jumper and was delighted when two of the Great Britain selectors approached me after the game. The selectors stated I was to be selected for the 1970 tour to Australia and New Zealand. They told me I had to keep this news to myself. Seeing as though there were only three members of the selection committee, I went home convinced that in two months' time when the tour selection was named, I could pack my bags for down under.

At least I kept my part of the bargain. The selectors didn't.

Once again Yorkshire selected me before Peter Flanagan. It appeared that Great Britain was happy to do the same and blood some youth for the future. This they did by selecting a young guy called Malcolm Reilly. Sadly for me, the powers-that-be hastily put together a Wales side to play a Great Britain squad to help in the tour selection but they picked Flanagan ahead of me to take on two roughhouse Welsh players, Jim Mills and Tony Fisher, who were on the fringe of being selected. Both were Welsh through and through and also the prop-hooker combination for Bradford Northern at the time. Despite having already been told by selectors I was on the tour, they left me out. They went for experience and gave the Welsh pair the nod. Flanagan also played well in this game and, like Mills and Fisher, he got selected for the tour.

I was dumbfounded. I had to accept the selector's thinking that the tour would be a tough baptism for me and that the two Welsh boys could handle such pressure. These were facts that nobody could deny for Fisher and Mills had a solid reputation for not taking a backward step and were only too happy to take a few steps forward as well!

Having seen film of that tour I feel the selectors were right in taking Fisher. He was a strong presence in the tests and went a long way to help win the Ashes. I accepted the decision in good faith and went about playing the best I could. Instead, I set my sights on being selected to play against the Kiwis who were about to tour England in 1971. A few weeks before Great Britain flew out to New Zealand, it hit the press that Mills had turned down the chance to tour and had accepted a chance to play under Roy Francis at North Sydney. This was another slap in the face! To his credit, Flanagan approached me after a clash with Hull Kingston Rovers and said I deserved to have been selected before him seeing as though he'd had his time. He said I should be on the plane rather than him. It was a great gesture and one I will never forget from Peter.

I couldn't believe how my luck had deserted me. The fact

that Roy Francis was involved made it even worse. Francis had made a name in Australia as a coach. Four years earlier when I was just starting out at Dewsbury, he had arranged to meet me at the New White Bear restaurant at Tingley, near to Leeds to discuss emigrating to Australia to join Norths. So my new wife Patricia and I took two bus journeys in the nervous hope of making a career change. Francis never showed up and I never received even a phone call from him again.

After such a confusing time in my career the previous year, my chance finally came. My name was in the *Yorkshire Evening Post*, I bought four copies just to make sure it wasn't a misprint! Again the match was at Castleford. This was the scene of my first representative debut in Great Britain's under 21s against France. I hoped and prayed it would prove a lucky ground again. Pulling on that Great Britain shirt was beyond my wildest dreams. I had to take refuge in the toilet to pull myself together as the tear drops ran down my cheeks. I looked at the badge and cried. It didn't help either when I opened telegrams from my parents and my old Shaw Cross coach, David Bradshaw. David's telegram read quite simply 'Don't lose the scrums 18–0', referring to my fateful first game at Hunslet Juniors.

I was selected as a substitute and I wouldn't be out there for the kick off but to me that didn't matter. All I wanted to do was get on the paddock as soon as possible.

It's hard to describe the feeling as I lined up for the National Anthem. I was in a daze as I went back to sit in the dug out. I was just sorting out the blankets and preparing to put on my tracksuit when the whistle blew for the start of the game. The next words I heard were, 'Quick, you're on.'

'I'm what?' I replied. I then saw Bob Haigh on the far side of the ground leaving the field clutching his arm. He'd broken it in the impact from the first tackle after catching from the kick off. Only seconds had gone by and I hadn't even seen the incident. Sadly for Bob it was a bad break and kept him out of the game for quite some time. I took his place in the second row and played there until half time, when, after giving away far too many penalties, hooker Tony Karalius and I changed places. I packed down in the front row for the next 40 minutes.

We were losing at the break and Alex Murphy, playing in his last ever Great Britain test left nobody in doubt about what should be done. He screamed that we needed to stop being penalized in the scrum. No one argued, least of all me. I never said a word because although Murphy wasn't the coach, he was in charge. Nobody else got a word in edgeways!

We lost the game, yet should have beaten them when a clever piece of play from Murphy sent winger Joe Walsh over in the corner. This would have given us the lead for the first time in the match. We all watched in horror as the Leigh speedster decided to get nearer the posts to make the conversion easier only to slip and put his foot over the dead ball line. I didn't think anyone could swear so much. Murphy gave him both barrels whilst the rest of us just stood there in a daze. Within minutes the Kiwis hit back. They sensed this was going to be their lucky day. It was, and they won the test series for the first time ever on British soil.

The deciding break came from their skipper, Christensen. He beat the first line of defence and then avoided my desperate cover tackle. This left him with only full-back Derek Edwards to face. The Kiwi captain's strength proved too much for the talented Castleford full-back. He couldn't stop him. Some of the papers blamed me for missing what they said was a crucial tackle. It was a crucial tackle but some other players missed him as well! Not surprisingly I got dropped from the team as did nine others when the selectors went to town.

Losing the test series for the first time on home soil was hardly going to have the selectors at Chapeltown Road rolling about laughing in the aisles. They created a record by giving no less than seven debuts for the dead rubber at Headingley where Great Britain put the cleaners through the tourists. But it was too late; the Kiwi's had been celebrating ever since that final whistle at Castleford and their singing drifting down from their dressing room after the match still sticks in my mind. Our changing room was silent. Not even Murphy said a word.

It could be said that it was an eventful series. I was pleased to see that Tony Halmshaw got his Great Britain cap for that third Kiwi test. He had been playing well for Halifax at the time and deserved selection. Tony and I grew up together in Saville Town. It was some achievement for two guys from the same area to win an international cap. I was convinced I was going to join that long list of 'one test wonders', despite becoming the quickest substitute in international rugby league, and playing in Alex Murphy's last match. It was no consolation to think I bowed out in good company. After the match I sadly pulled off my jumper, looked at the badge and comforted myself with the knowledge I at least got the chance to wear it and play for my country. When I tried to put the shirt in my bag, it was taken from me. 'We need them for the last test,' I was told. I was a one test wonder with not even a shirt to keep! I refused to take off my shorts and socks. At least I was going to keep something from the match.

I wasn't in the best of moods, and I was pleased I didn't have a dog at home.

The newspaper clippings showed it had been a bad day at the office. I kept the clippings in my bedside table as a daily reminder to ensure that one day that I would prove the doubters wrong. I struggled to come to terms with my failure. I had blown my chance to prove I was good enough to stay on the international scene for quite some time.

Not many people realise that at the time we had to play twice for Great Britain before earning our international cap. Playing one game only earned us a blazer badge! The badge arrived by post not long after. I opened the mail, looked at it and placed it in a drawer without showing anyone. I wouldn't be putting that badge on a blazer until I felt I'd deserved it.

6

MAY I BORROW THE SALT AND PEPPER?

Despite receiving the elbow from the Great Britain selectors, I looked forward to the 1971–1972 season with even more confidence than before. My team mates at Dewsbury were fantastic and I knuckled down and worked even harder. That season brought about a new coach and a different attitude to our game plan. Tommy Smales had been a shrewd player in his time for Featherstone. He brought plenty of experience to our club. He also had the ability to listen to the players and discuss various aspects of the game with the team. This made us feel involved. It was a bit like a teacher at school treating their class as adults.

He also brought with him an assistant coach, Keith Goulding. The pair set about turning the side into winners with a killer punch.

Goulding was unbelievable. He was the most interesting coach I've ever been involved with. He lived and breathed rugby league. He must have been a relative of one of the founders way back in 1895. He didn't talk about anything other than league; breakfast, lunch and dinner, rugby league was non stop, 24-7. We would sit down in a restaurant and even before ordering food, he would have the ashtray as the scrum, salt and pepper as the two half-backs and he'd be showing us the angles we should run. Then he'd lean over to the other table (excusing himself) and borrow knives, forks, spoons, salt and pepper and proceed to inform all and sundry where the players should be positioned, where they should run and when they should run. He was a rugby league freak.

Both coaches came from Featherstone each training night and I'm sure poor Tommy would hardly get a word in. Tommy was shrewd and knew a lot of Goulding's ideas would work so he fine tuned them and turned Dewsbury into one of the most exciting set move teams of the time. Our stand-off, Alan Agar was also from the same area and swore blind that some of the moves they came up with were bordering on insane. They were mad maybe, but they worked! The coaches pushed us hard at training and we continued to practice these obscure moves time and time again. The moves all had different names such as 'Pork Pie', 'Egg and Bacon', 'Union Jack' and other outrageous titles. I wish I could remember them all now, but sadly my brain packed down in far too many scrums for that. I do remember that the more outlandish the titles, the more they gelled. We knew it confused the opposition when their defence shouted things like, 'Watch for Bates running the angle!' As much as the opposition tried, they just couldn't work out the moves. This wasn't surprising as we struggled to understand them at times.

There were so many variations on one set move that often a runner would get confused, appear in the wrong place, but still score because I had forgotten and gone the wrong way too!

All of us would stay close after each training session to continue discussing tactics over a few pints. There were a few times when a few pints turned into many pints. We'd get home late and blame the coaches for keeping us at the training ground to fine tune our tactics. I know Tommy Smales copped plenty of abuse from many an irate wife. They even suggested to the coach it was a disgrace to keep the players training until the early hours. One guy even convinced his wife that he had to stay back for treatment for a leg strain because the atmospheric pressure changed after midnight, which helped the muscles respond more!

It was part and parcel of our routine to have the odd beer after training on a Thursday night. It was thirsty work having to do a full day's shift and then go training. We felt so fit we reckoned we could handle it. But I never drank two days before a game, except for one wintry Christmas when it was iced over for days. Most of us worked on the morning of Christmas Eve, packed up at lunchtime and went on a pub crawl. Every pub bounced with good cheer and beer. Normally because we played on both Christmas Day and Boxing Day, I would just have a couple and go home but outside was so frozen with huge drifts of snow everywhere that it was impossible for any game to be played over the festive season. Games in football and league were being cancelled by the hour. Consequently I went on the razzle big time.

I love rugby league fans. They are so knowledgeable about the sport and will do anything to get their fix of league each weekend. Little did I know we had some eager little helpers working their socks off to get the pitch at Crown Flatt ready. They had braziers and straw spread out across the grass. The fans, including my four aunties, worked throughout the night to stave off the frost. Meanwhile, I was filling up with Christmas cheer. I got home late, and didn't even make it upstairs to the bedroom. I decided it was safer to sleep on the couch downstairs. I was awoken by my wife just two hours before kick off. I was still in my working gear, stank like a brewery, and felt like death warmed up.

'Look at the state of you, go and get changed quickly.'

'Don't be silly, look outside,' I moaned, 'the game's off.'

'No, I've just heard it on the radio and the club phoned to say the game will be played,' was the reply.

I went into panic mode. I didn't own a car and couldn't drive anyway. The roads appeared snowed in and I knew I was in the shit. Feeling like death warmed up, I showered, grabbed my gear, ran out of the house and stopped the first car going towards Dewsbury. In the car were a startled old gent and his wife. They kindly accepted my apologies and drove me to the ground. I arrived just in time, shoved my boots on and went out to take on Huddersfield.

The first scrum was a nightmare. There were 12 heaving bodies all full of drink, sweating like pigs and smelling like beer that's been left in the sun for a month. I threw up as did three others, and that was only on our side. I'm sure it's the first time a bunch of players were more drunk than the fans. We all felt dreadful and yet I scored the one and only hat-trick of my career, won the man of the match and ended up with winning money! It's a funny old game.

I vowed I would never do that again and despite it being Christmas Day I didn't have a drink that night. Instead, I went to bed early and prepared for the return match at Fartown on Boxing Day morning. I produced probably one of my worst performances for the club. I was shocking. I dropped balls, missed tackles and got a real hiding in the scrum count. Not surprisingly, we lost. The loss brought back memories of my first game at the ground where our A-team started the match with just 12 men. We had 13 men on leaving the dressing room but nobody took into account the antics of one of our players. He took the coach's advice to the letter after being told to hit their key ball player the first chance he got. So whilst passing the key player (who was also their skipper), he did what he was told and knocked the bloke out in the tunnel!

Thankfully the club had become more professional since then. Antics like getting boozed up at Christmas were frowned upon. Despite this, when I bump into past players they hardly ever talk about what went on in the games tactically. The usual subjects of conversation are the amusing incidents that happened on and off the playing field. Former Great Britain scrum-half Alan Bates often recalls when hailstones as big as billiard balls started bouncing down just 10 minutes into the second half. Our away opponents, Hull Kingston Rovers were leading 6–5. It was shocking weather. The forwards were more than pleased when the next scrum was formed.

Alan refused to put the ball in the scrum and sheltered under the two prop forwards. The referee screamed at Alan to feed the scrum. Again Alan refused. If he had fed the ball in, I wouldn't have struck for it. Flash Flanagan (my opposition) and I knew what was good for us as the poor three-quarters were being pelted.

'I'll abandon the game,' the referee screamed.

'Do what you want, I'm not moving and neither is the ball,' said Alan. At which point the referee blew his whistle and declared Hull Kingston Rovers the winners.

We didn't care. It was so cold we rushed inside to the dressing room and jumped straight into the huge bath. We still had on our boots and all. We stayed there for well over an hour until we got some feeling back in the bones. Why didn't we think of summer rugby league in those days?

I also have painful memories about playing at Whitehaven on a bitterly cold day. I had a long gash above the eyebrow from a mistimed tackle that left blood pouring down my face. I rushed off to get stitched on the sidelines. After a quick four loops, I set off to rejoin the play only for the doctor to come with me. His hands were so cold he'd stitched his own finger onto my eyebrow. He didn't feel a thing!

Having achieved my dream of playing for Great Britain I was aware of what it entailed to get there. I have to thank many players and people for helping me along the way. Those old heads who in the early days took me to the cleaners, probably never knew that they were helping me get to the top. My first encounter with Castleford Prop Dennis Hartley was a case in point. I was a cheeky youngster desperate to strike for the ball and gain possession the best way I could. All through my career I could only strike with my right leg. Even when they brought in the rule of only striking with the furthest foot for a while, I still didn't change. I continued to use my right leg and (believe it or not) only got penalized once! My left leg could have been cut off for all the good it was. To win possession I had to cheat. That's what I did against Dennis and his hooker, Dickinson at the first scrum. I slipped off the loose arm, scraped across the floor, gained possession and didn't get penalized by the referee. 'How easy is this?' I thought, 'Swinging with a loose arm and getting away with it!'

Dennis even picked me up off the floor and suggested what a fine young prospect I was (or words to that effect) and finished with a polite, 'Do that again and I'll break your bloody hand.' In the next scrum I did it again, and Dennis was true to his word. I still glance at my mangled finger to this day and think what a nice chap Mr Hartley was in that match. It taught me to stop being smart and cheeky. It also taught me to take advice from a 17 stone prop forward with feet larger than Coco the Clown's.

Most of the hookers doing the rounds when I first started playing were big, rough and tough. They were from the old school, where they virtually walked from scrum to scrum. The likes of Bob Dagnall and Tony Fisher were great strikers of the ball and hard to shift about in the scrum. None were harder to shift than Don Close at Huddersfield. He was another international and the first few times I scrummed down against him, all I saw was his number nine pushing into my nose. I realised there was more to this hooking game than just being a fast striker. Close's positional sense and the angles he packed down in the scrum just blocked me off from seeing daylight never mind the bloody ball. I knew I had to do something to survive.

Like a youngster eager for an autograph, I started searching for these guys after each game. Over a drink I asked them, 'How do you do this . . . ? How do you do that?' Not one of these guys ever refused to tell me. It was great to think they took time out to help a new kid on the block. I started to write down all the tricks of the trade. I noted which hooker did this and that, how he blocked me out and so on. This is how my little black book full of hookers arrived. Granted it didn't have the same ring perhaps as boasting about 'Randy Rita' and 'Blow Job Betty' but it contained hookers none the less.

Fans from both sides of the world like to ask players a

number of similar questions including who were the best, toughest and meanest players I faced in rugby league. It's hard to relate that question to different eras. The toughest is a difficult one to select seeing as though not many players could be regarded as soft. The likes of Malcolm Reilly, Dennis Hartley, Tony Fisher, Cliff Watson, Jim Mills and my old prop forward at Dewsbury, Harry Beverley were hard men but the man who took the biscuit was Frank Foster. Frank wasn't just tough, he was cruel. They said he was temperamental: 50 per cent temper and 50 per cent mental! He was a tall, rangy player who started life in the back row and finished in the engine room, the front row, much to the chagrin of hookers throughout the game. One of my first (and lasting) memories of Frank was when I faced him just after he'd transferred to Hull Kingston Rovers. In that game he wouldn't have made much of an impression on *Come Dancing* as he seemed to spend his time stumbling all over my body at every opportunity. His lack of balance created some fine designs all over my head, limbs and torso. Here was an artist who used studs rather than a regular paint brush to create a masterpiece of Aboriginal proportions or even a Picasso. Either way my skin canvas was badly in need of restoration after the match. The following morning my mother came into the bathroom with a cup of tea as I soaked the latest entry for the Turner Prize and she burst out crying. She was obviously not too fond of modern art!

Playing Frank was like Chinese torture. The opposition's blood went drip, drip, drip until they faded away. Despite my best efforts to hurt him, he seemed oblivious to pain.

Several years passed and Frank was near the end of his career (playing not painting). He played as prop for Oldham when I finally snapped. I decided to bend the rules a bit. Perhaps a more accurate description was that I decided to seriously break the rules and give him a bit of his own medicine. It was one of the very few times that I actually intended to really hurt someone by foul play. I asked Brian Taylor, my prop, to get underneath him after the scrum had broken up and offer me a superb target. He did and I let fly with a beauty. Frank wobbled, looked shaken and at that moment I prayed he'd fall down. He didn't. He just rubbed his jaw and congratulated me on such a sweet blow. Shit, I was in trouble.

Half time came and the coach was furious that we were getting no possession at the scrum. He asked what was going wrong. I pointed my head towards the coach and showed him two slits that deep inside contained two eyeballs. 'Having a bit of trouble seeing,' I barked back.

The coach quickly blasted the two props for not looking after me, and they in turn displayed a remarkable impression of Siamese cats with matching slits for eyes, 'Having a bit of trouble ourselves,' came their reply.

Amazingly after being guided into the Oldham club house after the match, Frank slapped me on the back, offered to buy me a drink, said 'Well played,' and suggested I may have broken his cheekbone. I would have loved to have seen the swelling on his face. I contented myself instead to listening to my team mates describe how he looked and that he was in obvious pain. 'That will teach him,' I thought as I stumbled blindly towards the toilet, hurting with each movement.

Sadly, Frank retired soon after and was a great loss to the game. Some suggest that doctors in the north of England still raise glasses in tribute to the man who must have helped turn stitching eyebrows into an art form. To my knowledge no one ever got around to sending Frank a 'Happy Retirement' card but the thought was there from most within the game at the time. Not that Mr Foster was lost to the game for he eventually took over as coach at Workington Town and held the position for quite some time due to the fact (or rumour) that no one was brave enough to tell him he was sacked! I don't blame them.

With all the tribulations, injuries and effort, I felt it was time for things to take a turn for the better, and they did.

7

QUITE HOT, ISN'T IT?

It had been a long wait. Yet with hard work and tremendous help from my team mates, I was selected for Great Britain again. Dewsbury was no longer being described as a mid-table team anymore. Because of the way we won and displayed some outstanding rugby league, the selectors couldn't avoid our efforts. No less than six of our players picked up their county caps during the season of 1971–1972. Because Yorkshire was county champion for the third year in a row, this added weight to the claims of me, Nigel Stephenson, Alan and John Bates, Dick Lowe (his real name is Trevor. You work it out) and Jeff Grayshon to be selected for Great Britain. It was quite right that eventually most of the players obtained international recognition. They were great, talented players. It was through their efforts and the efforts of coaches Tommy Smales and Keith Goulding that kept us in the spotlight.

In my next game for the country, Great Britain played France at Odsal Stadium. We ran riot over the French and won with ease. I crossed the line for my first international try in a little run from dummy half. The try was nothing outstanding but it was a big moment for me.

It would have been hard for the selectors to have gleaned much from the match because France didn't click at all. Yet we all felt confident we were in with a chance to go to the World Cup in France in October and November 1972.

Dewsbury finished the league in a high position and we were pleased with our performance. Again we didn't win anything. It irritated us all. We had to somehow handle the pressure, show composure, learn to cope in tight games and not get excited. We knew we had a good side but our eagerness and inability to steady nerves was letting us down.

Goulding and Tommy were still shuffling salt and pepper pots and anything else they could lay their hands on to extend our range of set moves. It proved an experience for not only the players but for those lucky, or unlucky, to be dining at the same time. It was fun and helped my understanding of the game so much that Keith nagged me to join him and study for my coaching certificate at Lilleshall where the RFL held a yearly skills program.

We had also recruited yet another Leeds cast off in Cumbrian Harry Beverley. He was a rough no nonsense prop who never took a backward step. He added more spice to our defence and attack. Harry watched the antics of our coaches in quiet amusement and though he rarely said anything, he would rub his chin from time to time. He was a man of few words but on one occasion he stopped Tommy and Keith and demanded to know who he was. 'You're a prop, Harry,' was the reply.

'I want to know where I am on that table!' he cried.

'You're the wine glass, Harry,' Keith replied.

Harry just walked away went to the bar and returned with a pint pot, slammed it down and replaced the wine glass. 'That's better. Now I understand.'

It was all great fun for us, but not for the opposing defences because we started to improve these moves. This was the same time big Harry Beverley lost his temper with me. Since joining the club from Leeds he'd made a real name for himself as an uncompromising forward with a running action of lifting his knees in a high, unusual manner. Oh how the crowd would roar when Big H. got the ball. He had a laconic way with words, short and sweet but his knees did all the talking.

For a few months Harry would trot to the scrum and enquire whose head it was. I always gave the same reply,

'Ours of course, Harry,' even when it wasn't. This resulted in some rough contests between him and the opposing props. He never knew the rules. It was only when he'd been penalised for head butting and threatened to be sent off by the referee that he suddenly gave me a weird look. As we trotted off for the half time break, Harry pulled me to one side and raised his voice for the first time and claimed, 'You've been telling me porky pies.' He then proceeded to clip me round the ear and trotted off inside. He never said a thing at the break but I felt him staring at me. After the restart at the first scrum he asked me again, 'Whose head is it?' Then he winked at me and head butted the opposing number eight!

Nothing had changed, but it left me wondering for years about who had been kidding who.

I was working on a building job in Leeds at the time they selected the World Cup squad. As we stopped for breakfast, I found it difficult to eat my bacon sandwich due to the fact I had all fingers crossed. I quickly scoured the morning papers and read the pundits' slant on who would and who wouldn't get selected. Two scribes even suggested I was on the plane to France.

My workmates were fantastic at keeping my spirits up, but I had experienced the disappointment before at the hands of the selectors. I took nothing for granted. All day I walked around in a trance and to my knowledge, only managed to plumb in one toilet pan in the entire shift! (My trademark was based more on style than speed.)

I'm not overly superstitious but I begged the guys to stop at the same café on our way back to town. I ordered tea and rushed next door to the newsagents where much to my relief my name jumped off the page! 'This time I won't blow it,' I thought.

The squad met at Headingley a few days later for a photo shoot. We were also fitted out for blazers, pants and training kit. I was in a dream, although I knew I wasn't nailed on for the starting spot for the World Cup tour to France. This was because my arch rival, Tony Karalius, was also included in the squad.

The RFL also arranged two trial matches to bond the team. The first match was at York and the second match was at Oldham. We then flew out to Paris and on to Perpignan for our first game against hot favourites Australia. We had a solid team lead by Hull winger Clive Sullivan. We also had the experienced centre, Chris Hesketh as vice captain. I was told early on that I would start each warm up game and that Tony Karalius was on the bench. Tony and I had some great scraps over the years. He was such a funny guy, always cracking jokes. Each time we met, he pretended to feed me a sugar lump, patted me on the head and said, 'Good horse'. I remembered from the Castleford test against New Zealand when I was second string to him how difficult a pill it was to swallow. Yet Tony supported me throughout the World Cup campaign. He showed not one ounce of resentment. That typified the team spirit in the camp.

The two trial games were put in place to ease us into top gear for the competition. Whilst many of the squad thought perhaps it would be like a training run I knew it wasn't going to be plain sailing. Both hookers at York and Oldham were themselves on the fringe of selection and I knew they were not going to take this lightly. They had a point to prove which, when I look back, helped steel me for the up-coming crunch games in France. The trouble was that Peter Dunn, the York hooker, took it far more seriously than expected. He came out throwing everything bar hand grenades. Each scrum was a mess with legs and arms all over the place. Each strike for the ball in the scrum became a matter of life and death, so much so the bloody referee sent us both off for persistent infringements in the scrum!

Bloody great. Here we were on a build up mission to lift the World Cup trophy and I was sat inside the York dressing room after just 30 minutes. I threw my boots all over the place in anger. The poor boot man tried to calm me down. What possessed the referee to lose the plot was anyone's guess, and he evidently wanted to show he was the boss. He did nothing to help me prepare for the Kangaroos. 'It's a bloody trial, not a cup final,' screamed one RFL official, 'we need game time for all the squad.' It was a farce. I watched the second half from the stands and I wondered if I'd blown it again. Our coach, the great Jim Challinor, quickly put my mind at rest and stated I would start the next game against Oldham.

The publicity of the York fiasco reached the ears of the Oldham players. This included another firebrand number nine called Clarke. 'Here we go again,' I thought. 'Another night to prove your worth.' It was a rough, tough affair which certainly beefed us up and lifted our intensity. No longer did the lads feel it was going to be an easy trial match. It wasn't either, and we even lost the game! My open side prop, Terry Clawson, cracked a smile and giggled after just the third scrum and said, 'Quite hot isn't it?' It wasn't, it was freezing cold but I knew what he meant and I also knew here was a man who wouldn't be bailing out when things got rough.

Sadly one of our squad, Ken Kelly, the Saints scrum-half, broke his arm in his club game the previous weekend. A young, raw kid from Wakefield called David Topliss replaced him. The more experienced players ribbed young Topliss incessantly saying that he'd only got the nod because he was the only one who could fit into Kelly's blazer and pants. I think he started to believe it. He shouldn't have, David had burst onto the scene with some outstanding performances and was soon to become one of the world's best players. I'm sure that the experience he gained on that World Cup tour was a major reason he became so good. Even at a tender age, he gained the respect of the best judges in the game, despite him not even getting a run on the subs bench. Just being with the squad was a great learning curve for him. It was the same for me.

Surprisingly, coach Challinor wasn't upset that we lost to

Oldham that night due to the many changes he made throughout to try out different combinations. He was confident and so were the more experienced players as we boarded the coach back to our Manchester hotel. We flew to Paris the following morning.

As usual throughout my entire playing career, I was shattered after the match. I had a couple of drinks and went to bed. This amused some of the squad who 'snuck' out to a nightclub in the city. Frankly I was too knackered to join them. All I wanted to do was to get some rest, board the plane and start some serious training. We only had a week to get things working in unison before the first game.

On the flight I sat next to John Walsh. He was a remarkably gifted centre who stunned me by completing *The Times* crossword well before we started our descent into Paris. I had seen *The Times* before of course but it usually contained fish and chips.

We changed planes at Paris and had plenty of time to eat lunch. We all ordered steak and we all sent it back when it arrived virtually raw. Minutes later, we sent it back again, much to the disgust of the waiter. On the third attempt, we finally ate it but the look on manager Bill Fallowfield's face indicated he may have to find a fish and chip shop on the south coast of France.

The league press flew with us. John Robinson from *The People* newspaper sat at my side. He was great with the team. And he was the only press guy who used his expense account to buy the lads a drink throughout the entire tour. It must have been a bit unsettling for some of the press guys who had bagged the selection of certain players in the squad, including myself. They suggested we were well below top class. Without a doubt, some great players were missing. Frank Myler, Malcolm Reilly, Roger Millward, Cliff Watson and Tommy Bishop were just a few who had either gone to play in Australia or were injured. Subsequently the press boys gave us little chance against the might of the Aussies who had rebuilt a great side after their Ashes loss to our Great Britain side in 1970. Despite this we were really motivated, lifted by tales of the 1954 side. They, like us, had gone to France with a side lacking their top stars and yet went on to win the trophy against all the odds. We also fired each other up; Clive Sullivan was amazing. His energy was infectious. He often called for extra training runs and ensured we ran past the hotel where the Australians were staying. It was a great ploy as the Aussies had been training in France for nearly three weeks. They defeated New Zealand the week before which confirmed their favourite status. They were walking through the town like peacocks on heat.

The first night nearly undid everything. We'd trained hard and the manager allowed us the first night off to shake off the flight and relax. Sadly John Walsh took the liberty of forgetting the word 'few'. He returned to the hotel drunk as a skunk and walked over to the RFL officials in the lounge bar. A few choice words on the lines of 'You're just Eddie Waring's puppet,' to boss Bill Fallowfield did little to smooth the way, and made John a candidate for the 'Prat of the Year' award.

The RFL officials were furious and wanted to send him home on the next plane. Walsh was a great player and we didn't want to lose him. We knew sending him back home would not help our team spirit or confidence. Once again Clive showed tremendous leadership by calming things down and personally offering his assurance to Bill Fallowfield that no further outbursts of this nature would occur. John publicly apologised to all the players and officials, and we pushed the incident to one side and forgot it. I was also impressed with the press guys who witnessed his antics and yet never filed any copy over the incident. I dread to think what would happen today. To be fair to John, he didn't do anything stupid in public. Bill Fallowfield went up in my estimation by accepting the apology. To be honest, the incident did have a positive outcome as it seemed to make a closer bond in the team. We were lucky the incident happened at the start of the tournament. We then all kept our off field activities very discreet. After John's outburst we made sure that if we wanted a drink, when we returned to the hotel we went via the fire escape and not via the front door.

The team spirit in the Great Britain camp was amazing. We seemed to be forever singing a song called *Mardi Gras* with George Nichols' broad Liverpool accent leading the way. Irrespective of the time of day, he just wanted to sing all the time and even threw in the odd, *In my Liverpool Home* from time to time, which informed me that Liverpool really had two cathedrals and one to spare.

All in all we enjoyed our underdogs' tag, but we were deadly serious about winning. What better way to start than by beating hot favourites Australia. The day before our clash with the Kangaroos, a bunch of Aussie fans stopped us in the street. The fans were actually wearing green and gold shirts, something we found weird. Of course now nearly all fans walk the streets sporting their team colours. Way back in the 1970s this was unusual to say the least. These fans proceeded (in good humour) to inform us about the size and strength of their beloved national side. We left them laughing over the fact they'd tried to convince us that all their players had ribs of steel and hands as big as cornflake packets. When we came out to face the Australians the following day, we soon found out these comments were true rather than humorous. The team was bloody huge.

Again I was a nervous wreck before the game. I visited the toilet at least a dozen times. Then I turned around in horror to see Terry Clawson with a cigarette in his mouth! Coach Challinor calmly suggested it would a good idea to stub it out because we kicked off in less than 10 minutes! The 'Claw' was the calmest man I have ever seen on or off the playing field. Nothing bothered him. He was a real 'Mr Cool' with class and a sarcastic, witty tongue to match. I had been ready for over 45 minutes, strapped up, boots on and ready to rumble. Clawson was still walking about the dressing room in his jock strap when the call for us to walk out cut the air.

Clive led us out and we all followed in the true Great British tradition of one, two, three and so on. We all left in regulation style and were surprised to be stopped by an official. He waited for Australia to join us in the tunnel. There we stood side by side, trying not to look at each other. I glimpsed the giant frames of John O'Neil and Bob O'Reilly. I could see Graeme Langlands at the head of the line. One guy confused me. I'd never seen him before and he stood well over six feet. He was built like a brick shit house and I swear blind he had hands ... the size of cornflake packets! I nudged Clawson, who at number eight was just in front of me, 'Claw, who the hell's that guy?'

Clawson glanced at the big brute. At this time he turned his back to us and displayed a number five on his back. 'Christ he's a winger,' I murmured!

'Bloody hell,' said the Claw, 'What are the forwards going to be like?'

The number five was of course Mark Harris from Eastern Suburbs. He was, and still is, one of the ugliest men I've ever met. His nose is living proof that when he went on one of his block busting runs he didn't always fend players off with his hands. His nose was like a kid's piece of Play Dough stuck on his face.

Finally we stood in line for the national anthems. First came a rousing rendition of the host nation's anthem, followed quickly by *God Save The Queen* which even to this day leaves me with a lump in my throat. Hearing it on this momentous occasion was no exception. I was pleased to run away to my position ready for the kick off as I was shaking like a leaf. Again I was surprised to see Terry walking slowly away from the band looking confused.

'A bit rude that,' said the Claw as he finally took up his position.

'What?'

My Mum and Dad, Alice and Albert.

Auntie Mary and Mum.

Aged six, I could always tie a good knot.

Me with my brother Derek, wearing a suit that came in the post.

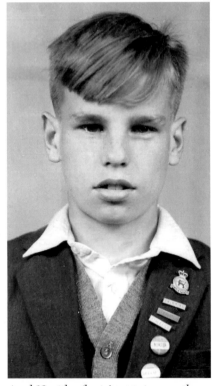

Aged 13 with a 'basin' cut to impress the girls.

On holiday at Butlins. This wouldn't be the last time I worked with a dummy!

Dad had a great voice and a moustache to excite the ladies.

Meeting the Duke of Gloucester, St James Palace 1964, presenting a goodwill message on behalf of the Yorkshire Federation of Boys Clubs.

Receiving County Championship medals with Nigel Stephenson and Alan Bates.

Aged 19, looking through my huge Jazz collection.

The 'Master Plumber'.

Voted Dewsbury Player of the year in 1969.   *On the run with no teeth!*

Receiving my Yorkshire Cap from Mick Lumb and Roy Harter.

Lilleshall Coaching Academy 1971. I'm on the middle row, second from the right.

My first try for Great Britain against France at Odsal in 1972.

Getting set for a scrum against Wigan at Crown Flatt.

Training for the 1972 World Cup at Headingley. Left to right: Phil Lowe, me, Clive Sullivan, David Redfearn.

The GB team arrive at Paris Charles de Gaulle for the 1972 World Cup.

Coach Tommy Smales preparing us for the 1973 Championship Final.

'They never played *Waltzing Matilda*.'

'Silly sod, *God Save the Queen* is their anthem too.'

When the match kicked off, the Aussies went berserk in the opening scrum. It just exploded with fists flying all over the shop. It was like a bomb going off with low flying aircraft everywhere. I didn't take French at school, and it was obvious to all that the French referee hadn't taken up English either which allowed the fracas to last a while and set the scene for an ugly match for the full 80 minutes. We knew that if we could master their forwards, we had a chance. We also needed to ensure we never gave Bobby Fulton space to move. Fulton was magic, we all knew it. He was the big star in Australia earning heaps of money both on and off the field. In fact, he was the first real superstar of the modern game. I played against Fulton a few years before when he came back to play for his town of birth, Warrington. Back then he was just a young, raw kid sent over by the Aussie club Manly to gain some experience. Our Dewsbury coach at the time was David Cox who made it quite clear before kick off that if we belted the young Aussie early doors he'd just freeze. 'He'll shit himself,' I think was the final comment before we went out to kick off.

By half time the young Mr Fulton had scored a hat trick. Coach Cox was far from impressed, 'I thought I told you to give it to him. The kid's running riot!' It's one thing belting a young kid. But it's quite another thing trying to catch him. We just couldn't get near him, he was so good.

We kept a keen eye on Fulton and held our own with the pack. This gave scrum-half Steve Nash plenty of space to get the three-quarters moving. Sullivan and Atkinson, the wingers, created plenty of chances. In fact John Atkinson's try in the left-hand corner created one of the funniest passages of rugby league farce I've ever seen. Atkinson dived in for the try, got up to celebrate, raised his arm in triumph and then got stiff armed with such power it not only nearly knocked his head off it forced him over the fence into the crowd. The culprit was a delightful chap called John Elford, a man noted for his ability to knock people down for fun. But this was no laughing matter, Atkinson could have been seriously injured such was the ferocity of the blow. The all-in brawl lasted quite a while. Officials ran all over the place in an attempt to calm things down. Terry Clawson decided to release his grip on Elford's throat in time to attempt the conversion. He kicked the ball sweetly over the cross bar with a huge grin on his face which put us in the lead and we never looked back.

Aussie skipper Graeme Langlands brought the ball back for the kick off, placed the ball on the spot and stepped back. Every time he attempted the kick off, the French referee, Claude Tissiere, stood over the ball and pushed him away. Langlands obviously hadn't learnt French at school either and screamed at the official to get out of the way so he could restart the match. The air was blue. After a few minutes both sides gathered at the kick off spot to try and work out this problem.

An interpreter was called for but the chaos continued and whilst broken English was being offered to Langlands and his team, Terry Clawson approached skipper Clive Sullivan and suggested, 'I think he's giving us a penalty.'

'What for?' I asked.

'I don't know but he keeps pointing to their sticks so I'll grab the ball and kick for goal.' To everyone's amazement, the referee nodded his head and started to push the Australians back to the 10 yards line....Great Britain was awarded a penalty. Terry didn't argue and kicked the two pointer from the half way line.

Imagine what the Aussies said at this point. The referee raised his arm, blew the whistle to indicate the penalty was successful and then ran to the scoreboard end. He shouted to the bloke holding the numbers that Great Britain had indeed scored another two points. Referee Tissiere had just created the seven point try! It took another 18 months before the rule was officially brought into the game. From that point on, the Aussies were more concerned with trying to knock our heads off than playing open rugby which played into our hands as we kept breaking out wide, and even I sneaked over for a try.

There had been plenty of fun and games but we were the only ones laughing. Sadly after the match many of the Aussies wouldn't shake hands and Langlands decided to spit at me instead! They ended the game rattled and we ended up pissed. The French hosts were just as pleased with the result as we were. Australia's loss gave France a better chance to reach the final. As a result, they sent taxis to the hotel and took us to a 'special' restaurant to celebrate. It was special all right. The tarts at the bar left us in no doubt it was a brothel. I don't think I've seen as many ugly women in my life. Instead, we all decided to hit the drink. We joked about how the ladies might start to look more attractive as the night wore on. I'm sure a few of us would have got involved if it wasn't for one British journalist claiming he had grabbed what he thought was a women only to feel his wedding tackle! The 'she' was a 'he'. We all charged out of the establishment like a herd of elephants.

My roommate Steve Nash and I got lost and walked for half an hour trying to get back to our hotel. We had little success and finally flagging down what we thought was a taxi. It turned out to be the police who, to their credit, drove us back to safety. I've always enjoyed going back to the South of France ever since. They are nice people and so different from those snobby upstarts in Paris.

Our next match was against the French in Grenoble. If it hadn't been for Phil Lowe we would have lost. He played a blinder as we were stung by some weird refereeing from a guy called Francois Gril. He tried his best to give his country the edge. At one scrum the French half-back didn't even put the ball in the scrum. He threw it directly to his centre standing out wide! To be fair, the French team played with plenty of guts and effort. French rugby league players are different to most. If things are going well they can play some outstanding rugby. Yet when things go against them, they lose control and revert to kicking, spitting and shouting abuse at even their own players. To give some idea of the lengths they would go to, we were told that Adidas wanted to shower us with new boots, track suits and polo shirts. One of their representatives took us on a walk that they said was just a few hundred yards away. As it was the day before the game, we decided it would be alright. We didn't bother using the coach to drive us there. The walk would do us good. It was only after about three miles that we suspected we had been tricked. We threatened the bloke to take us there quickly or he would come off worse for wear. We then phoned to ensure the coach drove us back!

It was my first insight into sponsorship and I couldn't believe the amount they gave us. We were given heaps of clothing. The coach was full to bursting when we returned to the hotel. Most of the French players were used to such gifts and had also been supported financially by a big sponsor. This enabled them to prevent union clubs from snaring the best league talent. It was hard to keep hold of a good player in rugby league when rugby union was openly paying their 15-a-side players huge amounts of money. They just laughed at the so-called amateur tag that other countries covered up. Many a star league player has been transferred to union in a blaze of publicity with full details of their financial reward made public. Yet the stuffy union officials from the rest of the world continued to live the myth that their players never received any payment. This is still a huge problem for rugby league in France especially now the barriers are down between the two codes. Union has so much cash to throw around that it's always a struggle for France to field a team at international league level. At least we can sleep easy in the knowledge that the gin and tonic brigade is paying tax for a change. But I wonder what happened to the factory that produced brown paper bags?

The French were devastated at losing the game. They worked hard and fully expected to beat us by hook or by crook. We were confused by most of the French antics of slowing things down, throwing the ball away and arguing with officials. The scrums were a farce and it was only the blockbusting style from Lowe that swung the game our way. To be fair to the French they tackled like demons and obviously were on a huge bonus. We struggled in the stop-go game and were somewhat relieved to hear the final whistle and take the match 13–4.

Two wins on the trot left us confident as we drove to the little town of Pau. The town is steeped in history, castles and vineyards. I was in my element as I started to get a taste for the local wine. Again the authorities rolled out the red carpet with tours of the local sights. We even had time to visit Lourdes and the shrine of the Virgin Mary, which would impress even the most ardent non-believer. Sadly it was spoilt for me by the commercialism of the town. Nearly every shop sold holy water in different size plastic bottles and trinkets that made Blackpool souvenir shops look classy.

We also encountered our first serious injury on the tour. This was when stand-off Denis O'Neil suffered a bad knee problem at training. The press chased a story that he had fallen off a pyramid of chairs in some bar room antics. Whatever the story, it was a blow. O'Neil was a sad loss as he was a key player. His combination with Steve Nash was outstanding in the opening two matches.

The selectors decided against giving young Topliss a chance in our quest for the trophy. Instead they launched Leeds utility player John Holmes into the fray. John was a classic three-quarter. He had good balance, a strong kicking game and the ability to glide past the defence with ease. We were more than happy with his record breaking effort against New Zealand. His 10 goals and two tries (26 points) were a world record at the time and ensured we won easily. I nipped over for yet another try before I was rested late in the game.

That win ensured we were in the World Cup Final with only the France versus Australia match to decide who we would play. It also took the pressure off us to find a new stand off if Dennis O'Neil didn't recover in time. It left coach

Challinor with a huge headache if O'Neil was declared fit. It was going to be hard to leave out a guy who had scored two great tries and kicked 10 goals! The win also helped me erase my memories of my nightmare debut at Castleford when the Kiwis clinched the series. This time the Kiwis were flying all right ... straight back home.

The following weekend we drove to Toulouse to watch the French play Australia in front of a partisan home crowd. They were confident they could upset the green and gold to reach the final as they had done in 1954. English referee Mick Naughton (sadly not with us anymore) was in charge of that game and found himself embroiled in yet another fiasco in the tournament. Australia came out all fired up, yet the French held the early onslaught and started to play with confidence. For a while, we felt there could be a shock on the cards. Australia had been given plenty of stick in their press who were calling for coach Harry Bath's head. The Sydney press suggested Harry couldn't control the team. Because the team went to France three weeks before the tournament started, the fans down under expected more from the Kangaroos.

After 20 minutes, Australia made the breakthrough they had been searching for. Brannigan split the defence to serve winger Harris with a clear run to the line. Whilst Harris raced under the sticks, the French touch judge came onto the field with flag raised. Naughton was bemused and through yet anther interpreter, the flagman called a forward pass.

'He can't call a forward pass, that's my job.' The touch judge then changed his mind, said he'd made a mistake and that Harris had put a foot in touch.

'He was nowhere near the touch line,' blurted a by now frustrated Mick Naughton.

This was explained to the flag waver who stood his ground before pushing his flag into the pitch and starting to walk off in disgust. He was persuaded to come back and poor Mick had no option than to disallow the try. Australia was furious.

After the fiasco in Perpignan it looked like the entire team were about to leave the field in protest.

Talk about poking a man in the eye. The Australians played like men possessed and blasted the home side away in all departments. Some of the tackling was cruel and the standard of football unbelievable with Fulton, Langlands and the rest running riot.

We knew the Aussies would seek revenge and would be one hell of a side to beat in the final.

8

ARE YOU THE BLOKES THAT WON A CUP IN FRANCE?

Making that first final in my professional career was something I never forgot. When the final happened to be the World Cup it added that little bit of charisma. Irrespective of what sport someone plays, be it draughts or tiddley-winks, when the potential outcome of a game will mean that they can boast they're the world champion, it makes them feel more pressure. The RFL thought so too because they decided after watching the France-Australia clash, that we should fly back home and spend a couple of days with our families. We should then fly back to France three days before the final in Lyon.

I don't know if this was a cost cutting exercise to save on hotel bills and food, but I think it was a master stroke because suddenly we were back sleeping in our own beds. It sort of kept our feet on the ground. We didn't get much publicity apart from in the northern press. It wasn't as though we'd come back home in a blaze of glory, more like we'd slipped back into Manchester, jumped on a bus back home, then gone to buy the bread and the milk and popped into our local for a couple of pints! The spin doctors of today would call it 'low key', which it was. Yet no spin doctor could feel or describe how the inside of my guts felt. They were churning with anticipation, excitement and fear.

As I've explained earlier I'm far from Mr Cool when it comes to preparation for games. My routine was to visit the toilet umpteen times complete with dry retching. This time I started to get the symptoms with five days to go. I tried to put a brave face on it but underneath I was a nervous wreck. We had beaten the Aussies, France and New Zealand and were at the top of the table with maximum points. We all knew the Aussies would be tougher to beat this time around. The newspapers down under were hammering the Aussies and we knew they would be determined to prove a lot of people wrong. I felt our build up for the game was top class. Jim Challinor was a fine coach. He was calm and collected and made us work hard to ensure we operated as a unit. We also knew what bad press could do to help motivate players, 'Remember,' he would say, 'Our own media didn't give us a chance either.' Meanwhile the Sydney press especially went to town saying the Kangaroos were letting the country down. We also knew that most of the supporters from down under had teased us in France by saying our win was a one off and that Australia didn't play well in that first encounter. They thought that the Kangaroos would correct this blip in the final.

The one thing about the Aussies is that they are a confident mob. I liked their attitude and easy style but our team was also determined to ensure our own press never had the chance to say we were a flash in the pan.

In the four weeks we'd spent in France, I roomed with scrum-half Steve Nash. This was a smart ploy by Jim Challinor to ensure we got to know each other. It helped both of us on the field, particularly around the scrum. Nash was a magical player. He was tough, tackled like a demon and ran himself into the ground each game. He was a non-stop worker with guile and brains to match, although he wasn't using either when I caught him soaking his feet in the bidet! Being a plumber, I knew exactly which part of the anatomy he was supposed to wash in the damn thing. I just smiled and let him enjoy the moment. Living in the same room with a bloke for lengthy periods can be challenging. Not Steve though, he was a bundle of fun and always smiling. He had a strange fashion sense though. He always dressed in black when he went out. Even his underpants were black!

People often talk these days about psychology playing a big part in modern sport. However back then, Jim Challinor wasn't without some sharp ideas to get the best out of the team. On returning to France, the team management put me into a large room with the other front rowers, David Jeans and Terry Clawson. This helped me as Jim knew how nervous I became in the build up to games. It was a master stroke. Clawson was so laid back I swear he slept for most of the day and David was just as easy going. Front row forwards are a breed apart. In my opinion forwards have to be mad to play up front. It's not an easy way to make a living when forwards have their brains bashed out each week. But both Jeans and Clawson put me at ease.

The team trained well. We awoke on the morning of the match at ease and full of confidence. Sadly, as so often is the case with the administrators of our game, the French decided to use the World Cup to lift the country's awareness of the 13-a-side code, 'Rugby a treize'. This ploy failed badly and less than 10,000 people turned up to watch the final played at the Stade de Garland. It was an impressive soccer stadium but when we walked out all we could see were empty seats, not a soul in view. It was only when we turned around for the national anthems that we saw all the tickets had been sold for just one stand.

If you ever get chance to watch the video of the game, there looks to be nobody there. All the viewer can see is a mass of concrete. This is because the cameras were positioned in the main stand. It was a huge gamble by the French but because their team didn't make the final nobody in this major football playing area bothered to turn up. Not that it mattered to us. We had our minds on other things.

Before we left the dressing room I wandered over to Steve Nash to discuss last minute instructions of how I wanted the ball put in the scrum. Unfortunately, I could see he was in considerable pain. This wasn't surprising when he dropped his shorts to display three of the hugest boils I've ever seen.

'The doctor's going to lance them in a minute and that should make me feel better,' he said.

Christ, it was ugly. How he played is beyond belief. Anyone who has had the displeasure of a boil will know the surrounding area feels like they have been branded with a hot iron. Steve had three of these buggers. I didn't know how to strap a man's backside until that day. I knew how legs, arms, ankles and fingers were strapped, but I soon to found out as the medic somehow created a figure eight that left Nashy looking like a Sumo wrestler.

Not once during the entire match did Nashy complain, including throughout the 20 minute's extra time. We could all see the blood trickling down onto his legs. He was one tough cookie that day and his courage lifted us all.

We also knew that Dave Valentine, the successful captain of Great Britain's 1954 World Cup winning team was attending the game. Coach Challinor made it clear that he led a team of 'no hopers' to victory. He also told us that this was the same stadium where Great Britain beat Australia in 1954 in the first game of the series. Australia was defending its world crown after beating Great Britain in the blood bath final at Headingley two years before.

Despite us beating them five weeks earlier they were odds on favourites to retain the trophy. Like most finals it wasn't a classic. Both sides were so intent on snuffing out the opposition there was little chance for open play. Tension and nerves affected everyone yet the game was electric throughout. The Aussies scored first when John O'Niell went in mid-way through the first half with a great run into the corner from 30 yards out. Ray Branighan converted the try from out wide. Australia then started to open out and test our defence time and time again while we struggled to get into their half.

At 5–0 down and close to half time we hung on in defence only for Australia's Mark Harris to have the ball dislodged by a huge tackle from George Nicholls. It proved to be the moment we were looking for. Sullivan sprinted clear and raced 80 yards down the touchline to score in the corner, just beating an amazing feat of cover defence from prop forward John O'Neill. O'Neill prevented our skipper from turning towards the posts to give Clawson an easy conversion. Not that it mattered as the 'Claw' banged it over from the touchline to send us in level at the break. Without that quick thinking from Sullivan we may have folded against the pressure Australia applied. It would have probably finished us off late into that first 40 minutes if a little bit of luck hadn't gone our way when scrum-half Dennis Ward kicked high into the corner from 35 yards out. From nowhere, full-back Graeme Langlands dived full stretch over the line and caught the ball in mid air. It was an incredible sight. It should have been a try. Later, video evidence proved Langlands was on side and the freak try should have counted. If Sky TV had been around in those days we would have lost the World Cup. It was a freakish effort, beyond belief and, sadly for the Aussies, the French referee Mr G. Jameau thought it incredible also. He disallowed the try claiming the Aussie skipper had been off side and in front of the kicker. The Kangaroos went crackers and it took quite a few of his own side to restrain Langlands who not for the first time in this tournament wanted to rip an officials head off. I often smile over the fact 13 players were screaming what was probably one of the few words we all knew in French. 'Non!' whilst the other 13 players were shouting 'Oui!'

After the game, the referee explained that no man could run that fast. Unfortunately for Langlands he should have got the try which would probably have left us too much to do.

Soon after the restart for the second half, Lady Luck returned to the green and golds. A neat passing move sent big prop Artie Beetson over out wide. As he turned to place the ball nearer the sticks, I came from the back and dislodged the ball only for it to drop straight back down into his arms for him to score.

At 10–5 and with just seven minutes remaining, Sullivan came running inside on a weaving mission to try and pull the defence out of position. His angled run and off-load to Brian Lockwood persuaded the cover defence to go for the big Castleford forward. I knew Brian's game inside out. He was one of the best off-loaders around and I screamed for the inside pass. He stepped and dummied to pass out wide then swung the ball back into my hands. The rest was history. I'd crossed the line for the most important try of my career. I was beside myself and yelled and screamed. The joy was overwhelming and I was happy as a pig in shit. The joy soon passed as skipper Sullivan wanted to know why I hadn't gone around under the posts when I should have. I realised straight away why, the soccer markings were still visible in the in goal area, and I'd panicked and got the ball down as quick as possible. The try was 20 yards out from the nearest post and I was horrified to think we could miss the conversion that would tie up the game.

'Don't worry, I won't miss,' came the comforting voice of Clawson. True to his words, he didn't.

Both sides attempted drop goals at either end in the final five minutes but, to no avail and we went into extra time. The players on both sides could hardly walk. We were all shattered. It was the longest 20 minutes of my life. We knew before the kick off that a draw would be enough for us to lift the trophy. We kept shouting to each other about keeping our defence solid and not be tempted to run out of a solid straight line. It worked. We held on and danced with glee when the whistle blew. The faces of the opposition will stay with me for life. They were stunned.

Sadly a couple of the Aussie's refused to shake hands. One player spat at me and even Steve Nash, who had exchanged his shirt, was requested to exchange it back by the Aussie dressing room. We went wild in the dressing room as you can imagine. Yet we soon quietened down when witnessing one of the most sporting gestures I've ever seen. Aussie coach Harry Bath played with our coach Jim Challinor for many successful years at Warrington in the 1950s. The respect each man had for each other was amazing. He must have swallowed lot of pride to enter our dressing room and congratulate all of us. He was a truly great man. Little did I know that within a few months I would befriend him in Australia.

I don't know how many times we filled up the trophy back at the hotel but I never saw it empty. It did disappear for quite some time as a couple of the blokes thought it a good idea to take it down the road to where the Kangaroos were staying. Evidently a couple of our blokes added something extra to the beer that day and I don't think it was vodka!

We boarded the plane the following day still drunk on a mixture of beer and emotion. We wondered what sort of reception we'd get when we arrived back home. Unfortunately the answer was that we got no reception. Our flight landed at East Midlands airport where only one local photographer greeted us. He was a local freelancer who on seeing a mass of blazers come out of customs had to ask, 'I'm sorry but are you that mob that's won a cup in France?' A couple of photos later, we boarded the coach back up north to reality. We didn't expect a ticker tape parade but we were left thinking that nobody knew who we were and that nobody cared that we had won the World Cup. I smile when I think what happened when England won the Rugby Union World Cup in 2003. All the squad, including the baggage man, got a gong for their efforts. We were like strangers going into a foreign country. The BBC televised the game but we wondered if anyone was watching out there. Little did I know that 12,000 miles away one club watched the game and they dramatically changed my life.

Amazingly we didn't even get a winners' medal that day. It took the RFL nearly 30 years to eventually present our squad with a medal each. This was after I suggested it would be a fitting tribute to those long ago heroes and would also be a build up to the 2000 World Cup. After discussion with John Huxley from the RFL and the World Cup sponsors' Lincoln we finally got our just reward. We did receive a plaque from the RFL as a memento of that great day and we were paid £50 for our efforts. It arrived by post a few weeks after the final in Lyon with a note of thanks for our great win. It also informed us that they had kindly taken £10 out of the bonus to pay for the plaque! What more could we expect for being World Champions.

9

IF AT FIRST YOU DON'T SUCCEED...

The 1972-1973 season had already started back in England when we returned from the World Cup and Dewsbury had kicked off quite strongly. Confidence was high and so was I but I had to erase my World Cup glory very quickly. This was no time to ponder past exploits. It wasn't just about me and I realized what an advantage it had been to have a group of men at my club who worked hard to offer me the chance to be selected in that World Cup squad. I couldn't have done it without the entire Dewsbury team playing well and ensuring the selectors took notice of me. I also knew that a poor season in the build up to that World Cup could have left me struggling.

I enjoyed the moment when Clive Sullivan picked up the trophy. But deep down my thoughts were with my team mates back home. I wanted more success and realized that my club also wanted a taste of glory. I hoped that my good fortune would prove to all at the club that we were a great outfit and that international selection was on offer not to just me but to the rest of the side. In the long run this proved correct, for both the Bates brothers, Alan and John, went on the Great Britain Lions tour of 1974. Their success was followed shortly by Jeff Grayshon who went on to play for his country many times in a long, illustrious career and Harry Beverley and Nigel Stephenson who were selected for England. Unsurprisingly I was confident at our prospects of snaring a club trophy. I wondered if this would be the year.

A good run in the early season Yorkshire Cup took us to the final against mighty Leeds, the League Champions the previous year. The venue was Odsal Stadium and we got thrashed! Leeds legends Atkinson, Holmes, Hynes, Batten and company took Dewsbury to the cleaners. We were devastated over our poor showing. Nobody on our side performed. We were like rabbits stunned by car headlights as the well oiled champions breezed through at a canter. At least we got a medal. It was a losers' medal granted, but nobody on the team wanted to even open the box to see what it looked like. Our return trip on the coach to Dewsbury was dismal.

The defeat knocked our confidence for a while. Coach Tommy Smales decided to make a few changes including giving me the captaincy. Alan Bates, the scrum-half made it clear for quite some time that he was uncomfortable with the job and wanted to play his normal game. With my World Cup experience behind me, Tommy thought it would do me and the team good. He was proved to be right. We started to shake off the slump. Then suddenly we were firing again. Not that we had lost any team spirit through our bad spell. Quite the opposite, and to be fair we all knew what had to be done. It didn't matter who was nominated as skipper. I was proud to be skipper and felt it was a good move as I was playing the best football of my career.

The cup loss to Leeds helped us dig deep. Not many teams came to Crown Flatt and won in those days. It was also the season when Dewsbury was the elected team to play in the Lancashire section of the League table. This meant we played all Lancashire clubs twice and Yorkshire clubs just once. Many pundits often suggested it was the harder of the two sections. To be honest, having to play the likes of St Helens, Wigan, Widnes, Oldham and Warrington gave us vital mental strength. We also had a great run in the Challenge Cup competition and found ourselves 80 minutes away from reaching Wembley. We were drawn against

Bradford Northern in the semi final at Headingley. For the first time Dewsbury went into the game as favourites. Poor Bradford was going through a bad period languishing in the bottom half of the table.

Wembley fever hit the town again. Could we surpass the 1929 side who played and lost to Wigan in the first final at Wembley? We felt we could. However, we still remembered two recent failures at Swinton seven and eight years ago. We also remembered our poor showing against Leeds in the Yorkshire Cup final and trained hard and prepared well. Yet the semi final curse wouldn't go away. Bradford fully deserved its shock win.

We shouldn't have taken anything for granted. Sadly a couple of team mates decided to have more than a few beers two nights before the game. I don't use this as an excuse; I'm just stating a fact. When the players admitted it days after the semi final loss they were in tears. Full credit to Bradford, they came out and played rough, tough tactics whilst we went out like baby lambs. We knew we could beat them if we played anywhere near our form and displayed the set moves that had the rugby world buzzing. Unfortunately teams have to know when to start these tactics. Semi finals aren't about fancy stuff. These games are about knocking the opposition's confidence. That's what Bradford Northern did. They hit us with the kitchen sink. We threw nothing more dangerous than bloody washing up liquid. From the kick off, Bernard Watson, a former Leeds star and an experienced campaigner in cup ties set the ball rolling, or should I say set Nigel Stephenson's eyes rolling. Watson hit him with a ball and all tackle in the first minute that left our star centre out like a light. I mistakenly thought Nigel was kidding and I urged him to get up and not show the tackle had made its mark. I can remember running to him and screaming for him to get up as though nothing had happened. I soon realized he was in Disneyland. We got the penalty but they got the ascendancy and never lost it.

Nigel was a key figure in our attack and could kick goals

from all over the park. He was a fine, crafty player. After that initial clash he never looked himself and neither did the rest of the team. We looked like stunned rabbits again. The spark we had shown all season just wasn't there. Again we struggled when the pressure was on and were lucky not to be swamped in that first 40 minutes. Coach Smales tried gamely to lift us but I felt we were all chasing a lost cause. The writing was on the wall and we didn't show enough guts to try and wipe it off. I sneaked over for a try soon after the resumption and thought just maybe it would spark up the team. It did for a while until winger David Treasure crossed for his hat trick and sent Bradford back into the dressing rooms singing 'We're off to Wembley'. The glum faces in our dressing room indicated that the only bloody place we were going to was a nightclub in town. It was owned by one of the club's directors, Billy Mann. He had expected it to be a night of champagne. It was more likely to be a night of flat beer.

Tears streamed down some faces and other players just stared. We all felt we had 'failure' tattooed on our foreheads (it should have read 'duped' or 'stupid'). Tommy Smales was speechless and had to be persuaded to go back to Dewsbury with us. I couldn't blame him for wanting to be alone with his thoughts. We played badly and Tommy didn't deserve such an ending after all the time and effort he'd put into the build up. We had shit ourselves on the day and knew it. There was just one glimmer of hope, the playoffs that following week against Oldham at home.

We hardly did a thing at training the following Tuesday night. A gentle jog was about all we could muster. We weren't just hurting physically. It wasn't long before the rumours about the antics of our two drunken players leaked out! Both players apologized for spending more time socializing than preparing before the big game. We cleared the air and Tommy left no one in doubt that the playoffs for the championship were our last chance. We looked at each other and knew what plonkers we had been. I take nothing away from Bradford's performance. The team deserved to win and showed us how to win in tense semi finals. Looking back, the loss did us a huge favour. At the time we thought the club would continue to be dogged by our inability to complete the job in hand.

The playoffs loomed and the door was there. This time we wouldn't be politely knocking on the bloody thing, we wanted to rip it off its hinges. We hit Oldham with a whirlwind of moves that split their defence like an overripe melon. They couldn't handle us. We were confident that our concentration was back.

The league structure was so big it was impossible for teams to play each other twice. It was only fair to have a top 16 playoff. We finished eighth in the table which enabled us to have a home tie against Oldham. This proved a bonus. Many of our fans were still angry at losing out to Bradford in the semi final and so most of them turned up and cheered us to victory. Not many supporters 'bagged' us. A few supporters lost substantial wagers but I can only remember one person going into full hate mode and giving me plenty of abuse. I honestly wanted to kick seven bells out of him. I would like to think that my professional outlook and level head prevented me from doing so. Sadly the truth was that he was over six feet tall, had a face that only a mother could love and a pug nose that had seen many a boxing glove in its day. I decided diplomacy was a much better option!

It's hard to explain how players can be down one minute and then up with the stars the next. I sensed a good feeling in the side mainly due to the fact we were all honest about our feelings. A few harsh words had been exchanged between some players but it was quickly forgotten and we set about training like men possessed. We went into overdrive in perfecting our set moves.

As I mentioned earlier, our game plan included some weird names and I often wondered if we all understood them! One of those outrageous moves included our full-back, Adrian Rushton, charging into the three-quarter line so wide out that he was nearly in the crowd. Yet he would start his run up from the opposite corner to fool their defence. At the same time, I would use the forwards to run at different angles all around me at the play the ball. After throwing umpteen dummies, and at least two twirls I would throw out a speculative pass towards the touchline. It was without doubt the most bizarre ploy imaginable. To put it mildly the whole plan was crazy, plus it left me exposed to the best stiff arm in the business. Seconds count when plying a trade in amongst the big boys. Those likely lads got great pleasure from seeing the odd tooth fly out or hearing the tender crack of a jaw or cheek bone. With this move a good hiding was more than likely. Coach Smales thought the exercise was crackers too, yet decided it was so out of left field that it might just work against our next foe, Featherstone Rovers.

The boys from Post Office Road had achieved what we failed to do in getting to Wembley. To be fair to them, they had one eye on the twin towers when we arrived at their ground. We also knew that they would be keeping two of their key players, Steve Nash and hooker Keith Bridges, on the subs bench. We guessed that most of their players would perhaps hold back and not go into the tackles with the same bite as usual. Playing against the tiny mining village side was never an easy task. They had rugged forwards, crafty half-backs and willing workers for the full 80 minutes. So we set out to upset them early, take the lead and tighten the screw. Right from the kick off, we tackled like tigers. The first time we got the ball we called for 'that' move. I knew there were only two things that could happen. Either we scored or they put me in hospital! Thankfully, it worked. Don't ask me how it worked. Don't bother asking the rest of the team because they wouldn't know either, especially full-back Rushton who plucked the ball out of mid air and sailed over.

Featherstone looked stunned but not half as stunned as we were. As Nigel Stephenson kicked the conversion, we all looked at each other and grinned. 'It bloody well worked!'

was the cry.

The home side struggled to get into the game. They even sent out Nash and Bridges early in the hope of pegging us back. But it was our night. We were awesome. Well that's what one of the press guys wrote afterwards, 'A display of set moves that were a delight to watch, in this mood Dewsbury would have beaten anybody.' He was right, we would have. Little did anyone know in training 'that' move was practised no less than 10 times. On each occasion it had been a dismal failure. Yet Smales asked us to produce a rabbit out of the hat that not even Tommy Cooper would have attempted.

And so we were in the last four. We reached yet another semi final. We all knew our track record at the club when it came to a crunch game. Our trip to red hot favourites Warrington was going to test our nerves. The 'Wire' was under the magic of Alex Murphy as player-coach and his ruthless attitude and will to win rubbed off on his side. Murphy is without doubt one of the best players I have seen and could motivate those around him to run through brick walls. He was a ruthless leader and probably a pain to referee. Murphy had put together a team with a rugged pack and speed in the backs. This coupled with his guile and kicking game left them confident about reaching the final. It turned out to be one of the most nerve racking games of my life. We had snapped up a former Welsh Rugby Union A winger called Greg Ashcroft who had speed to burn but, would have starved if he had to make a living out of being a juggler. Greg was the first to admit his handling wasn't the best. When he did catch the ball he was dynamite. These days, coaches pour over tapes of the opposition to find a weakness and although this game was before the advent of video tapes we didn't have to be Einstein's to work out Mr Ashcroft's Achilles heel. We knew Murphy had sent out scouts to watch our past few games and that his kicking game would be aimed at Greg's wing. This was confirmed before kick off when Murphy and I tossed the coin and he quietly suggested our Welsh Wizard would soon find out what a 'bomb' meant.

All that week at training, we had full-back Rushton playing virtually at the side of Ashcroft. They were so close they were like twins. But Ashcroft played the game of his life as Murphy rained bomb after bomb towards his wing. Somehow he took each kick with so much confidence onlookers would have thought he had buckets for hands. It was fascinating to think that 26 players watched the ball go skyward, and that all 26 held their breath wondering if Dewsbury or Warrington would collect the bomb when it came down. Yet time and again, the ball stuck to Greg's hands like shit to a blanket.

I had a quick word with Greg at half time and suggested he keep up the good work. He shocked me with his confident reply, 'Don't worry about me, you make sure the rest do their job.' The rest did their job and we held on by our fingers, or should I say Greg's fingers, to make it to our second final of the season. Murphy was far from amused that Greg had confounded everyone with his agility and eagerness to climb high and defuse each bomb. But he had the grace to congratulate us on our win and even suggested our team was the better side. This was high praise indeed. Greg was a hero. He didn't pay for a beer that night which confused the Welsh lad no end because since joining the club he had always joked that Yorkshire men were tight as a fish's backside. He's right; we are. But that night none of the team objected to digging deep into their pockets (albeit through gritted teeth).

Ultimately I believe the real difference with this win was that we used our tactics and brains. We played tough and concentrated on our defence. We took our chances early, never forced the ball and kept it tight because we knew Warrington expected us to come out with the fancy stuff. We displayed our set moves but we kept them to a minimum. At long last we'd got it right, and reached another final. It wouldn't be long before the result came through that Leeds had won the other semi final to set up a repeat of the early season Yorkshire Cup Final. We celebrated into the night but we didn't drink like there was no tomorrow, because this time there was! The week's build up would prove crucial and we had to overcome the psychological advantage that Leeds would carry into the game.

Each of our early training sessions ended with a good talk about where we had gone wrong before. We boosted each other's confidence so much that we just couldn't wait for Saturday's final to come. I arrived home on Tuesday night feeling a bit tight in the chest. This was nothing new as I was asthmatic. By Wednesday lunchtime the tightness turned worse. The doctor conformed bronchitis and ordered me to bed. He refused to let me train with the others. I was devastated. It was one of my biggest games of all time and I was in bed looking and feeling like a 70 year old. The doctor allowed me to run on the eve of the match to fine tune our set patterns. It was only a light workout and yet I still knew I wasn't 100 per cent. I took some more antibiotics, jumped into bed, crossed my fingers and dreamt of Odsal glory. Thankfully it was a bright sunny day, unlike the week's build up when it was damp and windy. The mere fact the sun was out cheered me up no end.

The old dressing rooms at Odsal were at the top of the stadium and like so many teams before, we had to walk down that famous track and then down the stand steps to reach the ground. It was a walk of at least 200 yards through the spectators. It was so steep that both sides didn't return to the dressing rooms at half time because by the time the team got there they had to come back again! Besides the walk was knackering anyway. The sanitary arrangements for half time were a problem. Both sides stood in front of the main stand in full view of the fans. A discreet blanket was wrapped around each player whilst he pissed on the grass.

In the dressing room, the look on each player's face indicated this was going to be our day. The odds were against us. Leeds was 10–1 on but a few of us took great delight in taking a couple of the local bookies, who thought Leeds were special, to the cleaners.

I started to feel good as we set off into the crowd and onto the winding goat track to the pitch. I turned to our physio, Jim Greenhall and passed him my teeth wrapped in my handkerchief.

'What the hell's this?' he asked.

'My teeth. We're going to win that trophy and I'm not lifting the bloody thing without my gnashers.'

Jim roared with laughter, shoved my teeth inside his tracksuit and followed us down into the arena. He could see from our actions that we were all very confident.

Leeds had a glut of star players. I was the only international in our team whereas the boys from Headingley had no less than 12 capped players in their 15-man squad!

The bookies had written us off despite our courageous showing at Warrington because the memory of the Yorkshire Cup loss still lingered in their minds. We reckoned the Leeds players would feel the same way and give us no chance. Yet full credit to coach Smales, his tactics paid off again. Unlike our game plan for Warrington, coach Smales pleaded for us to live the moment. 'Don't be tense, enjoy it, let's play our set moves, all of them and early too.' So we did. We pulled off one of the biggest upsets ever seen. It was certainly on a par with the Sheffield victory over Wigan at Wembley many years later. We had a ball with run-arounds, inside passes, angled running, cheeky little under and over passes and all with a will to win that was second to none. I scored two tries that day and won the Harry Sunderland Award for man of the match. Whilst I'm proud of winning such a prestigious honour, the simple fact is that it could have gone to any of the other players. It was a team effort that had the star Headingley outfit and defending champions gasping for air. Sadly the great player Alan Hardisty received his one and only red card from the referee for a stiff arm tackle on second rower John Bates. It was a reaction tackle that looked a lot worse than it was. John was running upright with his head held high as though his nose had just smelled some dog shit. When Alan's arm touched him, Mr Bates swung up and down like a pub sign in a strong wind. But the game was won well before that incident and all the Leeds fans, even to this day, confirm that view. I couldn't believe it. In the space of one season I was involved in winning a second piece of silverware. Not only was I part of the World Cup Champion team, I was also part of the British Rugby League Champion team.

When the whistle went for full time the players and fans danced with joy. The Dewsbury fans stormed the field in their hundreds. It was bedlam. Even the Leeds players had trouble getting near us to shake hands. But they did, a sign of a proud team that accepted with dignity the better team had won on the day.

The police were concerned that none of the team could get near the steps to receive the trophy. The fans were everywhere. Unfortunately, Jim Greenhall, the physio, was nowhere near. Whilst being pushed and escorted towards the presentation, I could see Jim a good 30 yards away waving my teeth in the air. I thought 'Shit, there's no chance he can get near me.' And so Mr Michael Stephenson, captain of Dewsbury walked up those steps and received the cup from Lord Derby with mouth firmly closed. I mumbled my thanks, kissed the trophy, and lifted it towards the fans. Not once did my lips part company until we hit the dressing room. Every photo taken that day shows me with my mouth tightly shut. Not only that, I knew the BBC was televising all this live and I wasn't prepared to flash my gums at anyone.

We finally caught the team coach back to Dewsbury expecting a few fans to greet us. Yet there were thousands in front of the town hall. All looked happy and pissed. We weren't far behind them in the drinking stakes. Lifting that trophy was sensational and it was even better to do it on the balcony of the town hall for the civic reception with my teeth in and a huge grin from ear to ear.

I know many players have won several trophies and teams like Wigan, Leeds, Bradford and St Helens have cornered the market for silverware for years. This was a local team, a bunch of hard workers who combined together and produced the goods. It was a proud moment for team and town. I made a quick speech thanking all the fans for their support, which was followed by a speech from club chairman Mick Lumb. He told the supporters that this was going to be the start of something big and that Dewsbury was now going to build for the future and become a major force in the league again. Little did I know I wouldn't become part of that plan. I'd played my last game for my hometown team.

10

THE COMMITTEE WANT TO TALK TO YOU

It was a few weeks later when I finally went back to work after shaking off chest problems. It was a blessing as my £100 win money (which we all got for becoming champions) was dwindling away. I needed to earn a crust. Don't get me wrong. In those days £100 was a huge earner. The gloss was taken off it when it became known Leeds players were paid £110 for losing!

We had become the champion club. We knew things would have to improve if we were to stay at the top. The committee suggested they would be looking to strengthen the side. With the added revenue from the cup win, we started training for the 1973–1974 season in good spirits.

On my second week back at work I was in Harrogate demolishing the inside of a huge house that was being turned into flats. We had just taken out the staircase when through the dust I made out a bloke standing amongst the rubble, shouting out my name. I soon recognised the strong Aussie accent and replied he was looking at the man in question. I scampered down the ladder to confront a Mr Wally Ward from the Penrith Panthers.

'G'day mate. Any chance we can talk?'

'Sure. What about?'

'It's a bit dusty in here. Can you come back to our hotel?'

And so I did. In my dirty clothes and steel toe capped boots, I sat in the Dragonara Hotel in the centre of Leeds eating a juicy steak and washing it down with a nice drop of white wine. I just hoped the Panthers were picking up the tab.

I knew that a few Aussie clubs had representatives in England scouting for new recruits. Only two days earlier, Penrith had equalled the world record transfer fee of £15,000 in buying Wigan's second row forward Bill Ashurst. The publicity was enormous and all clubs started to worry that their star players were going to be targeted.

Wally Ward was the president of the Panthers club. Along with business manager Bruce Wellesden, he started to explain what was on offer: house, swimming pool, flights, car and even a job with a guaranteed hefty wage. It went on and on. My head was swimming and I was flattered they had taken time to offer me such a wonderful opportunity. I was quick to stop them going any further by saying they were wasting their time. Dewsbury had already informed me they would never sell me. The team was in the process of building a better and bigger squad to retain the trophy we had won a few weeks earlier.

'We have spoken to them already and they say the same thing, but money talks all languages,' Wally said.

He was right and they were both talking a language that soon after I learnt quickly. I thanked them for their time and explained it was nice to be wanted but the club would never sell me.

'We don't just want you to go to Australia as a player, we're looking to the future and hope your skills and profile will help our area and the club. This is a long term thing. We want you the player, the captain and eventually the coach. We finished last in the competition last season despite having a great junior development in our area. We are still newcomers in the Sydney competition yet we want to be at the top one day, and we know you can help us get there.'

It was devastating stuff. Not many people would give a thought about going from a champion-winning side in England to join the wooden spoon team in Australia. I asked them to give me time to think it over and discuss it with my wife. I parted with them on good terms and as they picked up the bill, I left them with some extra knowledge that stunned them somewhat, 'I Just better warn you my father-in-law is a Dewsbury Director, and I can't see him wanting to see his little daughter up stumps and emigrate down under.' I thanked them for the meal, walked out the door and crossed the road to get the bus back home.

I was in a daze. As I stared out of the window of the bus, I kept thinking, 'Bloody hell the buggers are keen, I'll give them that.' The double-decker slowly found its way into Dewsbury bus station. I wanted to run around all the pubs and shout out that an Aussie club wanted me. But I knew the meeting had to be kept quiet. I calmly walked home thinking about what to say to the missus.

I'd hardly walked 100 yards when someone shouted out from a passing work van, 'Are you going then?' I was flabbergasted. At the first newspaper stand I bought the *Yorkshire Evening Post* to see my photo and the headline, 'Aussie club swoops for Stephenson.' Thankfully my wife had not seen the paper so at least I could break the news personally. We sat up until well after midnight discussing our options.

The following night during training, Tom Clarke, the club secretary summoned me to a meeting. We were midway through a sprint session.

'The committee want to talk to you.'

I entered the board room, nodded to my father-in-law, Roland and listened to Chairman Mick Lumb outline what the papers had said and how Penrith had requested to speak to me. He added that the club would be turning down any offer and said I would receive a bonus if I continued playing at Dewsbury. I didn't say a word and glanced at my father-in-law who smiled as they told me the bonus would be £500. So that was it, I'd be a little bit richer and I set about sprinting again.

Ten minutes later I was called back into the boardroom,

where the same thing was spelt out to me. This time they added that Penrith's new offer would still be turned down. I thought it worth a try to demand another bonus to go on top of the last one. Surprisingly they upped the anti to £750.

Once again I was back on the sprint track even richer. By this time all the lads wanted to know what was going on. They, like all the fans, had read the reports in the paper.

'Don't worry, the club's not selling, you're still stuck with me.' I said which raised a laugh. It soon disappeared when secretary Tom Clark summoned me for the third time. This time his face was etched with gloom.

It was becoming a farce. I consoled myself, thinking I would cheekily ask for another bonus. I had nothing to lose. I walked into the room to find glum faces.

Chairman Lumb cleared his throat, sheepishly glanced at my father-in-law and announced, 'After due consideration, the committee feel they don't want to stand in your way.'

'Christ you've sold me?' was my reply.

'Erm, yes!'

'But I haven't made a decision yet if I want to go.'

There was silence. They had taken the cash. Wally Ward had been right when he said that money talks all languages.

I was still in shock. I blurted out that I hadn't asked for a transfer so therefore I was entitled to 10 per cent of the transfer fee. It was my right, and they agreed, although I had no idea what that transfer fee was. The directors sent me into the private players' bar to meet Wally and Bruce. They welcomed me on board the good ship Penrith Panthers.

'How much did you have to pay?' I asked.

'£20,000. A new world record.'

'Bloody hell, you must be mad.'

'We'll be the judge of that. Anyway we would have gone higher. Like we said before, we want you.'

'You've got me.' I replied.

The day after it became clear what had transpired in the board room that night. Dewsbury continued to turn down any offer Penrith threw at them. In desperation, the

Australian delegation suggested, 'Everyone's got a price. What sort of money would change your mind?' Wally and Bruce had left the room to let them mull it over.

After a short discussion, one committee member suggested a huge figure that would scare them off, £22,500 (which included VAT). The fee was well over 25% more than they'd paid Wigan for Bill Ashurst. Wally and Bruce returned to the meeting and were told the price tag. At this time they queried the weird figure. The board told them about the new VAT regulations. Wally calmly pulled out his cheque book and asked who they make the payment out to. He signed the cheque, passed it to Tom Clark and requested they talk to 'their' new player.

The cheque was only written for £20,000 and the board was quick to remind them about the new VAT regulations. Bruce was quick to inform the board that international transactions were void of VAT. He smiled and ushered Wally out of the boardroom. It was as simple as that. The look on my father-in-law's face wasn't a pretty sight. His daughter was on her way down under and he'd been part of the bluff that didn't work.

Tom told the players I had been transferred to Penrith. The lads took it well, especially physio Jim Greenhall. He later whispered that six weeks ago he'd applied and had been accepted to work in Sydney with handicapped children. He was on his way down under too. That cut-price fortune teller was right.

Sadly my transfer didn't go down well with the fans. For weeks afterwards I received abuse from all sectors. I was spat on a couple of times. This didn't amuse Pat, my wife, who was still coming to terms with the whole thing. The Australian rush for pommies had begun. Phil Lowe, Brian Lockwood, Dougie Laughton and many more players were targets. The RFL panicked and stated that any player going down under would never play for his country again. Taking abuse from fans was one thing but for the RFL to take away a player's chances to represent Great Britain again was another thing. On top of that, the RFL took great delight in backing clubs (Dewsbury included) in not paying players the 10 per cent cut of the transfer fee.

I'd been banned, abused, and was now without a huge amount of money that, according to the laws of the game, I should have received. I was pissed off to say the least. After all, the club chose to sell me! Dewsbury received a world record fee for a player that cost them £200 eight years earlier. They had the cheek to refuse to pay me a penny. In those days £2,000 could buy you a three bedroom, detached house. One high-ranking official at Chapeltown Road's RFL headquarters took great delight in calling me and saying I could well have captained the next touring British Lions team to Australia and New Zealand. The rugby league hierarchy were running scared. They were worried that more top British players were going to follow me to the land of barbecues and sunburn. They were right when Lowe, Lockwood and Laughton signed new contracts with Aussie clubs. I thought, 'Bollocks to them all.' It made me even more determined to do well down under.

By this time the new season in Sydney had already started. I was far from amused to be awoken by a reporter who had read the sports results from down under. He said Penrith had just been beaten by Manly to the tune of 70–7. I thought it must be some mistake. No team could lose by that much. I quickly called the AAP news service in London to confirm it had been a typing error. A charming bloke took the call. He politely told me to hold the line whilst he checked. He came back and started reading out the full results from the Sydney Premiership. It was true. Even he was surprised at such a score line and through a half-whistle exclaimed, 'Imagine playing for a club like that, they must be hopeless.' Imagine indeed. I knew this could be a harder job than I originally thought.

It looked like Dewsbury had done a good deal. Unfortunately it wasn't long before the transfer money had gone. It wasn't surprising as they persuaded one hooker to take my place by giving him money under the table tax free. They probably gave him the same amount they owed me. To make it worse, the bloke never even turned up for training, never mind to play for the club. It wasn't the last stupid transaction the club made over the next couple of years. Ironically several years later, the club had squandered the entire transfer money. They were so much in debt that in desperation they decided to auction off sections of the field to raise funds. They even sent me a letter in Australia requesting that I dip my hand in my pocket to help my home town club that was struggling. I couldn't believe it. I read the letter three times before I realised it wasn't a joke. I don't know if the club ever got my reply which suggested they purchase the entire playing area, plus the bowling green and the car park with the £2,000 they owed me. I told them to keep the change!

Anyone moving house knows it's a nightmare. Emigrating to the land of Kangaroos makes it even worse. We had to have medicals, complete forms, pack and then arrange shipping. We had to decide what to take, what to leave behind and what to sell. It drove us all mad. It took so long to organise that the new season in England was underway. I went with my family to watch the first game and was stopped at the gate and asked to pay! I suggested to the gateman that he go forth and multiply. I then pushed him to one side and said he'd better take up the matter with my wife's father, Roland. He was on the committee and paid his bloody wages. They even made me sign into the club house. Technically I was no longer a member. They then refused to allow me into the players' lounge! Again a few choice words ensured I burst through the door to meet my old team mates. Petty wasn't the word for it. Yet they did call me up to be included in the official photo shoot before the game with the championship trophy.

It was strange to get stripped and pull on the team jumper

and know I wasn't going out to play. I was glad I could take a team photo to Sydney as a souvenir. Little did I know that after I went back inside to change, they took another team photo without me and that was the photo they used to grace the club's walls.

Not all the fans were angry I was leaving for distant shores. One ardent supporter, a friend, actually gave me some cash in my hand. He gave me £200 the week before I flew out to Sydney. He was appalled at how the RFL and club had handled the transfer. He forced me to take the money whilst swearing me to never reveal his identity. I never have, but that gesture made such a difference. It taught me a great lesson that I could count good friends on one hand. For most people I was just a number soon forgotten. I had to take what opportunity came and enjoy it whilst I could.

I may have been a lost identity in Dewsbury but I was determined to be reborn in Australia. The pommie was on his way.

11

BOUND FOR BOTANY BAY

It was 14th November 1973 as we pulled away from Wakefield Westgate train station to London Kings Cross. It was the same day as the royal wedding of Princess Anne and Captain Mark Phillips. My wife Pat and our two children, Craig and Hayley, watched the procession pass by as we waited for the coach to take us to Heathrow airport. As the rain lashed down outside I thought it odd that I didn't have any regrets about leaving England. Considering the treatment some of the fans and officials had meted out, I was determined to make a go of it in Australia.

The flight was a nightmare, as most people who have travelled with youngsters will know. It was a 26 hour flight to Sydney. We arrived in Sydney on the morning of the 16th to be greeted by a mob of press writers, photographers, TV cameras and the works. I was bewildered by it all. Tired and jet lagged, I tried to answer all the questions as best I could, including the very first which made me smile.

'How do you like Australia?'

'I don't know, I've just arrived,' I replied, which brought a titter. Most of the questions were about why I signed for a bottom club rather than one of the established top clubs like Manly, Cronulla or Eastern Suburbs.

'To have a better life style and, I have to admit, the chance to earn a decent living from playing rugby league!' I said. At this point I could detect a look in their eyes suggesting I would have to work hard to earn a living. It wasn't the only reason. I believed I had a job to do that would challenge me.

The Penrith club had been honest right from the start. I was eager to meet the players and begin the job in hand.

We had a warm welcome from all concerned. There was no pressure from the media yet. I genuinely thought they meant it when they thanked me and wished me well. There was one nice guy at the customs' desk that went out of his way to welcome me to Australia. With a smile, he handed me a little gift. 'How kind,' I thought. It wasn't until later when I had chance to open it that I discovered a bar of soap! Sadly, most Aussies think pommies don't wash. I don't know why. This may have been true in the olden days when I was a kid and had a bath once a week. Nowadays hygiene is pretty high on the list of the British. Still it's all good banter and even to this day the Aussies come out with things like, 'I'm as dry as a pommie's towel.' They still insist on calling me a pommie bastard despite the fact I've now lived in Australia for over 30 years!

Driving into Penrith was strange. It's a small town with a long high street. A couple of older mates in England who had spent time in Penrith just after the Second World War suggested I avoid the tumbleweed when the wind blew on the boardwalks! It wasn't Gotham City, but I liked it straight away. There was warmth about the place. Did I say warmth? More like hot. Bloody hot. The heat took its toll on our family straight away. Being over 50 miles from the coast meant there was no sea breeze. There was plenty of humidity and when the wind blew it was like opening an oven door. Getting out of the air conditioned car in front of our new home was an experience never to be forgotten. I turned bright red within seconds and I thought the kids were going to faint (my youngest, Hayley, did two hours later). I swear we all walked around with frozen peas on our heads even with the air conditioning turned on.

As we walked up the driveway we burst out laughing as we saw two brand new cars shining in the sun.

'What's the matter?' enquired Wally Ward, 'Don't you like the colour?'

'It's not the colour. We can't drive. We couldn't afford a car back in England.'

Wally was stunned. 'But you're an international Stevo!'

'Maybe, but we didn't get paid well enough for such luxuries.'

It was the first time I'd been called Stevo. This name has stuck so much that I feel many people don't even know my first name. In fact if anyone shouted out Michael, I wouldn't turn around I'm so used to Stevo. Everybody in Australia has a nickname: Smacka, Fog, Sumo, Wary, Dumbo, Fettucini, Salad Bowl and so on. They just have to give each other a nickname and quite often they refer to each and everyone with this moniker, so much so they lose track of their real names. Only a couple of years ago a close friend, the Ghost passed away. I wanted to send a sympathy card to his wife but couldn't for the life in me remember his real name! No decent person could send a condolence card to Mrs Ghost.

Ghost earned his name because of his ability to find and slip in unnoticed at a house where a party was going on! He was a great character. When he was told he hadn't long to live, he decided to have his own wake before he died. It was a full house. He paid for a full on farewell party and passed away two weeks later. It just about sums up what great people the Aussies are when even in sad times they can enjoy a party.

For the first two days every time we looked outside the house, we admired our new status symbols parked outside. One car was green the other was blue. On the third day we woke up to find they'd been replaced by two different coloured cars. They were a red and a yellow Ford. I was beginning to think they changed colours each week when Welsh 'Taffy' knocked on the door and introduced himself as our driving instructor. He said he would pick me up at 2.30 pm for my first driving lesson.

The club had changed the cars from manual to automatic to make it easy for us. We learnt to drive quickly. In fact very quickly as after just two lessons, Taffy failed to turn up. A new bloke arrived. He didn't say much to start with and then stopped outside an official looking building in the centre of town. He went inside and came back with a book of questions. I answered each question and then he promptly congratulated me on passing my test. He said to tell my wife that she would pass same time next week! Taffy must have been one red hot driving instructor. We were red hot too as the end of the year approached with temperatures reaching the 90s. Added to this, training had just started.

It was an unusual first meeting with the players. Roger Cowan the boss of Penrith introduced me to them as a group. He no doubt felt I would get to know each guy as the training session went on. The session began with a five mile run! The humidity was high and so was my blood pressure. I found it hard to keep up but I managed to stay with the pack of runners. I thought it would give me a chance to have the odd chat. Not many runners came by and introduced themselves. In fact a total of three runners introduced themselves. These were the two prop forwards, Terry Geary and Tim Sheens and sadly some other bloke whose name I still can't remember. He didn't turn up for the next session and I haven't clapped eyes on him since. It was plain to see the resentment within the camp. They weren't a happy bunch of toy soldiers at all.

I was disappointed to discover Penrith had appointed a 'head coach' over and above Roy Masters. After a successful tour to England with the Australian schoolboys, Roy was appointed the first team coach. I'd met Roy on the schoolboy tour when his squad were guests at a Dewsbury game. Little did I know we would turn up together in the Panthers' lair. I was impressed with Roy and happy to think we could work together. It was a blow when the officials informed me the committee had decided to follow the style of Jack Gibson, the guru coach in Australia at the time. Gibson established a different attitude to training and coaching. He had spent many months working under American grid iron coaches, and he put these methods to great use in Sydney. So much so that Penrith also decided to appoint a senior coach who would have an overview of the three grade coaches: first, second and juniors. The aim was to impart the same success big Jack enjoyed. Unfortunately the man they selected to do this was Jack Claire. Claire was an unknown to me and I was soon to find out that he was not recognised by anyone at the top levels of coaching either. Jack had previously coached the Balmain Juniors. After the first training sortie I wish he'd stayed there.

After our five mile run, we trouped into Penrith Park. He introduced himself and shook my hand as though he had a point to prove. Then without warning, stood back and requested that I show all the guys all the moves that had become such a smash hit with Dewsbury. I couldn't believe it. There had been no conference about this, no tactical discussions made, no deciding the team's aims, no training schedules put in place, no structure and no targets. To say I didn't hit it off with him is an understatement. I thought this behaviour was rude and unprofessional. I stood in the middle of a park with a 40-man squad staring at me, expecting me to produce the goods like bloody magic. What's more, I hadn't even been introduced formally. I was furious. I was left with no option but to suggest that last year's three-quarter line up and pack should take up an attacking position on the training pitch. I then decided to make up two moves on the spot. I had forwards running all angles and the half-backs running either side of me. I threw a dummy to them all and strolled over under the posts! It was crazy but he clapped at this outrageous tactic. The players were bemused. They obviously thought the club had signed a lunatic. After this episode, I walked to the stands and suggested we didn't do any more because I didn't know the players enough yet. He nodded, shook my hand with a vice like grip and congratulated me on such a fantastic showing. He thought it was Christmas. I thought he was crackers!

At each session from there on in, it became clear he was out of his depth. The only thing he repeated was, 'Be tough, be fit, wear down the opposition, tackle them hard.' Thankfully after I'd had several discussions with the committee they allowed Roy Masters to take control. We were all relieved. Roy knew what was needed both in training and on the park. Because the club was embarrassed to admit it had made an error it still continued the saga of allowing Jack to be the boss in front of the media. After each trial game, Jack would pontificate for the journalists. In truth he had nothing to do with the team's build up for the matches.

As you can guess, I didn't get on with Jack Claire. I knew he wanted to punch my lights out. He called me all the names under the sun. The truth was I hadn't flown 12,000 miles to play rugby league under someone who had never been involved with top grade footy in their life. Claire was in his late 50s and a fit looking guy for his age. Despite our mutual dislike, I really felt sorry for him. I couldn't blame him for accepting a lucrative position. Business is business and it's not surprising that Mr Claire hung around the entire season taking his money, and talking to the press. The media quickly latched onto the fact that poor Jack was just the front man. It wasn't fair to Roy Masters who was doing a wonderful job. It was a difficult time and I realised why so many coaches had come and gone at the club. Not for the first time camp morale wasn't good.

Slowly and surely the other players started to thaw. Even some of the hard nosed pros realised I brought some knowledge and value to the team. Much had been splashed all over the sport pages about my transfer and I knew many of my team mates were upset about the huge sums of money I was supposedly paid. 'Footy' is huge news in the Sydney papers. It gets a spread similar to football in the UK. Like most journalists, the Sydney press knew how to blow up a story. If they saw a player visiting the toilet three times in the day they'd swear blind he had a bad case of the shits!

I was happy with my contract. I have never made its details general knowledge but the press was outrageous at times. They would pluck a figure out of the air of what I was supposed to be earning. Within a month of arriving, I upset the head coach, riled some of the committee members, still irritated a few players who didn't want to talk to me and the season hadn't even started. My fellow pommie, Bill Ashurst hadn't even started either. He was having immigration problems and wasn't expected to join us until just before our first trial games in late January.

I needed a mate badly. The club was rife with in-fighting and a bit of support wouldn't have gone astray. I was looking forward to seeing Bill again, even though my last encounter with him had not been under happy circumstances. We last saw each other when we played at Wigan the previous year in the playoffs. Bill decided to hit Alan Bates off the ball, cracking his jaw. This led to a nasty punch up between the two sides. When the incident happened, Wigan had just scored another try on their way to an easy victory and Alan was walking back to the goal posts to stand behind the sticks. Rugby is tough enough when players are hyped up whilst the game is in progress. Players don't need to be clobbered when they're off guard as well. This is uncalled for. I knew for the sake of the team that Bill and I had to push the past behind us and knuckle down to some hard work. Sadly I was soon to find out that hard work was something Bill couldn't quite come to terms with.

12

BRING A PLATE

When Bill finally arrived in Penrith, it was clear that the support I needed to turn the club around wasn't going to be forthcoming. His attitude towards training was poor. This in itself didn't help the younger players. Often he sneered at the methods Roy Masters was using and to put it mildly he didn't run the risk of breaking into a sweat at most training sessions. Unsurprisingly many of the younger players noticed his 'relaxed' approach to nearly everything. The result of this was that they held back when they should have been busting their guts to improve their performance. The trouble was that Bill was a gifted player who could produce a brand of football that was breathtaking at times. I know he often boasted to the players that it didn't matter if they didn't train hard because, 'The proof is in the pudding.' This may be so, but someone has to turn on the oven and give it heat to rise. Young players are often led astray. The players at Penrith thought they could emulate Bill and his extremely laid back style. Who could blame them? For when Billy Boy turned it on, his game was a delight to watch. Unfortunately not all players have the fortune to have been born with natural high skill levels. The majority have to work damned hard to succeed.

It was difficult for the coaching staff and the other team members who were putting in 100 per cent effort both on and off the field. It became quite clear that Bill hated the fact I was captain. He proved the point at an early team meeting where all players were allowed to express their thoughts. He asked why I had a column in the *Sydney Daily Sun* (usually referred to as the *Sun*) and he didn't. I calmly waited until the meeting was over to tell him that what I did off the field was my business. I suggested that if he wanted to write a column, it would be a good idea if he got off his backside and asked one of the Sydney papers to give him a chance to write one. Bill, like many other people, thought I picked up the phone and spoke to a journalist ghost-writer. This was far from the truth. I became friendly with the great Australian journalist, Ernie Christiansen, during the World Cup in France. Within days of arriving in Oz, I gave him a call and asked, 'Would the *Sun* newspaper want a pommie writing a different style column for them?'

'There's only one way to find out. Come into Sydney and ask the sports' editor,' was his reply.

And so I did. Just two days after passing my driving test, I ventured into the big city a full 50 miles away. It was a sheer fluke that I didn't kill somebody on that torture run as cars passed me on both sides with horns blaring. A few suggested that I stick my head where the sun don't shine. Sydney drivers have a habit of not being understanding on the roads. Eventually, I made it to the Fairfax building, parked the car, walked into the lobby and asked to see the sports' editor. I shook like a leaf as I was introduced to a Mr John Benaud. I did wonder if he was the brother of cricketer and commentator Richie. I kept my mouth shut and found out later that this move helped my entry into the journalistic world. John was fed up with being asked about his famous sibling. John was charming and straight to the point. He asked me if I had written anything before. I replied proudly that I had written a couple of pieces for the world famous *Rugby Leaguer*.

'The what?' He said in disbelief.

I quickly changed tack and suggested to him that no, I hadn't written anything of note in my life. He summoned his PA and sent me into a conference room with pen and paper and told me to write a column. Just like that!

Two hours later I emerged from a mountain of screwed up paper and proudly walked back to his office.

'Christ, Stevo, I'd forgotten about you. Sit down and let's see what you've done.' He looked it over and declared, 'Shit!'

I was about to stand up and head for the door when he said, 'It's good shit. Are you always prepared to be so honest and straight to the point?' I nodded.

'Good, you can start next week. $50 a column.'

I was stunned. Not only had I been given a column, I was being paid more for each piece than I had earned each week as a plumber in England! My mouth must have dropped open for he quickly suggested an increase.

'Okay, $55 and that's my final offer.'

At this point his knuckles and fingers looked quite tasty, but rather than bite his hand off I shook on the deal. Little did I know this was a handshake that would change and shape my life for many years to come.

I was eager to sharpen my pencil and get on with the job, but John wouldn't have anything to do with handwritten copy. Nor was he interested in me just picking up the phone and talking to a ghost writer. Within minutes, he arranged for me to collect a typewriter.

'Take it home and learn to type. I need your copy by next Tuesday. Nice to have met you.'

I was still stunned. I walked out of the Fairfax building in a dream carrying this huge sit-up and beg machine to begin a career on the side. Within weeks I was invited to meet the staff at the newspaper and soon became friends with them all. I enjoyed more than the odd drink with many of them at the local pub, the Great Western. The Western was well named for it often got wild as it was the haunt of some of the funniest journalists in the world. If I'd saved all the money I spent in the pub in the 15 years I worked at the newspaper, I could have retired to Barbados years ago. I could probably have taken a few friends with me! Of course this wild behaviour occurred after my retirement from the game. I rarely went overboard in the drinking stakes whilst playing. I must say I've made up for it ever since!

Bill and I knuckled down and tried to produce the right effect to lift the side. It wasn't easy due to the bad atmosphere about the place. The press didn't help either. Because I was at the *Sun*, the opposition afternoon paper, *The Daily Mirror* (referred to as the Mirror), was quick to stir up the dirt. They targeted Bill in a big way. They didn't offer him a column but they knew Bill was quick to offer a quote without thinking. One day I was stunned to find my photo alongside Bill's photo on the back page. Bill stated that he wouldn't play under my captaincy! He went on to add that we hadn't spoken to each other for weeks. This was an out and out lie. I rang Bill straight away and demanded to know why he had done such a stupid thing. He pleaded innocence, claiming he hadn't said anything to that effect. The club was furious and I wasn't too impressed either. The damage had been done. Our feud was born and would never go away. It lasted right up until Mr Ashurst's hasty departure two seasons later.

As I was now involved with the press, I tried to explain that the press would use any off the record comments. My warning fell on deaf ears. Unsurprisingly Bill became quite friendly with the opposition newspaper journalists and on a slow story day they would dig up the so-called feud.

Our feud became a huge story. After 12 months we would often appear at the local shopping centre on stage and re-live this 'hate' we supposedly had for each other. In all honesty I never once gave Bill any cause to blast me in the papers. Even when I confronted him about it, he shrugged his shoulders, smiled and said he was misquoted. The one time he wasn't misquoted was in the build up to our pre-season competition game against Manly at Brookvale. Much to everyone's shock, in the papers Bill raved about what he was going to do to Phil Lowe. Bill claimed Phil pinched his spot on the previous tour to Australia. I couldn't believe what I was reading as Bill claimed he'd show everyone who the best second rower was in England. He also said he had a few surprises for Lowe.

The press wrote it up as though a Third World War was about to erupt. The comments ensured a sell out crowd but did little to help our cause. Malcolm Reilly was quick to ring me at home and enquire why on earth a fellow Englishman would stir up the shit. 'He'll soon find out that it's tough enough in Oz without having a grudge against a fellow countryman.' Malcolm rightly claimed.

Reilly was livid. When Malcolm got excited he was man to stay clear of on the field of play. The former Castleford and Great Britain legend had made his name in Sydney and was regarded as being one of the toughest and most skilful players to leave British soil. I knew Bill would receive a torrid welcome at Brookvale Oval. Needless to say that from the kick off, the opposition targeted Bill. Within minutes both players were on the ground rolling about like two wrestlers. The publicity had not been wasted on the referee either. He was eager to warn them and threatened to send them both off. Sure enough, after the next scuffle, two of Britain's finest players were heading for an early shower.

I can still see a seething Mr Reilly pointing the finger at Bill and suggesting a meeting behind the stands may be in order. Thankfully the officials steered them in different directions. They tell me the air was blue in the Manly dressing room for quite some time.

It's a brave man that mixes it with Malcolm. Malcolm was a true legend within our game. Without him, Manly would have never won their first premiership.

I hoped the fiasco would get the message through to Bill that we had to stick together in the big league and not start shouting our mouths off. Sadly it didn't. The press knew he was a 'story on a stick'. Just one phone call and they had a back page lead. Even after I retired five years later, the *Mirror* scribes couldn't resist getting on the phone to Bill in England in the hope of discrediting me. The *Sun* newspaper was running my life story over five days. The *Mirror* was not going to be outdone and concocted the most ludicrous story imaginable that Bill deliberately knocked me out in a scrum whilst playing against St George and that I had to be taken off the playing area on a stretcher.

At least Bill got the bit about me being carted off right as I had twisted my back in a scrum collapse. How he could have given me an uppercut when he wasn't even playing in that game was anyone's guess! He must have the longest arm in the world to have hit me whilst watching in the stands. It just shows what newspapers are prepared to do at times to get a story. As a result of this, the *Sun* arranged a link up with Bill when I rang him the following day. They recorded the conversation and Bill yet again admitted he had been paid to tell the 'little white lie'. Our back page slammed the *Mirror* for running a story that was sheer fabrication. This left the journalists of the *Mirror's* sports section with more than a little egg on their faces. Many years later the journalist who rang Bill that day admitted he was ashamed of his actions. Not that I lost any sleep over the affair. I'm sure he didn't either. I knew first hand that the media have a job to do. The press just weren't helping a club that had struggled for years. I had signed a contract to get Penrith up with the big boys and I was determined to ensure we at least gained some respect for a club that the media had declared a disaster zone. We were only 50 miles away from Sydney, yet many rugby league writers were quick to point out it was a pain in the backside to travel there. To them we were 'Hicksville'.

Peter 'Zorba' Peters was a *Sun* journalist who had played in the successful Manly Premiership winning sides of 1972 and 1973. He made sure in no uncertain terms that Penrith were outcasts and easy beats. His thoughts were obviously buoyed by the fact he had played in that infamous match in 1973 where Manly thrashed the Panthers by 70 points just days after I'd signed for Penrith in England. But it's amazing how things can change. Now there are teams from Queensland, New Zealand and Melbourne playing in the elite rugby league competition. It was justice when a few years ago, Penrith defeated Manly by over 70 points. This was when the said Mr Peters was manager of the Manly team.

Zorba, named such because he has a Greek background, was a talented writer who could sniff out a good story. He was amusing to be with. He could tell a good yarn, although he did have a reputation of stretching the imagination. I remember that one journalist suggested he was the world's best fibber. It was clear he didn't rate Penrith at all.

Another character was Geoff 'Pinky' Prenter, who launched the then famous *Rugby League Week*. This was a trade paper prone to declaring exclusives that ran along the lines of 'I know who gouged my eye out'. It sold well, and major players such as Bobby Fulton wrote for Pinky's publication. Pinky earned his name from the fact that his face went pink when he'd had too much red wine. We soon learned that it wasn't the only thing that changed after a good drop of the grape. He arranged to meet me at Penrith Leagues Club for dinner so we could discuss a deal about me writing for his publication over a nice steak and lobster. Naturally, the wine was of good quality and as the night went on we both started to feel the effect. This was not a good move as we had not yet discussed terms. When the time came for him to offer me terms, I wasn't seeing things too clearly. I suggested that I sleep on the offer and would get back to him shortly. At which point his attitude changed and he told me he'd driven a long way, and I was getting exactly the same amount as the real stars of Australia! I told him to stuff it, stating I wouldn't want to work with such a cranky bugger. He stormed off. I was quick to remind him that he'd not paid the bill. He responded by throwing money onto the table and declaring for all to hear that he ran league journalism in Sydney and I would **never** get a job in the press world! My column at the *Sun* came out the following week.

Our first action at Penrith came in the shape of trial games.

The first game was at Wyong on the central coast. Bill and I were invited there the night before the game to do some PR work which involved talking on stage and being polite throughout. We met our opponents as they filed past us as if we were the generals congratulating the troops. One by one we shook their hands. When one guy tried to squeeze the living shit out of my hand, I quietly suggested he was the hooker I would face the next day.

'How did you know that you pommie bastard?'

'A wild guess,' I replied, knowing full well this wasn't just going to be an easy warm up match. It proved difficult on the day when the crowd booed both Bill and I when our name was called out. One lady even attacked us with an umbrella as we ran down the tunnel. In the first scrum, my vice-grip friend from the night before decided to re-arrange my face with the help of a few of his mates. It was what I expected and I gave more than I got.

With the warm up games against amateur sides out of the way, it was time for the big boys in a pre-season competition called the Wills Cup. Four teams from four leagues played each other. The table toppers went into a sudden death semi final followed by the final the following week. Our first trip was to Cumberland Oval, the dust bowl of the Parramatta Eels. It proved to be an eye opener to say the least. The ground was like concrete and as I waited in the tunnel to lead the side out, the photographers asked me to wait a moment whilst they took pictures. I obliged and so did two delightful 'ladies' who decided to spit on me. I was covered with the stuff but trotted out unfazed and was amazed by the amount of people who suggested I didn't have a father.

The former great Australian scrum-half, Keith Holman, was the referee. He wore a starched, blinding white shirt with a huge metal badge pinned on it. The badge stated he was the referee. The thought, 'Doesn't he know he's the ref?' flashed into mind.

After the toss I shook hands with Eels captain Dennis Pittard. Then I grabbed Mr Holman's hand and wished him a good game.

'What you do that for?' he demanded

'I'm sorry, we always shake hands in England,' was my reply.

'You're not in bloody England now.' Then he panicked, shouted for Pittard to return quickly and shake his hand also for fear the crowd would go bananas. I didn't know it wasn't the normal thing to do.

The kick off by Parramatta was somewhat unusual in the fact that all the forwards were grouped together at the centre spot. I knew straight away where the ball was aimed … at me! In those days the hooker took up the position 10 yards in front of the kicker and as I expected, the ball was kicked ever so softly. It rolled until it just came over the white 10 yards line. It was shit or bust. I got both when I dived on the ball. I finally emerged from a gang tackle with blood streaming from my mouth and eyebrow to play the ball. I gave the referee an evil eye. His response didn't surprise me. 'Play the ball. You're not in Bradford now.'

He was right. This slab of concrete they passed off as turf was so dry that the dust and grit blew into our eyes. The 85 degree heat did little to help. The stand was so old it looked like it would fall down and most of the spectators sat on the outer with picnic baskets and 'Eskeys' full of ice and beer. The Aussie fans get value for money by watching three games on the same day. They start with the junior game at 11.30 am and the main game kicks off at 3.00 pm. Imagine the state some of them are in once the sun and booze take effect. Despite the fact that heavy drinking does go on at the grounds, the crowds are not as rowdy as in England. In England the excitement is with players for most of the match. In Oz, they only go over the top when a score is on the cards. Sometimes this makes for a lack of atmosphere. This lull is the main reason players often hear the 'Wags' in the crowd. The deep voiced fans who sarcastically hurl abuse in what the Aussies call an expression of fondness!

'If they put shit on ye'r mate, you're accepted as a good

digger,' is a phrase they use often. It translates as, 'If they take the piss, they think you're okay.' I can honestly say that most times it's true. People ask me what it's like to be a pom down under and I say that the majority of pommie bashers use their abuse as a compliment. Just stand up to them and give back just as much or even more and you'll be 'as happy as a dog's dangler'. It doesn't always work. I remember standing up to one big Aussie bruiser who was a dustbin man, or should I say in Oz terms, a 'Garboligist' in a pub in Redfern. He brought me over a beer and suggested we drink it then go outside to fight to see who would pays. I enquired as to which beer was mine, picked it up, told him I could afford to buy my own beer and poured it into the huge rubbish channel that runs the full length of Aussie bars. He quickly gulped his beer, grabbed hold of me and started throwing punches like a mad man. I knew I came off the worst when the fight was stopped and I had blood trickling from my mouth. The big sod just smiled, stuck out his hand and said, 'Welcome to Australia mate,' and we have been friends ever since (with his size I didn't want to become his enemy on a long term basis).

In a new country it is important to learn quickly. Otherwise it's possible to get swamped. The first major game at Parramatta helped a lot. Amazingly I enjoyed playing at the old Cumberland Oval over the years, even though it was a dump and badly needed some repairs. The fans loved it until the Eels won their first ever Grand Final. Thousands made their way back from the SCG that day and promptly set fire to it. They burnt it to ashes, posts and all. For years the local council promised a new stadium and after this little episode they had no option but to concede to the power of the people. Within three years the council had built what is now the Parramatta Stadium, a ground worthy of any sporting venue.

If there's one thing that sets Aussies apart, it is their honesty. They don't stand on ceremony, they just tell things straight. They are a bit like northerners in England, which probably accounts for the fact that the majority of people who emigrate down under and return to mother England are from the South! It took me a while to settle into my new way of life ... about two days I think. After moving into our new home I was given the conducted tour of the Panthers Leagues after just 48 hours and was introduced to my first Aussie beer. It was bloody awful and tasted like cats' piss. They gave me what they described as a real man's drink, called Resch's, which I struggled to get down my throat. 'Thirsty!' came the cry. Someone ordered yet another. My mind went back to a guy I met on the plane going to Sydney who had told me the way to get on with the locals was to smile, say everything was fantastic and I would settle in just nicely. So I gritted my teeth and declared it was fantastic and enquired, 'How long has this been going on?' I was also quick to prevent the barmaid from giving me the same brew. I suggested that because I didn't know much about their beer it would be a good idea if I tried all the brews!

Aussie slang and different sayings often left me confused and sometimes embarrassed. I walked into a café and ordered a cup of tea and a bun from an attractive lady behind the counter. She dropped a tray full of sandwiches at my request. She was shocked and I was bemused. She soon composed herself and whispered in my ear that a 'bun' had a different meaning entirely in Australia. I had proudly ordered a cup of tea and a gang bang! Another shock came when one of the girls in the office waltzed over to her girlfriend to ask if she had any Durex in her drawer. 'Second drawer down, help yourself,' came the reply. Two days later her mate asked if she had returned the Durex back to her drawer! Thankfully, Durex in Aussie is sticky tape and not a condom. Not that the Aussie girls are shy when it comes to talking sex. Far from it. One female pulled me to one side after training and asked for my autograph on the team photo. I obliged noticing crosses on at least half of the side. She quickly suggested I could also join this 'hall of fame' or should that be 'shame'? She then passed me her phone number and asked me round for coffee some time in the near future. I had never seen her before in my life and here she was asking me to give her one! The amount of crosses left me in no doubt this was one fan to stay clear of. Another shock came after one of the long training runs. I could only see two players in the showers when I knew at least half a dozen players had finished ahead of me.

'Where're the others?' I asked.

'Out by the van,' was the reply.

'What van?'

'The one with the girls in.'

It amazes me how anyone could have the energy after an eight mile run to then drop their shorts and perform in the back of a van in full view of their mates. I had known about groupies that followed pop bands, but groupies in rugby league? My eyes were opening wider by the day. Another red face moment came when I was invited to my first barbecue where the host told me to bring a plate. So I did. I took cutlery as well. When I arrived everyone burst out laughing.

'What're these for?'

'You said bring a plate.'

Little did I know that 'bring a plate' means 'bring your own meat to cook on the hot-plate'.

I soon got used to Australian foibles and customs. I will never get used to Australian wildlife, especially the mosquitoes. They are a nightmare. They bite, the bite itches then I scratch the bite which in turn gets infected. The end result is that I look like Mr Blobby. I hate spiders. I'm frightened to death of them. I didn't take too kindly to watching a TV show whilst eating dinner that informed all the family that the funnel-web spider bite will kill within minutes. Back then they didn't have an antidote. I worked out that if I was to be bitten, I could just about boil an egg before I said my last goodbyes. Add to this the fact that Australia has the 10 most deadly snakes in the world and I sort of thought … 'Oh, what a great country.' Even the horses gave me trouble. Our home backed onto a paddock full of highly strung trotting horses, one of which decided to look for food in our kitchen. I was showering at the time when my wife screamed out, 'There's a horse in the kitchen!'

I raced out of the shower stark naked to confront this huge, brown mare snorting and slipping over the floor tiles. The horse got in by forcing its way through the fly screen door in search of food. Now it was getting excited. I'm not sure who was shocked most. My naked body obviously had some effect on the animal as it reared up on its hind legs. This scared the shit out of me and forced the same out of our four-legged friend. It made a huge mess on the floor. In desperation, I slowly went towards the bread bin and started to place slices of bread on the floor towards the now shattered door. The bugger of a horse started eating each slice and I basked in the glory of such a bright idea. Unfortunately the horse refused to go outside and eat the bread I had laid out on the lawn. It knew where its bread was buttered so to speak and wouldn't budge from the kitchen. In desperation, I rang the club, 'There's a horse in our kitchen!' I screamed.

'Don't talk so daft,' came the reply, with more than a hint in his voice to suggest their new signing had gone mad or had hit the bottle. Fortunately they started to believe me when they heard the kids screaming in the background. I don't know if you've ever seen the film *The Horse Whisperer* but a short while later a trotting trainer came into the house. He talked calmly to the intruder, whispered a few sweet things in its ear, and blow me down, the bloody thing just walked out with him! I've never been near a horse since and I'm not likely to either.

Then of course there are the snakes, goannas, geckos, the frogs who keep you awake all night, the possums that nest in the roof, and let's not forget the bandicoot that rips up the lawn and it's easy to see why it's such a wonderful place to live!

On one coaching trip to Darwin shortly after I'd retired, I met a guy called Alex Gow. He was a mad league player who happened to be the authority on the world's deadliest snakes. He told me of one occasion when he was racing downfield to score a try when the flying doctor's helicopter landed on the pitch and whisked him away to some poor bloke in the bush who had been bitten by a snake. After identifying the snake and administrating the antidote, he flew back and played the last 10 minutes of the game.

Darwin is different from the rest of Australia. It sells the best Indonesian style kebabs with peanut sauce, gamblers can put on the biggest bet in the universe and has more people trying to kill themselves through drink than anywhere in the world. The amount of people who live there that are running away from life or a wife or girlfriend is staggering. Think, 'Stop the world, I want to get off,' and that's Darwin.

13

THE CHOCOLATE SOLDIERS

In the five years I played at Penrith, I had plenty of good moments and a few bad ones. The highlight was the fact that we avoided the wooden spoon in all five seasons and that we improved as a club each year, despite a few traumas. We actually made the final of the Amco Cup. The Amco Cup was a rip off of the English Challenge Cup competition. It was played on a Wednesday night in front of massive TV audiences. The media still hold sway in most sport and this was no different as they even played the game in four quarters so they could get more advertising on air. Like in the English Challenge Cup, amateur clubs were involved (or in Australia's case, different country zones). We surprised everyone by making the semi finals, where against all odds we beat the red hot favourites, the Eastern Suburbs Roosters. They had the likes of Beetson, Brass and Harris playing for them. They also had a young union convert called Russell Fairfax. He went on to take the league game by storm. We had a depleted team with five of our regulars, including Bill Ashurst, missing and had to throw in a handful of inexperienced youngsters.

The one good thing about playing four quarters is that energy levels keep high. Knowing there was a break midway through each 40 minutes was a key factor in our shock win. We tackled them off the park. Even Beetson's famous off-loading skills were nullified. East's famed three-quarter line never got a chance to move. The youngsters did us all proud and we couldn't believe we had turned over the big guns.

The other semi final created an even bigger shock when the previous year's premiers, Manly, were held to a 10–10 draw by Western Division. Western Division was coached by ex-green and gold hero John King. The teams played the game in a snow-storm in Bathurst. It was bitterly cold. These were hardly conditions for exciting open play and Bob Fulton's side tasted defeat despite drawing the match. Some obscure rule stated there would be no replay and after a count back on penalties, Manly was out. Neither the sponsors nor the NSW rugby league were happy at the outcome. They wanted the top teams participating in the first ever knock out final. What they ended up with was last season's wooden spooners playing a team that wasn't even in the top flight. Thankfully for the TV executives, the viewing figures were outstanding and air time was already sold.

It wasn't what the league wanted, but the ticket sales went through the roof for the final. This new competition put some spark back into a game marred by unsavoury incidents. The press had started to call it 'Thugby League' and demanded the officials got tougher and handed down longer suspensions. Unfortunately for many, including me, they failed to do this until a few years later. As the years went on, some clubs decided not to risk their star players for fear of injury. What started out as a great competition was undermined by some top clubs putting out a bunch of youngsters and lesser lights to play in the mid week tournament. In the first season where prize money was high and expectations were at the same level, the clubs gave it their all.

So the dream final of the two big hitters, Easts and Manly, had gone out the window. It left for a fairy tale ending. Well, for Western Division anyway. They shocked us by using the same tactics of pressure defence. Coach Roy Masters had prepared us well and we had no excuses. They were the best team on the night and despite the game being low scoring and defensive, the sell out crowd at Balmain enjoyed a thrilling encounter. It was the first major final the Panthers had been in. I'm still certain we would have won if we had played the same enthusiastic youngsters for the final that won the semis. It's hard not to miss a final and I can't blame the major guys for fighting back from injury to ensure they were selected. I had my doubts that most of them were 100 per cent fit. This fact was borne out when a couple missed the next weekend's game.

It was a sad night in our dressing room. I made sure I went into the opposition's dressing room to congratulate and shake hands with every winner. They were over the moon naturally and coach King had a smile so wide I could have put the harbour bridge on his top lip. It was a tremendous effort from them to beat full premiership sides from the Sydney competition. Without doubt the Sydney competition (and with the highest respect for British rugby league) is the hardest in the world. It was also a great boost for the country rugby league and gave them something to aim for. At the same time, it put some of their young players in the shop window for Sydney clubs to take notice. It was big news, something akin to Hull Dockers or Dewsbury Celtic winning the Challenge Cup final. Imagine the pride out in the Western bush areas.

Years later when I took the Rugby League Express Museum train around NSW it surprised me how many ex-players introduced themselves as a reserve for that Amco Cup final. Now I know why they won, they had at least 50 players on the bench that night!

At least that first season finished on a high with a final under our belt. We also avoided the wooden spoon. We were, as the media put it, on our way up to the top. It was hard but we had a few laughs on the way. One day at Redfern Oval one of our second rowers was really trying to get into the mind of one of South Sydney's many star players by suggesting the player's wife was a good lay and how kinky she was in bed. It's an old ploy that normally doesn't work. On this occasion the opposition second rower became agitated and put off his game. Sledging doesn't normally get up a player's nose so at half time I said he should keep the bullshit going. He replied, 'It's not bullshit at all Stevo, I've been giving his wife one for ages.'

Many clubs suspect dressing rooms are bugged to catch what the coach says at half time. It was obvious that South Sydney had someone listening under the toilet window that day as straight from the kick off, our 'lover' was knocked out by the husband and had to be carried off! We kept our discussions pretty quiet in the break afterwards.

South's ground is famous for many things as it is one of the oldest clubs in the competition and it is also in an Aboriginal area of Sydney. Needless to say, Sydney South has a few characters. My first game there took me by surprise. A group of Aboriginals leant over the fence waving what looked like large dog bone at me and shouting some weird language. I asked Terry 'Dollar' Geary, my prop forward, what it was all about.

'Nothing to worry about Stevo. They're pointing the bone which means they're putting evil spirits into your body. If you don't drop dead within the next half hour, the spell's not working.' His sneaky grin didn't fill me with confidence. It was also the ground where I received a most painful injury.

Just before half time, a nice bloke called George Piggins (a hooker of note) decided when a scrum collapsed with me at the bottom that he wouldn't risk injury to one of his knees. He softened the blow by placing his knee into my groin. The pain was excruciating, so much so I could hardly breathe and was quickly taken back into the dressing room. The doctor thought I had a cracked rib penetrating my lung. He quickly cut my jersey apart and was about to check my chest when I motioned towards my private parts. After an inspection, they found my right testicle was missing and residing in the far reaches of my upper groin! I groaned and grunted like a stuffed pig. I didn't much care what medical science they would use to fix my painful problem. I needed help badly and was struggling for breath. The doctor asked the two strappers to lift me off the table and he told me to stiffen my body. They bounced me up and down like a rag doll. It took four bounces before the testicle dropped down. It was a great relief. The pain was still excruciating but at least I started to breathe freely. At this point the players came in for the half time break. Coach Don Parish enquired about my ribs.

'Not the ribs. A little bit more delicate than that I'm afraid,' the doctor said and pointed to my crown jewels. The swelling in my groin area was increasing.

'Can he still play?' Parish enquired.

'No,' said the doctor and explained that if the testicle made its way back inside it would create a serious problem. It wasn't worth the risk.

Before I could even explain the bloody pain I was in, one of the strappers suggested we strap them!

'Hang on, let's not get carried away here. You're thinking of strapping my knackers?' I asked, outraged.

The doctor and coach nodded. Before I could say a word, they stood me up, held my two testicles and strapped the connecting tubes above with insulation tape (green if you really want to know). They gave me a new shirt, shorts and jock strap, needled in two pain killer shots to either side and sent me out to play the next 40 minutes. Amazingly I won the man of the match that day but my radio interview with Frank Hyde, the commentator for 2SM, was of a high pitched nature.

It took me nearly an hour to remove the tape. It was bloody painful. I cut each pubic hair with a razor blade. So next time you moan about taking off a small plaster … think of my testicles.

Not all injuries are what they seem. We had a young centre called Ross Gigg who through the first half of a game struggled with a toe injury. He had no idea how he picked up the knock. When the doctor removed his boot at half time, out dropped his boot spanner! He'd laced up his boot before the game and failed to realize it was there. Talk about thick. Winger John Ryan was another to feel pain, sadly from gambling. One Saturday at an ABC TV game, John dropped down with injuries on a regular basis. I was concerned about replacing him, so I grabbed the physio to find out if he was okay to carry on.

'Sure, nothing wrong with him,' was the reply. So I left him out there. He did the same in the second half and it wasn't until after the game that I found out he wasn't injured at all. He wanted to know the afternoon's racing results! John went on to become even more famous by robbing TAB bookie shops so he could continue to bet. It was a disease for John. Just like an alcoholic he needed more. Unfortunately, he decided this was an easy way out. He got caught eventually and hung himself in the police cells. Some may say suicide is tragic. Others feel it's a selfish, easy way out to take one's life. It's hard to understand addiction and what it can do. John was such a decent bloke and his passing was a sad reminder of how gambling can ruin lives.

The club was so eager for success that they were willing to try anything. They even brought in a shrink before one game to build up our confidence and ensure we used our energy levels to the maximum. The shrink made the team lie down on the dressing room floor, shut our eyes, let our minds relax and picture the ocean with the surf breaking upon the shore. We had to imagine the cool breeze and how the sun's rays built our energy. We did relax and felt quite calm only for our scrum-half, Terry Wickey, to break the silence by snoring. He was fast asleep. The burst of laughter from all the players hardly helped. Neither did the shrink's session as we were so low key afterwards. Balmain scored three times in the first 10 minutes after that session. Needless to say we got hammered and no doubt the shrink went on to fool some other sporting organization.

Terry was a wonderful guy. He was as tough as teak and possessed plenty of guile and speed. Unfortunately he found it hard to grasp certain moves and tactics. Attention wasn't one of his strong points and he would often ask after a demonstration to have the move repeated. This was okay on the training field but not in the heat of a premiership clash. All teams have codes for different plays in the hope the opposition doesn't know what's going on. Unfortunately it was blown out of the water in one game against St George when I called a code to Terry to prepare for the next move only for him to shout back, 'What do I do on that one?'

Before I could answer him, Saints' hooker Steve Edge called out, 'It's where you run around Stevo and give it to the full-back.' We decided to let Terry play his normal game after that.

Aboriginals are famous for going walkabout. This is where at a moment's notice they disappear for days or weeks without telling anyone. For a league player, this can be difficult. Aboriginals often seem distant and most people find it hard to understand their makeup. I noticed for some time that Terry would never give anyone his autograph, even when pushed by the most fervent fan. It turned out he couldn't write. After many days' practice, our half-back suddenly started signing for all and sundry, although we often laughed about the fact I had to write his postcards when we were away on the end of season trips. I became quite fond of him and was the only one game enough to be his roommate. Drinking was not a strong point for Terry and he was a handful when he went over the top. Unfortunately some of the younger players would egg him on. They once convinced him to trash my room, put all the clothes into a full bath of water, and then add the TV as well (thankfully it wasn't plugged in). It was many hours later when I bumped into him in the hotel bar to find him laughing about the fact he'd trashed my room! It didn't dawn on him that he was sleeping in the same place and his clothes were taking a swim. Once in Hawaii he playfully requested directions from a huge cop on the beat by using an awful American drawl. Once the gun barrel touched his nose, I swear he went white!

End of season trips were amazing. At Dewsbury we took a coach to Blackpool for a day out. At Penrith and all the other major Aussie clubs, the world was our oyster. Most settled for Hawaii. It was a wonderful place. Fun packed full of sunshine and the best looking women I would ever wish to meet. Like most tourist places, the girls on the street corner do a roaring business. Even that has its drawbacks. I know of one official from a top Sydney club who refused to pay the lady of the night. He had evidently received poor service! The sound of a gun shot followed by the bullet hitting the bed just a foot away from his wedding tackle convinced him he'd better cough up. He added a bonus and took the next plane out of Honolulu.

I've mentioned before that the club was willing to give most things a try. It was becoming the done thing to copy anything from the good old USA. Jack Gibson's success from his trips to the Grid Iron teams had set the coaching ranks buzzing and the quest for that extra edge was well and truly on. One of the top Saturday night TV shows invited us to be hypnotized on live TV as we had hit a bad run of form and lost five straight games. The hypnotist was terrific and really had us thinking positive thoughts. When he started the swinging watch trick, we became edgy and all felt a bit uneasy about this being shown live on TV. We didn't know who looked the bigger idiots, us or him. They even arranged for a TV crew to film us in the dressing sheds and witness our resounding win over Cronulla. It all fell apart when the game was cancelled due to a waterlogged pitch.

Some doctor of an obscure American University Institute of Creative Science also had a turn. To prove his powers, he had me stretched out over the back of two chairs. He proudly claimed he'd got inside my mind and convinced everyone that I would still be horizontal when he pulled away one of the chairs. When he pulled away a chair, I fell to the bloody floor with an almighty crash. It left me in no doubt he was a nutcase. The experience also left me with a worse back than I had before. Yet the club employed him and his mind things for nearly two months! It was only when they checked out the so-called USA Institute and found it never existed that they gave him the bullet. We even had a doctor on board for the latter part of the season only to find out his qualification was as a part time nurse at the local hospital! My old Dewsbury mate, Jim Greenhall (the physiotherapist) often said he suspected the bloke was no good as he kept handing out aspirin to anyone with pain, irrespective of the symptoms.

It was a bundle of fun in those early days as the club reached far and wide for success. We all knew deep down that the only way to achieve was through hard work and buying a few top grade players rather than through employing cranks. The one thing about the whole scenario was that at least all at the club were trying. One couldn't help but admire Roger Cowan. He was the driving force who spent many hours plotting and scheming. It was nothing unusual for him to work between 12 or 16 hours a day. I liked his enthusiasm for the club, not just for the rugby side of it either. His drive is the main reason the Panthers is such a highly rated club now. The club has an empire that's leading the way in giving the general public entertainment and facilities second to none. Anyone visiting Australia should not miss seeing the magnificent leagues club these days with its cinema, hotel, theatre club, nightclub and top class restaurants. Roger had the power and with it came plenty of people who hated him. It wasn't surprising as his vision for the club was futuristic. He saw well into the new millennium back in the early 1970s. He was also responsible for taking the leagues clubs into a new era and turned Penrith into the Panthers. No longer would the club be controlled by a committee based around the football team. He turned the club into a mega business run by professionals. This upset many people, especially when he took away power from the rugby league side of the business. He broke the mould and from then on, the money spinning leagues club would control all finances. They made sure no silly money was wasted, which had been the case at all clubs in the past. Not surprisingly most other clubs followed suit and the raffle ticket days were gone.

One thing that didn't improve was the heat! In the early part of each season the sun still blazed hot. I found the humidity quite difficult to handle. It left the playing surface bone dry with little or no grass showing. Most grounds were ovals which meant cricket was played in summer. The centre of the pitch was made up of Bulli soil from the south coast of NSW. It provided the ideal concrete style cricket pitch. It was great for the leather and willow chaps but a nightmare for the rugby players, especially Parramatta and North Sydney. There the grounds were dust bowls and a danger to anyone silly enough to tackle low. Each tackle would see players pick up another skin scrape. Amazingly the Aussies refer to such scrapes as 'grass burns' (what bloody grass?) Christ it hurt and would often take weeks to heal due to infection from the chemicals used on the field. The injury would just start to scab over as the next game began and in the first tackle the bloody top would be scraped off. I still have scars to this day from simple but painful injuries.

It was at North Sydney where I noticed one of our players take a pair of women's tights out if his kit bag. The mind boggled and I asked him if he'd turned queer. I was half thinking about the old gag, 'How long have you been wearing tights?' Followed by the old chestnut answer of, 'Ever since my wife found them in the glove box.' The player was serious and explained that when he hit the hard ground the nylon film of the tights ruffled up rather than his skin. It worked as well and I used many a pair of tights to protect my lovely, soft pommie skin when the grounds were dry and hard. I always ensured the little nylon numbers were cut higher than the bottom of my shorts. It was one thing wearing tights and another showing them. I would often get ribbed by the blokes who asked that as I had the new-found thigh protectors and a corset (for my bad back) to boot, when would I go the whole hog and wear a bra?

The one thing the club did quickly was change the playing strip. No wonder the team was called the chocolate soldiers. Not only were the vertical brown and white stripe jumpers a mess to look at, each person attached to the club seemed to wear a brown blazer. They were everywhere. It appeared if someone swept the changing room or cleaned the toilets they were given a blazer! Whoever designed the strip didn't do the club any favours. The strip may look okay in black and white stripes for Newcastle United football club. The brown version was hardly trendy in Sydney. I helped convince the players and officials that when they walked down the main street of Penrith, it was possible to see other club jumpers being worn. Very few fans wore our jumpers. That swung it. In 1975 there was a new design of a white shirt with a brown and blue saddle over the shoulders. We also had a new dressing room built because all three grades had had to all strip in one large room. It proved a nightmare. The club played three games each match day and the dressing room looked and felt like a battlefield with bodies all over the place. I couldn't see the logic of the coach trying to ensure the first grade players focused on the job in hand, when other players were being stitched and treated for strains. At times even a few minutes before leaving the dressing room, the area was a heaving mass with bodies everywhere. Players couldn't think or move in the humidity and steam from the showers. It was certainly not conducive to good karma before kick off.

Another surprise was the fact the club expected players to wash their socks and shorts and look after their own boots. Even at Dewsbury, the club sorted that out for players. All players had to do was arrive with their jock strap. Yet here in the land where the rest of the world found the Aussies so far advanced in ideas, the club only washed players' shirts. Unfortunately the new strip included a touch of red here and there. Some of the single players living a bachelor's life didn't take much care with the washing. They turned up on match day with pink shorts and socks. The club decided that from then on a little old lady would handle the washing.

A further shock was when I was summoned into a board meeting to sort out the end of season trip! As I mentioned before, a day at the seaside was the norm in England. Imagine my surprise when the committee indicated how important it was for team morale that they could look forward to a trip overseas. All through the year we sold raffle tickets for the so-called 'Injured Players Fund'. This money ensured we had a bit extra to spend at the season's end. I had no idea what the players wanted to do or where they wanted to go. I asked if the trip was for just a couple of days or a week. 'No, it's a fortnight,' they replied. I was stunned. A 14 days all-expenses paid trip with pocket money to spend! I was left speechless when the committee suggested either a cruise or Hawaii. 'You're the captain Stevo, we'll leave it up to you,' they said. I went back to the lads and let them decide. They opted for a life on the ocean wave on the P&O cruise ship the Himalaya. This was okay until we tried to book the trip and was told there was no way a rugby team of any code would be allowed to sail on her. I couldn't blame them as some of the younger blokes went apeshit when away from home (so did a few of the older ones come to that). We applied again for the cruise as darts' teams who wanted to run a competition on board! They fell for the ruse but the team was greeted by the biggest bouncer as we walked up the gangplank. He demanded to see our darts! Most of our mob had never seen a dartboard never mind play the game. A quick wink and an exchange of the folded stuff sorted it out rather quickly. The blokes had a ball.

We sailed to New Zealand first then onto Fiji. We went through customs without a hitch until one of the silly young blokes decided to drop out his one-eyed trouser snake to a huge woman who asked to see his passport. She wiped the grin off his face when she stamped his cock with a visa print. Then she smiled and said, 'Next!' The print took five days to wash off.

I was still in a daze at such a luxury being offered to players. Each year the club would stump up the money to send us on yet another excursion. You had to earn the trip through playing so many first grade games or being a star performer in the lower grades. It was certainly a great incentive on top of our wages.

For the next four years after the cruise, the team went to Hawaii and the famous Waikiki beach. I could fill chapter after chapter with all the tales from our tours. Whilst the code of silence and the adage, 'What goes on tour stays on tour,' is a good thing, I would kick myself if I let the opportunity go without telling a particular story about the club's team manager, Ron Workman. Two days into one particular end of season break, Ron knocked on my hotel door, passed me all the tickets and money and said, 'It's all yours now and I'll see you back at the airport in 12 days time.' It was obvious that the part of a woman that's got more pulling power than a 10 ton truck had seduced our Ron into falling in love! We never saw or heard from him for the entire trip but he was at the airport waiting for us to board the midnight redeye back to Sydney. Most of the lads were saying farewell to new found friends and of course promising to write, phone or whatever. The crocodile tears flowed in bucket loads. I never went back with the team to Australia. Instead I opted to stay an extra few days before heading back to England via mainland USA. I had hardly walked 30 yards on my way out of the airport when a commotion at the departure lounge made me look back. It was Ron. On the spur of the moment he came crashing back through the immigration checkpoint to fall into the arms of his girl from the USA. It was like a bloody movie as they walked past me and left the building arm in arm. His poor wife was waiting at Sydney airport and enquired why Ron had missed the flight. Someone mumbled that he was a bit pissed and would surely be on the next available plane. It was nearly three years later when Ron came back to Australia. On his arrival, he rang his missus to pick him up. And guess what? She did! Work that one out.

Returning from one of the trips, we arrived at Fiji airport to find out Pan Am had overbooked the aircraft. Ten members of the party would have to miss out and stay on the island until seats became available on another flight. Because I was captain and staying anyway, I asked all the lads to put their passports into a draw to see who would get the available seats. Amazingly, after all the seats were taken, there should have been 10 passports left in the bag. There wasn't one left! All the young, single lads with no reason or wife to go back to hadn't even bothered to put their passports in the bag in the first place. They spent an extra four days on holiday with free meals and accommodation at the airline's expense. They even had the cheek to grumble when they were told a flight with plenty of spare seats was now available.

It was good fun. The trips did help bring the team closer together. Whilst we never threatened to make the playoffs, come the season's end we were never in the hunt for the wooden spoon either. I felt the club was getting there.

Bill Ashurst was proving to be a stumbling block. He was again swaying some of the younger players away from hard work. He even begged the Penrith club to give him a job at the leagues club. This was something all clubs were reluctant to do. They finally gave in and made Bill the odd job man about the place. He once took five days to paint the toilets in the men only bar and it took another five days to clean up the mess afterwards, so they gave him a desk job. Well it wasn't an actual coat and tie behind an office desk, more like a cushy number of bookings' manager for the club's squash courts.

Roger Cowan the head honcho at the club was a keen player and fitness fanatic. He was put out for quite some time because he could never book a court before 9.30 am even though the courts opened at 7.30 am. Bill filled in the first two hours with fictitious names so that he could lie in bed and not start work until about 9.15 am. It was a classic and even Roger eventually saw the funny side of it. He wasn't smiling when he enquired at the time of the pre-season team photograph why Bill was running late. He asked if I knew where he was.

'What time is it Roger?' I asked. Roger obliged by saying it was 7.30 pm.

'Oh, he should be just about landing in Singapore by now.' I replied.

Bill had had enough so he just left the club, simple as that. Bugger the contract, Billy boy was on his way home. The club sent out a scout to check out his house and found the place bare. A few days later, one of the committee men actually owned up to buying a TV from Bill three days earlier. He still didn't realise Bill was going to flit.

'He said he'd won it in a raffle!'

That was Bill. He did it his way. It was a shame as he was the most talented attacking player I've seen. He had a great kicking game, both long and short. He could offload and evade a tackle with such ease it made players wonder what planet he'd come from. If only Mr Ashurst had put as much time into training as he did trying to evade the hard slog, he would have been classed as one of the all time greats. I don't think anyone actually witnessed him at his best because he seemed to play like he always had a bit in reserve. Most of the time I had to use reverse psychology on him by demanding he kick a deep punt into the blind side corner, or kick up a high bomb. He often wouldn't even reply. He'd just side step, chip over the top of the defence re-gather and score. He was that good. Then he'd trot back for the kick off and shout out to me, 'What do you know?' It was hard to keep a straight face at times. I bump into him now and again up in the north and we meet each other like long lost brothers, which is nice. I think his calling from God has changed him for the better as he would rather read the bible these days than watch rugby league. A few years back he admitted that the hand of the Lord had touched him whilst sitting in a dressing room after being sent off for foul play. He's now a devout Born Again Christian, and to his credit went back to Penrith in late 2006 to be inducted into the Panthers' best team of all time. He apologised to all and sundry about his quick exit 30 years ago. He's a character, that's for sure. He's good company to be with, tells the corniest jokes imaginable but I still feel he wasted his God-given talents. He could have given more to the game.

Talking of wasted talent, Penrith certainly shunned one of Great Britain's finest attacking players. I persuaded David Topliss to join the club from England. His class would provide the team with some much needed strike power and we all looked forward to his arrival. Like all overseas imports, it takes time to settle and coach Barry Harris never gave him much time or chance to show his ability. The coach wouldn't select David because he never did much tackling. I argued that we had brought him over to win games not bloody tackle all day. But my argument fell on deaf ears and David, after playing most of the season in reserve grade, returned home with his pride severely dented. He proved a point two years later when he signed for Balmain and took Sydney by storm. He always put in that bit extra each time we played the

Tigers. It wasn't easy for Barry Harris who had taken over after my tragic attempt to be a player-coach.

Penrith's directors were eager for me to handle things in my second season. I tried to put them off by insisting they gave the job full time to the man who should have got the job in the first place, Roy Masters. Yet again Roy had to settle for being second fiddle. Roy took the news well and supported me 100 per cent as I tried to do the impossible by playing, captaining the side, planning the tactics, organising the moves and more. It was a disaster from the start. I think I was the last player in Sydney to be made a player-coach which isn't surprising after the mess I ended up in.

There are two ways to coach and handle players. Either become one of the players (which as a player was easy), or be aloof, stay clear and stamp your authority. When I did the job I was honestly on the verge of a nervous breakdown. I couldn't sleep, went off my food and for the first time in my life started to not enjoy the game I loved. It was the worst period of my career. The job affected my form and sadly I started to think everyone was plotting my downfall. I became uptight, angry and I started to think I was going mad. Add to this the fact that my wife and kids had gone back to England and it's easy to see what turmoil I was in. I was heading for a divorce, well on the way to the loony bin and I started hitting the drink. These were lonely times. My entire character changed. To put it mildly, I wasn't a nice bloke to be with and I was losing control. I was beginning to struggle to play through injury and lack of form and for the only time in my life, I asked for some advice from a chemist friend of mine; could he give me something to make me sleep? He did give me some tablets but emphasised I should only take them for a few nights as they could become addictive. I took the tablets and for the first time in weeks I started to get some deep sleep.

Later that season I went down with bronchitis. I felt shocking and rather than do the sensible thing and pull out of the team, I decided to battle on even though I was weak in mind and body. The chemist suggested he could give me a boost! I was shocked at the time but he persuaded me that the pill contained only vitamins mixed with herbs. I knew it sounded fishy but I was desperate to get the team and my game back on track. I popped the pill two hours before kick off.

Once before I had been conned into thinking I had taken an illegal substance when a physio handed me a tablet at half time. I went out and played a blinder, only to find out the pill was a salt tablet and nothing else! It was foolish, I knew that and even though drug testing hadn't been brought into our game at the time, we all knew some blokes were taking stuff because we could see it in their eyes whilst playing. I couldn't get to sleep the night before, even with the aide of a sleeping tablet. I toyed with the idea of taking the pill and it disturbed me.

With one hour to go before kick off, I felt dizzy and spent a long time in the toilet trying to get my bearings. I forced myself to be sick, knowing that whatever the bloody pill contained, my body didn't like it. To make matters worse, I played a shocker. I dropped balls, missed tackles and felt like death warmed up. I felt a little bit better in the second half and got more involved. It was obvious that whatever this boost was, it wasn't working. Not on the field of play anyway. Two hours after the game, I started to sweat and burn up. I went to the club doctor who gave me a sedative and sent me to bed. Forty eight hours later, I was still in bed with eyes so wide I looked like a comic cartoon character with ping balls for eyes!

From that day on I have refused to take any sort of medication not prescribed by my own doctor. Even then I swallow nothing other than what I need to take for my heart and bronchial problems. I don't even take a cold cure or a headache tablet. I have no idea what was in that tablet and didn't bother to go back to the chemist and find out. In some ways it helped me understand my plight. I was looking for answers to a question that was staring me in the face. I was the only person who could get me out of the shit. I had to face up to the fact that sometimes I was fragile. I needed to get back to basics, start all over again, build myself up, believe in my goals and accept that some things don't work out. Failure is not the end. It's the start of a new attempt.

A few days later an incident at training convinced me my time as a coach was over. One of the players walked off the park when we discussed tactics without saying kiss my backside or anything. I flipped and dropped him for the next game. I knew deep down I should have handled it better but he obviously thought I was a waste of space. Another restless night convinced me to stop the slide. I marched into Roger Cowan's office and resigned as coach on the spot. He took it well but suggested I come for a meeting that night.

They even offered me more money to stay in charge and I burst out laughing. It was probably the first time in weeks that my face cracked a smile.

'It's not the money. I just want my life back, my form back and most of all my sanity back.'

This was one time I wasn't going to be told what to do, despite the fact they were paying me good wages. It wasn't a finance thing at all; I wanted my pride and life back. They all looked shocked. This time they weren't pulling the strings and my mind went back to the early days at the Panthers when during the Great Britain Lions Tour, both hookers, Bridges and Ashcroft were injured for the rest of the Ashes campaign. Great Britain's tour manager, Reg Parker made a plea to the NSW and Australian rugby league for permission to draft me in for the upcoming second test at the SCG. I even went to the city to train with the side, only for the club to refuse to let me play. It hurt. I was desperate to pull on the Great Britain shirt, especially as the RFL had banned me from representing my country ever again. Reg ignored the ban and wanted me in the side. Because of the team's injury problems, I wanted to play.

Despite Penrith stopping me from playing, I have never felt betrayed by the club. They had every right to stop me playing as they had spent a few bob to get me to Australia in the first place. They didn't want to lose their new player through injury, especially when playing against the Aussies. I asked them to think again because of the plight Great Britain was in playing without a recognized hooker. They stuck to their guns. Penrith wanted their money's worth. The tour management was disappointed and so was I, but Reg saw the dilemma the club was in. Like the true gentleman he was, he shook my hand and thanked me for at least trying. I offered him the same compliment. It's on the record now of course that Great Britain had to take a gamble with Wigan's new Union recruit, John Gray, who came on tour as a prop! John kicked and played like a champion in that second test despite having a badly cut head and made himself a huge name by steering Great Britain to a famous victory. This was a game that alerted the Aussie clubs to his great talent and resulted in him being brought back to play in Sydney with North's and Manly. Sometimes players need that bit of luck; to be in the right place at the right time. I knew I wasn't in any place during my coaching days. When I walked out of the committee room I felt I was walking on air, like I was a man leaving prison. The euphoria was short lived despite the fact I soon started to hit top form again when Barry Harris who had taken control after I resigned thought I should stand down as captain. I did and he didn't have to tell me who would take my place. It was a Mr William Ashurst Esquire.

The media had a field day suggesting I was on the way out of the club. There were rumours that Cronulla and Manly were eager to sign me. It was all paper talk. I came to Australia to help build a club for the future and I was dead set on achieving that aim. The club knew this too and was quick to renegotiate my contract. Whilst the media rumours went into overdrive, I put pen to paper to keep me at Penrith for life! For as long as those ugly little legs of mine kept going, I planned to be with the Men from the Mountains.

14

THEY SHOOT HORSES DON'T THEY?

Neither Barry Harris nor I set the world on fire in the coaching stakes. It was a great relief to everyone to see the appointment of Don Parish, a former Western Suburbs star who loved the game and realised things needed changing fast. Don rang me in the off-season and informed me he was being given the coaching job. He asked if I would accept the captaincy again. I did. Don was a solid coach and did a fine job and we became close friends, spending hours discussing tactics. All the players felt at ease with the man and it reminded me of the old days at Dewsbury with Tommy Smales and Keith Goulding. Don was a calming influence on the team, especially among the younger players who had been influenced by Bill Ashurst's 'relaxed' approach to training. That was all to change and we all started to put in heavy work needed to become competitive.

Parish was the type of guy who never looked under stress. He may have been stressed deep down (I knew what pressure the Sydney competition can do to a man), yet he never showed it.

Bob O'Reilly (also known as Bear) joined us after several years at Parramatta. He was a great player who could offload and I looked forward to combining with one of Australia's best prop forwards. He certainly stiffened up the pack, although his first outing in a PR exercise hardly did him any favours. Roger Cowan had invited all the team to a riverside barbecue at his luxury house on the side of the Nepean River. We were on our best behaviour all day until the Bear cast his eye on a wonderful crystal glass punch bowl set with very expensive, delicate dipping cups hooked on the side. It must have cost a fortune. Bob asked what it was used for. I told him and showed him how to take a glass cup and ladle punch into it. Ever eager to try, the Bear grabbed the cup and was horrified to see the bloody thing disintegrate into a thousand pieces. Delicacy did not apply to Bob. Mrs Cowan took it in great spirit and acted as though the Bear had just simply crushed a beer can. 'Don't worry, accidents do happen,' she said. I later found out the punch bowl was unique and came from Hungary. It couldn't be replaced. Sadly Roger never invited us back after that day.

Bob and I up front coupled with Terry 'Dollar' Geary as the other prop formed a pretty solid unit. This gave Parish the green light to give the young kids a go. He often gave fast running forwards a chance on the wings. This was a ploy that other clubs had come up trumps with. All in all, the club was a happier place and the results started to show that. At one point we looked to have a chance of making the playoffs but sadly we dipped in form over the last few weeks. This was in no way the fault of one Mr Geary. Dollar was one of the toughest props I've played with. There was no fuss and no worry with Dollar. He could throw a punch with the best of them and had this strange habit of grinning after hitting a bloke!

'Want some more?' he would shout. Not many came back at him as he was a tough cookie.

He'd be one of the first players I would pick in my all time best team. Whilst I've never boasted about looking like Tom Cruise, having both 'Dollar' and the 'Bear' up front helped me keep some of my childish looks.

Playing in Sydney is a hard way to make a living. The five years I played at Penrith took its toll on my body. Struggling to get out of bed the morning after the game was one thing but, when I was still groaning on the Wednesday and Thursday, I started to wonder how long I could keep going. Playing in the front row was never going to be easy and that dreaded word retirement kept flashing through my head. I had become more involved in the media side of things. I was writing more columns and the *Sun* made it clear when I threw away my boots I could join the newspaper full time. I held all the coaching certificates but after my tragic time in charge of the team in 1975 there was no way this little bunny rabbit was going down that road again. Once bitten, 300 times shy!

My old bones were playing up. My bad back couldn't take much more, despite the corset, and 13 broken noses had left their mark on my looks. My knees were shot, my shoulder joints weren't crash hot either and my hands looked to be suffering from arthritis. In fact only my brain box appeared to be functioning properly and that was about to change soon.

Later on in that 1977 season whilst playing against the Balmain Tigers, I collected one of the worst late tackles seen in rugby league. One of their forwards, Dave Edwards smashed my head with a late swinging arm and knocked me out cold. I went down like a sack of potatoes. The force of the hit nearly took my head off.

Players learn quickly when offloading a ball to lift the arm and elbow to protect themselves from any oncoming traffic. I'd done just that after giving an inside pass to send one of my players through a gap. I could hear the crowd roar and knew we had breached the defence. I started to turn to watch the action when Edwards caught me with a coward's shot. I couldn't remember a thing and evidently was out for several minutes. I was taken to hospital and kept in a darkened room for several days. The impact left me dizzy and confused and I was like that for many weeks. The brain scan proved I had one but, that was the only good news. The surgeon was quick to point out that the impact had been so strong my brain had shifted and was badly bruised on the side opposite the impact area. I had to be sedated for quite some time in the hope it would settle down and repair itself.

The doctors showed me the x-ray and explained the problem. I was lucky in one sense because they explained that any sudden movement could send me to a life in a wheelchair or even prove fatal. It scared me rigid and I prayed to God and thanked him that I had escaped with my body intact and that I could move my arms and legs. The tackle messed up my brain box and for weeks and I had to go for therapy to encourage the old grey cells to start working again. It was a long, slow road to recovery that included tasks such as turning pages of a book and shouting out the colours, placing round pegs into round holes, square ones into square holes and so on. It might seem like child's play but it helped me regain my memory and kick started my brain.

Most people have been called thick in the head at some point in their lives. I can vouch that I have been there and done that. There are many who still think a few of my brain cells are dead and they are not far wrong. Even to this day I have to write down a 'trigger' word to help me remember what to say when we go on air at Sky; it's a little bit like having to use the choke before the engine fires up!

It was a tough period and the club was superb. It helped me be positive throughout. I missed only the last couple of games that season so I had the entire summer break to recuperate. It was slow and sometimes heartbreaking and I started to wonder if I'd played my last game.

Great Britain legend, Brian Lockwood, who was playing with the Tigers at the time, admitted years later that Tiger's coach Ron Willey singled me out for rough treatment before the kick off. He had even asked Brian to put me out of the game. This was a request he was quick to turn down.

Evidently Edwards was more than keen to get the pommie for not many Aussies sent me Christmas cards. I watched a replay of the incident many years later and I felt sick. It was the most gutless, cheapest shot I would ever wish to see. Amazingly Edwards only got four weeks' suspension which created a huge outcry amongst the fans and the media. It again prompted a call to clean up our game. The incident took place during a low period in Australian rugby league. Hundreds of parents stopped their kids from playing the game due to the poor image on TV. Nobody playing the professional game was safe and the referees appeared to have no control. Many actually enjoyed the rough stuff. It was open season and I ended up as one of the pheasants.

It was no coincidence that a few weeks later the NSW rugby league decided to clamp down on rough and dirty play by bringing in a top legal eagle. Mr Jim Comans was a well respected lawyer in Sydney. He was employed to shake up the disciplinary meetings. At the press conference Mr Comans stated that any player who didn't keep within the rules would be dealt with severely. He added, 'I can assure the good fans of rugby league that incidents like the Edwards' late tackle on Mike Stephenson will not be tolerated.' Chairman Comans kept his word and not long after he banned Les Boyd for a year. The message was clear, clean it up or be shipped out.

I honestly think the appointment of Jim Comans saved our game. It wasn't just because I was involved in a serious incident. I felt he gave confidence back to parents that he would clean up all levels of the game so that youngsters would be safe to display skills without fear. It was the start of a concerted effort by the NSW rugby league to change its image. They did this with a huge media campaign and I'm proud to say that a few years later I helped in some small way. Rugby league is a hard game without the cheap shot merchants. We need children to come through the ranks and enjoy playing the greatest game of all. We did not want the youngsters to be put off by brutes who display cowardly acts. I can proudly say I have never played a cheap shot on any player. I been involved in some fisticuffs, and I played tough but I never struck a player when his back was turned. Ironically the first game back for Edwards was a televised match against Manly. He took the ball from the kick off and was crash tackled by ace second rower Terry Randall. It was a fair, hard contact and Edwards crashed to the ground unconscious. It was only the quick thinking from a doctor that saved him from swallowing his tongue and perhaps dying. I didn't want revenge by seeing the bloke carted off in a wooden box but I did think at the time that life has a habit of striking back.

The long off season rest did me good. I started to put the bloody pegs and blocks into the right holes and identify red numbers from the green background. Even the doctors were happy with my progress; I felt in good shape and was yearning to pull on my boots again. One doctor suggested it was time to hang up the boots, another indicated I had recovered so well but I could still be at risk. Yorkshire men are stubborn and I was no exception. I came back the following season. Penrith showed even more faith by offering me extra bonuses. This offer was nice but I was determined to just take each game as it came. I'm sure they realised I wasn't going to be running around much longer.

Our season started well with a couple of good wins. I scored two tries in the opening few games yet I knew there was something missing ... timing. Coordination is important in any sport and I just wasn't getting things right. My support play was still good but I was a few yards behind where I knew I should have been. An inch in rugby can matter, so being yards behind was a big problem.

We went to Brookvale Oval full of confidence with more than just a slim chance of knocking off the top team on their own ground. We scored first which lifted us no end and Manly looked ruffled. I felt good, full of running and eager for the ball. 'Still life in the old dog yet,' I thought. Minutes later my luck ran out. Whilst coming into a tackle from the angle on Aussie prop Thompson, he turned at the last minute looking for the offload and smashed his elbow into my jaw. The impact forced my bottom three teeth back onto the tongue so hard it trapped it and left me with no option but to pull the teeth back quickly to allow me to breathe. As I gulped for fresh air, all three teeth dropped to the ground. My jaw was broken in a moon fracture, just below the gum line rather than on the side where most jaws come to grief. The medics said I could be back in about six weeks' time as it was only a hairline fracture. I smiled painfully thinking it had been a long time since I had boasted a hairline.

Two weeks later the club had a horror run with injuries. All four back up hookers were injured and we were scheduled to play a mid week televised game in the Riverina area. The game was part of the Knockout Cup (the Knockout Cup changed its name from the Amco Cup to the KB Cup after a famous Aussie beer). I stupidly said I would step into the breach and help them out. They thought I had completely lost the plot. My jaw felt much better and I was eating okay (slowly but at least I could chew some of the food) so I was confident I could get through the game. The club dentist fitted me with a weird mouth protector with a metal bar at the front to help support the crack in the jaw. Remember this was well before mouth guards were the order of the day. I looked a little like the ugly bloke in the James Bond movie who chewed metal for fun. I wore the mouth protector on the plane trip down south to get used to it. The rest of the team were more than happy as I could hardly utter a word.

Five minutes into the game at the first scrum I felt the jaw snap again. It felt just like I had crunched on a brandy snap biscuit. I finished the match in distress and looked like I'd been chewing on raw meat for a month. There was blood everywhere. Despite being hardly able to talk after the game, I grunted to Don Parish that I'd played against some good youngsters in my time but that the kid who played opposite me was all class. I suggested they snap him up and bring him to Penrith.

'Sign him up quickly, the kid's got it, and you'll need a replacement. That's me done.' I grunted.

I don't think Don was surprised and neither was the team. I looked shocking. So the last game I played was deep down in the south of NSW against a country side in the Riverina group area at the Eric Weissel Oval in Wagga Wagga. The Oval was named after one of Australia's great half-backs from the 1930s.

Amazingly several years later a relative of Eric Weissel presented me with his Australian jumper. It is proudly displayed in my museum at the George Hotel, Huddersfield; the Gillette Rugby League Heritage Centre. Each time I see the jumper on the wall, it reminds me of my final match and brings a smile to my face. This is somewhat different to the fateful night where I was a sight to behold. If I had been a horse they would have shot me. To make matters worse, we lost the game. We just hadn't played well and it was a quiet flight back up to Sydney.

For me it was over.

Sadly the club waited three days before offering the young hooker from down south a contract. It was too late; Western Suburbs had also been watching the game on TV and snapped him up the following day. Ironically West's coach at the time was none other than Roy Masters, the former Panthers' assistant. He became one of the most controversial team bosses the game has ever seen due to the psychology he used to out-smart the opposition and wind his own team up. He is now a well respected journalist and author. Roy knew straight away that the young kid had talent. His name was Ray Brown and he went on to play for

Australia and toured with the Kangaroos.

Amazingly I didn't feel all that sad about retiring. Maybe it was the relief that at least I was still standing. I threw a barbecue at my place for all my team mates to celebrate my retirement. They all turned up and gave me a send off to remember. They left with something to think about too as they said the steak tasted a bit different that day. Little did they know the fuel for the fire hadn't all been wood. My corsets, shin pads, jockstrap, boots 'n' all (now you know where we got the mid week TV show title from) were helping the blaze along nicely. All the players kindly said I would be a great loss to the club and that I would be sadly missed. This included the big prop Bob 'Bear' O'Reilly who was so moved by the speeches he fell into the barbecue pit. We quickly dragged him out of the burning inferno with his hair still smouldering and smoke swirling up his nostrils. I felt touched, for it's not every retirement party that can boast to have cooked a bear marinated in corset and jockstrap sweat.

15

FIFTEEN HEAD OF CATTLE

The ashes from my corset and jockstrap had barely gone cold before country clubs were offering me a chance to coach. I declined all offers, although one club south of Bega, famous for cheese products, couldn't offer me much in the way of cash. Instead they had done a deal with all the farmers in the area to give me 15 head of cattle each on 40 acres of land! I just couldn't see myself in a cowboy hat, trampling over cow shit so I accepted the post of development officer for the Penrith area. The area was huge and kids played rugby from the age of five. It was only a matter of time until Penrith took out the Premiership because the talent coming through the ranks was outstanding. This provided they could entice the youngsters to sign for their local club. For years youngsters had shunned signing for the Panthers because it wasn't fashionable. Now things had started to change. The team was no longer making up the numbers. Suddenly playing for the Panthers was something to be proud of and young kids were walking around town wearing Panther shirts rather than other clubs' colours.

My departure from the playing field also gave one youngster a chance to take giant strides within the game. His name was Phil Gould. 'Gus' was the man I recommended to take over my role as skipper. Despite being just over 18, his attitude was good. He had a mean streak running down his back and he had the ability to get things across to his players. He was a born leader. He wasn't the fastest and most skilful player but he was smart. He knew which options to take and when to bring them into play. It didn't surprise me when he went on to become a great coach at club and state level. He won both the Premiership and State of Origin titles and probably would have coached Australia if he'd kept his mouth shut. Phil didn't do things by halves and it was a pleasure to have him in the team. He was a grafter, gave his all and wasn't short of a word or two. He pulled no punches and that's probably why he never got a chance to coach the national side. Unsurprisingly he now does a similar job to me but on Channel 9 rather than Sky Sports and no doubt irritates some people.

Another kid who made great progress at Penrith was young prop Tim Sheens. Tim could read the game and knew what made players tick. I pointed out to the club that he would make the coaching ranks one day, and he did. He became a good servant to Penrith as a player and a coach and went on to win premierships for Canberra and recently, Wests Tigers. Like Gould he works hard at the game. Tim is the longest reigning coach in Australian history, just ahead of Wayne Benett at Brisbane. He's a deep thinker and few people know more about the game than Sheens.

I enjoyed the job of coaching and steering youngsters from around the area. It was great to see them come through into the top grade. Penrith has the largest junior team structure in the world. Over 400 teams pass, tackle and kick their way in a bid for stardom. Not many make it but the odds are in the club's favour that some will get a shot at the big time. Players like Brad Fittler and Greg Alexander are just two that were junior recruits. This gives some indication of how good the system is. In fact last season, Penrith won all three junior premierships available with the under 16, 18 and 21 squads all lifting silverware. It could be said that the future's bright but the colour isn't orange, it's black and red, with a touch of silver and purple.

Despite my fear of coaching again, it was different working with eager youngsters and I loved it. I found it was so rewarding. There are many areas of Penrith district that couldn't be called posh and like most cities in the world (Penrith has grown so much it is a city these days) drinking and drugs is a worry. Helping to keep kids off the streets was another reason I enjoyed working in junior development. But I yearned to spread my wings and I found travelling to Sydney to write my columns and match reports tiresome. Reluctantly I resigned from the club and sunk myself deeper into the world of journalism. Being a columnist is one thing. Working to a deadline is another. Although I still wrote two columns a week, getting a story out for a paper under pressure from editors and subs was no easy task. I found it hard to cope.

The famous racing writer, Bill Casey, stepped into John Benaud's shoes as sports' editor after the ex-Aussie cricketer became head of the entire *Sun* newspaper. I couldn't have wished for two better blokes to show me the ropes. Most people think the printed media is full of drunks. They're very near to the truth because the pressure can drive writers to the bottle. Some people in the newspaper business didn't like the fact I had forced my way into the scene without doing the hard yards of coming up through the ranks. To many I was given a dream run because I was a rugby league player. I had been given that chance, but it was far from a dream. It was bloody hard graft. John Benaud and Bill Casey fought hard for me to be accepted as a full Union member in the Australian Journalist Association at a time when the Unions were so strong. After nearly two years they accepted me as journalism was my sole career. Great sports writers such as Gary Lester and Ken Laws spent hours guiding me. I couldn't have done it without such men and I owe them. I still don't type fast, I'm a two finger and thumb wizard so it was a struggle sometimes to get copy in before we went to print.

I read the Aussie papers all the time on the internet. I smile when I read some of the former 'copy' boys who have gone onto become established sport writers. One character was Craig Young (not the same guy who played for St George and Australia) a stocky kid who loved horse racing and took great delight in accepting my copy and then returned grinning to tell me it had been 'spiked'. The mild definition of spiked was that the sub-editor thought it was rubbish. He was a cheeky lad who now writes about the sport of kings for a top class broadsheet newspaper in Sydney. Another top writer and former *Sun* copy boy (who will remain nameless) had a party trick where he would spring out from the pub toilet with pants down to his ankles and his testicles drooping down from his undies and emulate a kangaroo! He did it well too, I might add.

Peter Kogoy was another great bloke who helped me find my feet. His nickname was 'Monster' because he looked like one, acted like one and had a bad habit of tripping up and knocking things over. He was the most ungainly bloke I ever met and was often the butt of practical jokes. One day the young copy boys went too far by inserting an explosive pellet inside one of his cigarettes. After the paper was put to bed we all flocked to the Great Western pub to sit back and watch the action. As Peter smoked heavily, the 'doctored' fag would be smoked for sure. The copy boys became restless when Peter failed to turn up. They were stunned to be told he had gone to face the NSW Adoption Board. He was trying to adopt and change the name of his wife's offspring from a previous marriage. During the interview, a nervous Peter asked if he could smoke. As Peter answered the usual questions about being a good provider and father, the 'bomb' went off. Thankfully, one of the board suggested to Peter he certainly had a good sense of humour and it all worked out well in the end. He was furious and would have killed the culprit had he known who it was. Peter was so eager that he once heard a fire engine passing the Great Western pub. He raced out and ran down the street to jump on the bloody thing and interview the firemen as they drove to the fire scene! I still see him from time to time. On his last trip to London as we shared a pint, someone who had taken umbrage to his 'loud' manner walked past and poured beer all over him. Some things never change.

Ken Laws was a legend in his own lunchtime but never in his own dinner time as he couldn't remember much by the time it started to get dark. He enjoyed a drink so much that he was once given a hat with a holder that siphoned beer from the cap through a plastic tube. Despite his predilection for alcohol, Ken wrote an amusing sports column each day. It is nearly impossible to include humour on a regular basis. Ken wasn't the only journalist to often sleep under the desk at work to ensure he didn't miss his shift and no doubt won't be the last, but he was regular. He once caught a cab home knowing full well he hadn't the money to pay. He told the cab to wait and returned with a standard lamp from his lounge room as payment. The cabbie was more than happy to accept the lamp as it was worth five times the fare. Ken packed his own lunch after that episode and if my memory serves me correct, that was the start of his divorce. His column was a huge hit and gave the Sydney public much to chuckle over. It made him a celebratory around town, so much so he was invited to talk at his old school one evening for a handsome fee. I was invited too but Ken suggested we have a couple of drinks first to settle the nerves. Fifteen 'couples' later we struggled into a cab and fell out the other end. I was a mess, Ken was an utter mess and struggled to get to the head table. On reaching the head table, he shook hands with the principal, grabbed the microphone, grinned, grunted and fell off the stage! I spoke for over 50 minutes and sort of salvaged the evening whilst Ken snored away contentedly. Amazingly I found out later they had sent him a cheque before the event. It was not a smart move to pay Ken in advance but I did try and squeeze something from him seeing as though I did the speech.

'Stevo mate, you'd have only pissed it up against the wall,' he chortled, then proceeded to borrow $20.

Amazingly a week later the school rang me to say I had won a video recorder in the raffle. Ken wanted to sell it and split the money!

'You never even bought any tickets because you were pissed and slept all night,' I cried.

'But I was there,' came the reply.

Ken never could get the hang of paying his debts back. He did repay them in a fashion because he would repay the money on Friday and borrow it again on Monday! He got his just deserts one day when his oversized lump of a body struggled to cross the main road. A beer truck of all things mowed him down. It resulted in him being rushed to hospital with a badly broken leg. I dashed to the hospital after hearing the news and found him in great pain.

'It's so nice to think you care Stevo.'

'No worries, Ken I came soon as I heard the news.'

Despite his condition he still had his sense of humour and suggested it wouldn't have been a bad way to go if the beer truck had killed him. The poor bastard couldn't move so I kindly asked if he wanted me to look after his wallet, watch and clothes. I said I would drop them back at the office for safe keeping. Ken didn't know until weeks after that I snaffled his wallet (there was never any money in it) and borrowed his SCG members' pass to watch England play Australia in the Ashes test. Well he wasn't going to use it! It was when I was about to get married for a second time and Sam Morton and Walter Nelson came over from England for my wedding ceremony. They created all sorts of havoc at the Great Western pub. Sam, a former top class amateur rugby league player who looked capable of ripping someone's ear off at any moment, kept calling all the Aussies 'love'. This term is not uncommon in Yorkshire but it scared the shit out of the Aussies. They thought he was queer. Walter was a huge cricket fan who adored Geoff Boycott. When I introduced him to another of the *Sun* columnists, a certain Ian Chappell, he never blinked and obviously didn't catch on it was the Ian Chappell of cricketing fame. Ian had heard Walter spouting off about Boycott. He laughingly suggested he wouldn't cross the street to piss on the Yorkshire legend. At this point, Walter jokingly grabbed him and shook him around like a rag doll. No one knew that Ian had been for intensive treatment for a back injury before popping in to see sports' editor Bill Casey. Walter's antics did little to help Ian bat well the next day. Ian Chappell struggled in the early morning session and lasted 10 uncomfortable-looking minutes or so at the crease. I was in the members stand as Ian came back to the dressing room in obvious pain. He looked at me and said, 'I'll kill your bloody mate if I ever see him again!'

Sadly the SCG scoreboard was wrong. It should have read 'I. Chappell. Out for 3, bowled Walter'.

The Great Western was an amazing place. Over the years it had a few different landlords but there was no better time than when Doc, Bill and Charlie ran it. They were a trio of characters that sit happily in my mind forever. Before the advent of mobile phones it was hard to track people down. The pub had a wonderful idea where customers stated to the barmaids before buying their first drink if they were in or out in case anyone rang looking for them. I can't remember many saying they were in. The pub was full most of the time. The fun we had there was outstanding. Because the pub was a newspaper haunt, it attracted villains and politicians alike. Many a scoop has been created in the Great Western. It was popular with all age groups; borne out by the fact that on attempting once to select a few songs on the juke box I caught one of the young copy boys having it off with a bird from the typing pool, oblivious to anyone. Her legs were spread akimbo on the corner of the machine blocking out any chance of me selecting Sinatra or the Beatles.

The drinking sessions never stopped really. Many a time we would stay upstairs in one of the many bedrooms available. On a few occasions I would sleep in my van which I parked just around the corner. We often drank so long into the night that the three owners would take out the till, go to bed and leave us to it. They allowed us to help ourselves to drink and pay the next day for what we had consumed. I can happily say nobody cheated and often chucked in more money than they owed. We knew that when we had a local pub like this we shouldn't shit in our own nest.

Doc, Bill and Charlie drank so much we all wondered how they could make a profit but they must have. They sold the Great Western and went on to open a bigger place just out of the city centre. The sale did wonders for our health because the next landlord had to be persuaded to keep the pub open after 11.00 pm! One of the blokes had to carry a small bottle of brandy in his pocket to get over the shock of having withdrawal symptoms approaching midnight. The same guy proudly claimed at work that he was surprised to find out his bedroom walls were painted green. 'I hate green!' he shouted and vowed never to be sober again. We all went to his funeral later that year.

The new pub management changed a few things and also gave me an introduction to food. Not eating it, that is but serving it. I was about to enter the world of bistros and restaurants.

16

CUCUMBER, ANYONE?

A new wife and a new life settled me down somewhat. I started to concentrate on adding extra money to the pot. I still enjoyed newspaper work but I wanted to earn something extra. My new job came about through my brother-in-law, Brian Adams. Brian owned a bar called Fanny Adams, a famous drinking hole on Collaroy Beach which was a favourite spot for many of the Manly Sea Eagles stars. My wife Maureen was involved in the bar and encouraged me to help turn the bistro downstairs into a full on restaurant. The idea struck me as hard work but interesting. Because I enjoyed a challenge, I gave it a go.

It proved to be hard, enjoyable work. For once I saw the other side of the coin when it came to drinkers. I'm sure over the years I've irritated more than a few barmen and barmaids after having a few over the top. When the table was turned, I soon realised how bad it could be. We called the restaurant 'The Oxford Scholar', a play on words that the Aussies use to describe a dollar and a pommie. I wanted the restaurant to offer solid British fare. We served roast beef, Yorkshire puddings and all the trimmings. It worked out well. Naturally we also cooked steaks and fish. I was encouraged by how well the restaurant did.

One thing that didn't excite me was learning to cope with the chefs! If there's one industry that serves up more idiots, alcoholics, drug takers and psychos than catering, then I have yet to see it. Chefs are mad. They have to be to work in such a hot environment. On more than one occasion I had to jump into the kitchen and cook. I lost count of the number of times I had to throw out a chef slumped in the chair drunk as a skunk when just two hours earlier he was right as rain preparing food. Often a chef would just get worse as the night wore on. The food came out fine at 8.00 pm and then went downhill afterwards. One chef attacked me with a meat cleaver and accused me of having an affair with his wife. I could have understood this if he had been married, but he didn't even have a girlfriend! We had to hide booze from the chefs. Many pleaded that they needed wine, port or sherry to offer a good sauce. Proper chefs do. The ones I employed typically started out great which lasted for five or six weeks. They would have good reports and good reviews from the local press. This left me thinking, 'I've hit the jackpot with this one,' only for them to explode in a tantrum at the slightest thing. Fortunately I had picked up cooking techniques along the way. I realised early on that I'd better learn how to prepare the meals and make the sauces. I was lucky that my mother taught me the basics of cooking at a tender age. Adding the magic sauces over food worked a treat but I didn't want to spend the rest of my days cooking over a hot stove.

I enjoyed the meeting and greeting side of the business and had many good times with regular customers. I also had a few nightmares with some of the other customers. It's amazing how many couples would come into a restaurant, order their food, eat most of it and then complain when there was about one inch of steak left on their plate! 'This steak is off,' they'd claim, and then try to avoid paying for it. Others even promised not to tell the papers how bad the food was if I gave them a free bottle of wine! Some customers could be cheeky bastards. I'm not the prettiest thing on two legs, I certainly don't look soft and on a number of occasions I threatened these customers that either they paid or suffered the consequences! My racked body was still healthy looking and what is now flab in those days was muscle. As a consequence, not many customers refused to

The two tries that helped win me the Harry Sunderland man of the match award in the Championship Final.

What dreams are made of, lifting the trophy after beating red hot favourites Leeds.

Always up for free drink.

The last time I ever pulled on a Dewsbury jumper, 1973.

Dewsbury Supporters send me off to Australia with a huge farewell card.

Welcome to Australia, a tough baptism for the Pommie. Penrith v South Sydney.

One hairy skipper.

I did pass sometimes.

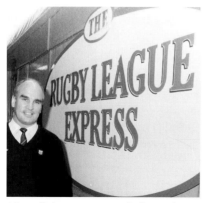

22 weeks living on a train! The Rugby League Express in 1988.

Let's get ready to rumble. Sydney Railway Station.

My old sparring partner, Eddie Hemmings.
© Sky Sports

Now there's a nice juicy, fat ear... On camera and about to be assaulted by an Ostrich!
© Sky Sports

Voted Dewsbury's greatest ever player in 1998.
© RLphotos.com

My old team mates dig deep. They threw a huge £1.10p on to the plate ... most are from Yorkshire!
© RLphotos.com

Championship reunion. Left to right, back row: Mick Lumb, Tommy Smales, Trevor Lowe, Harry Beverley, Keith Voyce, Jeff Grayshon, John Bates, John Clark. Front row: Adrain Rushton, Terry Day, Alan Bates, Greg Ashcroft, Myself, Alan Agar, Nigel Stephenson.

My aunts, Doris and Margaret, at my induction to the Dewsbury Hall of Fame.

I must have been on a diet! On location with Eddie and Shaun McRae.

The George Hotel, Huddersfield. The birthplace of rugby league and the home of my dream, the Gillette Rugby League Heritage Centre.

Phil Clarke and yours truly push our old mate Scott from Hull on the Outward Bound charity walk from Hull to Widnes.
© RLphotos.com

Trying hard to engage brain before opening my mouth.
© RLphotos.com

put their hand in their pocket. The food was good and we knew it because we ate there ourselves. It was good enough for us and I'd say that's the proof of the pudding.

My mother came to stay in Australia a few times. I knew the warm climate would do her good and sometimes she would stay for the full 12 months allowed by her visa. She often enjoyed working for me behind the bar. Mum enjoyed a gin and tonic like a horse enjoys water and even in her later years could drink me under the table. I asked her to come down to the restaurant for a couple of nights which proved to be good fun. This was until one night a bunch of South Sea Islanders started getting a bit rowdy. They'd paid their bill and decided to order a final drink before we closed. I served the drinks whilst we were cleaning up, only for them to start arguing amongst themselves. The argument became so bad I knew I had to get them out before they started fighting. I politely asked them to leave at which point they all started to attack me at once. I knew only one strategy to save my good looks and that was to grab one of them quickly and hold him by the throat. I did this and they backed off watching their mate getting throttled by the minute. If I had let go they would have killed me. I kept a bloody tight hold on the bloke's neck, whilst doing my best to put his Adam's apple behind his ears. Three of them went outside but one of the group decided to jump me. He pounced over the top of us, pushing both of us to the floor. My mother rushed from the bar brandishing a bottle and was just about to hit the bloke when she realised it was a bottle of gin. She did a double-take then changed it to a bottle of whiskey and smashed it on the bloke's head. To everyone's relief they charged out together leaving a more than a relieved son, mother and daughter-in-law. Later that night, the door was damaged. Two weeks later they tried to come in for a meal as though nothing had happened. I politely told them to sod off.

The bar upstairs was a fun place. All the top players who were playing against Manly ended up at Brian's place. The bar is still there. It's called the Surf Rock Hotel these days but Brian still owns it. The bar attracts not only big league stars but World Surfing Champions too. It's the place to be seen. Many of my old foes visited and stepped downstairs to say hello. John Dallas Donnelly was a regular, despite living way out in the Western Suburbs. Like most of the players, he knew Brian and I well. He had a habit of sneaking down the backstairs and helping himself to food from the kitchen. He amazed me one day when he joined me at the bar upstairs. He was chomping on a huge cucumber! He then proceeded to abuse me because I'd locked the fridge and that was all he could get his hands on. Dallas was a larger than life character who sadly died after having a fit whilst surfing. He was a great player and tough to play against. He was part of the era when Roy Masters coached Western Suburbs where they called themselves the 'Fibro' boys. The team was named after the so-called cheap material used in building houses out that way. Masters would call the posh Manly outfit the 'Silvertails'. It made for good entertainment but the clashes between the two clubs got nasty at times. Especially when coach Masters wound up his own players by getting them to slap each other's faces before they went out to play.

It was always rugged playing against Wests at their Lidcombe Oval home ground. I had the dubious delight of meeting up with a young kid from the bush playing his first game for the club. He tried to punch me on the nose the first time I tackled him. Thankfully he didn't connect on that occasion but the same Les Boyd made a name for himself by not missing that often in years to come.

Bruce Gibbs was another Western Suburbs heavyweight who liked to create havoc. He shocked people from the north of England whilst playing for Oldham. One Christmas he had two tons of sand delivered onto the street in front of his terraced house. He then plonked deckchairs down and had a barbecue with all his Aussie mates dressed in t-shirts and shorts. The rest of the area shivered.

During that period, some of the Wests players came over to the northern beaches for a boat trip. The boat trip sailed out of the Royal Motor Yacht Club not far from where I live. By the time they came back late that evening, they were worse for wear and decided to play darts in the back bar. They soon got fed up aiming at the dart board and instead decided to throw darts at each other's exposed backsides. There was blood everywhere, yet they calmly removed the darts from one backside and took aim at another. We don't have many characters like that in rugby league any more!

17

NICE ARSE!

The media side of my career was ticking over nicely. In addition to newspaper work, the radio station 2SM offered me a job joining the Frank Hyde rugby league team to cover all games over the weekend. Because it meant I would get to a designated game on a Saturday and a Sunday, the opportunity was hard to turn down.

Frank Hyde is one of the nicest blokes I've ever met. He is a true gentleman who was a great player in the 1940s for North Sydney. He then made fame and fortune as a commentator for the popular radio station. I was thrilled to think he wanted me to join the team (who were also a good bunch). It was another case of walking into a job with no experience. Again I took a deep breath and gave it my best. My best turned out not to be so hot! I struggled to understand the timing and phrasing needed on radio and when they first came around the grounds to listen to my reports, I mumbled, stuttered and often got the scores wrong. It was not a great start to my broadcasting career.

Frank was fantastic in helping me understand the industry. He told me to calm down, not to rush things and prepare well. It was sound advice but it took me a long time to adjust to broadcasting. I often think back and thank both Mr Hyde and the radio station for giving me time to settle down. I've never been short of words in my life but it was a different story when I realised I was talking to thousands of people that I would never clap eyes on.

Slowly and surely I came to grips with it all. I became

more confident in expressing my views and feelings towards the game. I began to jot down notes rather than write out a full script that I read. Reading off a script more often than not sounds like someone is doing just that. The flow of language just doesn't sound right. Using notes enabled me to relax more and I spoke to the listeners in a natural voice. I wasn't on air long, maybe 20 seconds. It's easy to think that speaking for such a short time is easy. Try it sometime and you'll find out that 20 seconds **is** a long time.

After two seasons, I was surprised to be approached by another radio station, 2GB. They offered me more time on air and involvement in a few discussion programs. I accepted the job in the hope it could lead to something even bigger. This time I was involved in interviewing the players and discussing the match after the final whistle had blown. I loved it, although it was fraught with danger sometimes. One player was so excited over the team's victory he dropped the 'F' word. He suddenly realised what he'd said and then went on to apologise for saying the 'F' word. He followed this by another attempt at voicing his delight which included three 'F' words! He then finished off by stating he should have said 'Bollocks' instead. Unsurprisingly he didn't do many interviews with the live media after that episode. It was great fun and it beat working for a living.

So there I was, offering my dulcet tones over the airways, writing regularly for the *Sun* newspaper all wedged in between throwing chefs, and the odd customer out of the restaurant. Life was breeze! Little did I know there would be an ill wind heading my way. Thankfully it took its time before blasting me flat on my backside.

The national radio station, ABC, snapped me up to become the summariser for all their league games. I teamed up with commentator Jim Maxwell, a switched-on broadcaster who had made his name in calling the cricket; something he still does to this day for the station. Jim was an easy bloke to work with. His very relaxed style suited my more robust approach and we gelled well as a team. He knew the game but I always suspected he had more of a soft spot for rugby union. I detected that he perhaps would have been happier calling the 15-a-side code. He knows broadcasting, has a great way with words and a wicked sense of humour. Little did he know that so do I. One incident ruffled his feathers somewhat. He rather foolishly asked me to take a parcel over to England and post it when I landed in London. Up until that point I never imagined that Jim was as tight as me. I was amazed to think he wouldn't pay the extra postage to send the parcel direct to the UK.

Because my two children from my previous marriage lived back in the north of England, I travelled home for two months a year. The extra weight of a small parcel was no problem. As the parcel was addressed to the BBC in Manchester, I decided it wasn't worth posting it. I decided to deliver it in person. Manchester is about an hour's drive from my parents' house in Dewsbury. It was no heartache anyway as the package had the name of a female written across it. Let's face it; I wanted to see what type of English lady was attracted to my mate. And being a nosey sod, I wanted to know what was inside the package as well. So off I drove over the Pennines to cast my eyes over this northern goddess.

She turned out to be a cracker and I could see why Jim had done his bollocks over her. She was the type of girl who could change a man's life without knowing she had! On arriving at the BBC, I was told that the lady in question was in a meeting and asked if I would care to wait.

'Of course I will,' I replied.

Five minutes later a tall, handsome character with a quiff in his hair that would have done Elvis Presley proud strode out of the lift and introduced himself to me.

'Hi, I'm Eddie Hemmings. Come up for a cup of tea, she'll be out of the meeting soon.'

'Nice bloke,' I thought and followed him towards the sports room where I presented the parcel. We all waited for her to open it. She did and the first thing that she looked at was a return ticket to Australia! Boy, Jim had done his dinner on this one and I couldn't blame him. We all had a great night out; a few drinks a good laugh and I left in the sad knowledge that Jim was going to get a 'Dear John' letter very soon. I hatched a plan to wind Jim up and asked his lady what her house was like. I found out whether she had a garden, the colour of her curtains and the type of furniture she had. I planned to have heaps of fun when I got back to Aussie. Before I departed I told Eddie that if ever he needed any help with anything regarding rugby league then he should give me a call. I gave him my number and drove back to Dewsbury.

At the start of the following season, both Jim and I were calling the opening game between North Sydney and Manly. Because it was a Saturday match the game commentary was slotted in between the horse racing.

I think it was during the 3.35 pm at Randwick when I suggested Jim take a good look at a lady with a short skirt in the crowd. I suggested her nice arse reminded me of the girl I took his parcel to.

'You met her?' he asked.

'Yes, it wasn't far to travel so I delivered it personally.'

'You took it to the BBC in Manchester?' He cried.

'Not only that, she invited me back to her place. Nice garden and what about the leather chairs?'

Jim went crackers and grabbed me just as the studio announcer was crossing to us live at the ground. I can still hear the bloke back in the studio saying '… we appear to have lost the line to North Sydney Oval …' We had. Jim was furiously trying to wrap it round my neck. Some people just can't take a joke.

It was two years later that I heard Eddie's voice again. He rang me to tell me he had switched from football to rugby league. He was coming to Australia for the Great Britain tour to Australia and New Zealand. He asked me if I would be his colour commentator for the three tests against the Aussies.

The rest, as they say, is history. Little did we know it was the start of a new partnership that would last a long time.

As the ABC didn't have the broadcasting rights for the internationals, I was available. I gladly accepted the offer and enjoyed working with him. It must have gone okay because I received a nice letter from the BBC head office that remarked on my professionalism and forthright comments. They said that any time they needed a colour commentator, I would be top of the list! Wow, it was one thing working in the media but it was rare indeed to get a letter of admiration.

Things just couldn't get any better for me at this time in my life. I progressed to doing live TV at the ABC with Jim despite the fact he tried to strangle me months before. We settled into a good partnership. Jim then moved up to start his cricket career in earnest and I was joined by Dave Morrow. Dave was an eager beaver who loved all sports and probably had a bet on each of them every day. He liked a wager, that's for sure and with the way my life was going, I was confident our partnership would be a safe bet. How wrong could I be?

To lose one job is hard. To lose two jobs is heartbreaking. Within the space of three months my life turned upside down. The newspaper war for afternoon supremacy between the *Mirror* and the *Sun* reached its climax. Two newspapers couldn't exist together. One had to go. Sadly, after 13 years with the Fairfax mob it was the *Sun* that went down. There had been rumours for months that one newspaper had to go. Then one day, the editor, John Benaud stood on the subs table to announce that after today's issue the *Sun* was gone. His speech was simple, quick and straight to the point. John ensured that everyone who wrote had to file copy as he wanted to include all our names in the last issue. I still have the last issue at home in Sydney. It's framed as a reminder that things can and do happen in life. It's not all a bed of roses in the garden. The paper had even had drawn up all the redundancy cheques for the staff!

When we walked out after the last edition, we were all

stunned. We probably didn't even notice the traffic on Broadway as we made our last trek across to the Great Western Hotel to drown our sorrows. I remember talking to one of our sub-editors who had been at the company for over 40 years. He cried into his beer and repeated that his life was finished. I cheered him up and suggested he look at his pay-off cheque, surely that alone would bring a smile to his face. It didn't but it should have. I think it was for $908,000 and yet the bloke cried out of sadness rather than joy. You may wonder what was in my envelope. After working there for 13 years you might expect a nice little surprise but because I was on contract I didn't even get an envelope!

To their credit, both John Benaud the editor and Bill Casey the sports' editor took my case to the union. After seven months of haggling, I was awarded a month's wage for each year I had been at the *Sun*. It wasn't a fortune but it was the principal that mattered. I can't thank those two blokes enough for forcing the union to squeeze something out of the Fairfax organisation.

The closing down of an established newspaper was a big news event. TV, radio and of course the opposition press were there in the pub waiting for us like vultures. We all knew they had a job to do and we gave them heaps of copy. The interviews were non stop. They went on for hours. So did we. We went on for three days in fact. At least six of us didn't go home. It was one hell of a bash.

Thankfully I still had my TV work at the ABC and I knew I could survive. I was better off than some of the others who drifted away and struggled to get regular employment. Then a few weeks later, I received a telegram at home telling me that my services were no longer needed at the ABC and that I shouldn't bother turning up at the weekend! There was no warning, no face to face explanation, not even a telephone call. Naturally I called them and asked what was going on. The ABC had just appointed David Hill as the new MD. He was a pommie to boot, and he had decided to make changes. I was one of them. They feebly told me that I was too controversial and the new 'broom' wanted to sweep clean. Off I went. Another company had given me an offer I couldn't refuse ... the sack! At least I had another four months left on my ABC contract which would give me time to look for other work. This turned sour when the ABC told me they would only pay me one month. They advised me it was a waste of time trying to take a government run organisation to court over such a minor issue. Minor! The bloody cheek of them. My legal advice was to take the money and put it down to experience. I took the money and vowed I would rise again and show them I was good at my job on TV.

One of my mates at my drinking haunt, the Royal Motor Yacht Club, knew I had been dumped and offered me a job straight away. This was kind as I had a wife and two young daughters to feed. I accepted the offer and the following Thursday I started my new life as a labourer. I drilled holes in the ground for a company that put in footings and foundation pylons for houses that were slipping. This was a major problem in our area due to the sand content of the soil. We were working on a huge house overlooking the water when the owner said I looked a ringer for that pommie bloke on TV.

'This is that pommie bloke. They sacked me,' was my reply.

As you can imagine, I felt low. David Hill was not mentioned in our household ever again. Yet it was another man with the same name that later on helped me get back on the horse and show me that the 'Sky' really was the limit. But I had plenty to do before that opportunity arose. My years of collecting old rugby league memorabilia revitalised my dream of creating a Rugby League Museum. The viewers would have to wait a while before this bald, ugly mug reared its head on TV again.

One thing that did come to light at the time was an offer from England to coach Fulham. Despite not wanting to enter the intense world of coaching, the invitation to go back to the UK was tempting. But whilst my vibes were running at a low ebb, I discussed it with a close friend of mine, Ron Carroll who was a sporting players agent. Ron was a shrewd man and a close mate so he drafted out a contract and sent it off to the club in London. To my surprise they rang me straight away and gave me the job.

Bev Risman had just been sacked at Fulham and I tried to track him down, seeing it wouldn't be a bad idea to find out why. Unfortunately I couldn't get hold of his telephone number. The club explained they just wanted a change and new ideas so I said I would fly over for six weeks and see how the set up worked. If it worked for both parties then I would sit down and discuss an extended contract for two years.

A flight was quickly arranged and I put my affairs in order, packed my bags and was just putting them into the car to take me to Sydney airport when the phone rang. It turned out to be one of the directors of the Fulham club who had been arranging all the flight details and my hotel in London. It soon became obvious the guy had been drinking and was slurring his words but he got his message across just the same. '...Don't think you're coming over here to tell us what to f****** do. We run the club and you will have to do what we tell you and we have decided not to put you up in a f****** hotel, you will be staying with me at my house so I can keep an eye on you...'

To say I was stunned was an understatement. Here I was kissing my wife and two kids goodbye with the luggage in the car and this drunk was abusing me over the phone! As you can imagine I told this bloke to stick his job where the sun don't shine. I unpacked, put the kettle on and had a cup of tea, explained what was going on to Maureen and the kids and rang a top class restaurant and booked a table for lunch. No way was I going back to the freezing cold of Britain in November and working for a mob like that. It was obvious why the club was in dire straights and perhaps why Bev Risman had flown the coup. Little did I know that whilst we were enjoying a nice lunch, this boozed up director was sleeping off the drink and had forgotten to tell his chairman that I wasn't going to be on the plane. Not surprisingly the following day I received an abusive phone call again but this time from the chairman and he wanted to know why I wasn't walking through customs at Heathrow.

'Why don't you ask your other director?' I replied.

It took a while for it all to sink in but I explained in a quiet fashion what had gone on and that I certainly wasn't going to be involved with a club who have directors on the bottle and abuse people over the phone. I didn't need a job that badly.

The Fulham club went to town and bagged me to the hilt in the press. The journalists had a field day. Some of them who had been friendly whilst I was playing in England got the knives out and called me all sorts of names, one paper suggesting I'd killed the club off!

I made sure they got a refund for their airline ticket and pushed the incident far from my mind. Plenty of papers rang me in Australia to find out why I had not boarded the plane and I just told them to ask the people that ran the club. Simple as that. I could have snapped back at all the shit that was being aimed at me but I didn't because I wasn't going to stoop to their level. In any case, I knew Fulham were not going to tell the truth about having a piss-head on the board.

18

THE 9.15 FROM SYDNEY CENTRAL

Drilling holes for a few weeks was one thing. It helped the cash flow, but I knew I didn't want to wallow in self pity, spend the rest of my life being a defeatist and end up with blisters on my hands and a bruised ego. The one great thing about Australians is that most of them don't care what people do for a living or how people go about earning their coin. There are a few snobs who think they are better than others but most Australians meet people on a level playing field. I learnt that lesson early when a bloke at the pub came in and announced he'd gone bankrupt. He promptly bought everyone a beer! There was no sniggering or talking behind his back about how he'd failed. The entire pub supported him and helped boost his confidence. He'd lost a lot of his money in a venture that just didn't fire and even had to sell his house and start all over again. He did start over and is now worth millions (or should I say his wife is)!

My mates were supportive and eager to help. I did odd jobs here and there, one job I did was painting flats for a rental company. I survived. I knew I had a lovely house with a swimming pool and the works. I was determined I wasn't going to cry the sad tale and allow it all to slip from my grasp by sitting at home and hoping the phone would ring to offer me a job in the media. I wasn't skint, far from it, yet I needed something to spark my life again. My ambition for years had been to open my own museum of rugby league history and memorabilia. I had heaps of memorabilia such as honour caps, medals, old photos and programmes. I longed for the chance to display it all. I purchased an old van and fitted it out to carry my first ever exhibition. The only trouble was deciding where I would exhibit and finding someone to help pay the costs.

Selling a product is not an easy job. Selling a dream is even harder. I quickly put together a small but effective exhibition to show to the world. Australia was the hotbed for our game and the loyal fans from NSW and Queensland were about to learn more about rugby league than they could get from books. That was my thinking anyhow. I set about trying to get the message across to the power brokers at Phillip Street, the head office of the New South Wales Rugby League (NSWRL).

Each year Sydney hosts the Royal Easter Show where all the country folk from the bush display their wares, be it cattle, sheep or produce from the land. The show is a fortnight of sheer fun and brings farm life to the city. It's also big business as thousands of sales are racked up during the show. Each category competes for big prizes. Exhibitors can win medals and hard cash. This brings prestige and exposure and as a result sales soar. Show bags for kids turn over thousands of dollars, not surprising when nearly two million people pass through the turnstiles during the two week jamboree. I convinced the NSWRL and Channel Ten TV network that an exhibition of my collection would be a winner. It would attract big crowds to the stand and help generate more interest in the game. So after one week of hard graft erecting the show, the doors of the famous Hordern Pavilion opened and we welcomed a huge crowd to the stage for the first day. The rugby league exhibition was an immediate success; children and parents swarmed all over it. We were all stunned by the response and excited about the impact it had on the fans, especially those from out of town. To say that manning the stand was hard work was an understatement. My trusty helper and good mate Bob

Dawson and I slept in our vans outside in the car park for three weeks. This meant we were up bright and early to prepare for opening time. The doors opened at 9.00 am and closed at 9.00 pm. Even though the hours were long and it was hard work, we loved it. I knew I had a chance to be involved in the game I loved again.

The Sydney Showground is huge. The older fans of our game will recognise the buildings from seeing wide shots of the adjacent Sydney Cricket Ground. In the showground it was like living in a new town. All were friendly and enjoyment was the name of the game. When the crowds dispersed for the day the exhibitors hit 'our town', as the pubs would stay open on site. We often drank into the early hours of the morning, grabbed a couple of hours' sleep on the mattress in the back of the van and started all over again the next day. All the Sydney League teams took it in turn to show up with their stars. It was my job to interview them on stage. It was great fun as I talked to the likes of Mick Cronin, Peter Sterling and Wayne Pearce. The fans loved it. Hundreds of supporters would rush towards the stage to shake hands, get autographs and take photos. It was a magic time and I felt proud to be involved in setting it up. One day there appeared to be more than the normal surge of fans. Over a 30 minute period people came from everywhere to get a good spot near to the stage. I was interviewing the Sydney Roosters' players at the time. As the Sydney Showground is in their neck of the woods, I thought perhaps they had more supporters than most. I only figured out the real reason for the crowds when one of the top marketing gurus from Channel Ten told me I would be interviewing two up and coming stars on television. I don't watch soaps at all but even I'd heard something about Channel Ten's new show called Neighbours which had been launched barely two weeks before. I had to interview two youngsters who, according to the marketing guru, were going to take TV land by storm. Looking out over the huge crowd, I felt they had achieved that already. It was madness. Young kids screamed out their names until the stars finally appeared, shaking like leaves and looking like two small, frightened kids. The fans went crackers. Of course Jason Donovan and Kylie Minogue went on to bigger and better things. It didn't surprise me after the way their fans treated them that day. The manager of the Hordern Pavilion couldn't believe it. He was a man who had watched the like of Stevie Wonder and Elton John perform on the same stage without receiving such a response. We actually had to stop the interview and appeal to the fans not to push forward as some youngsters were struggling to stay on their feet. Bob and I started pulling fans onto the stage in fear that someone would get hurt. The stars were promptly whisked away. Thankfully some form of order was reached when fans realised the pair had flown the coop!

I feel smug having trod the same boards as the likes of Miss Minogue and Mr Donovan. Not many people can honestly say they appeared at the Hordern Pavilion for three weeks straight! To put it into context, all the top performers appear at the Hordern Pavilion. It's a similar thing to big stars appearing at the London Palladium in England. Interviewing the two young *Neighbours* stars did wonders for the show. Many fans returned day after day hoping Jason and Kylie would appear again. They never did and they probably wouldn't remember me now anyway!

The NSWRL made a smart move by selling all the clubs' merchandise. It flew over the counter faster than we could think. The promotional guys knew soon enough that this was a winner as all the merchandise was a bargain price. Sadly Bob and I did not earn a percentage of what was sold. Not that we expected anything. The NSWRL paid us good money to run the show and rent out my memorabilia. We were happy.

After two days we had the idea to charge people to throw a ball through a hole. If they were successful they won a prize. Bob and I found some old timber, cut a hole in it, rigged up netting down either side and we had a real 'Roll up, roll up' fun fair attraction. As I had to run the show and do interviews, Bob had the job of running our new enterprise. He didn't like the idea at first. He openly admitted he wasn't too fond of kids. He was frightened to death he would end up kicking a few off the stage for playing up.

'Give it a try,' I encouraged, 'it may work out okay'.

Two hours later, he had a bag full of Aussie dollars. This soon changed his mind. He was encouraging the kids to dig deep and have a go. Suddenly he looked and acted like Santa and children were his best friends! I still wake up smiling over Bob's voice booming out, 'Three balls for a dollar,' and the occasional, 'Three dogs balls for a dollar,' or 'Dogs fart in a bottle,' over the loudspeakers in the vast arena. He said it so quickly that nobody picked up on it. We rolled about laughing all day. And why not, the coin was doing the same.

Bob and I became so close we were like brothers. It was a sad day when he retired from helping with the exhibition and moved up north into Queensland. He still lies around in Queensland contemplating his ever decreasing navel whilst throwing down a few tinnies of Tooheys New beer. I still see him from time to time and he still greets me with, 'Dog's fart in a bottle'.

We exhibited at the Easter show for three years. It turned the corner for me and I decided I wanted to go even bigger. I knew I couldn't afford to rent a place in Sydney to host a museum. I couldn't even afford to rent a place outside of Sydney, come to think of it. I decided to test the water and met the marketing men at the Sydney League yet again. This time I didn't just want to put on a show for a couple of weeks, I wanted to do it for more like a couple of months! Encouraged by the huge number of rugby fans who travelled from the country areas to see the show in Sydney, I wanted to take the show to the fans in the bush. At first we wanted to build a huge, portable system that we could put on a truck and set up quickly in each country town. Then came the idea that made us all smile, '... let's put it on a train.' So within two weeks we started to rip out four carriages and build our own moving museum. I hadn't realised how big carriages are until I ripped out all the seats. It gave us a perfect area for the display. I went round to all the leagues clubs and borrowed extra memorabilia and photos. As the Aussies held all the world wide trophies, the cups and shields made their way onto the train too. In fact if memorabilia could be moved, it was gone. Even a few screwed down items found their way into my trusty van, bound for the Rugby League Express Train.

The train had all the mod-cons and comforts including four bedrooms, a kitchen, a chef and a lounge for entertaining guests that was stocked to the eyeballs with drink. The idea attracted some major sponsors. This was good, considering the exhibition took just under a quarter of a million dollars to stage. We completed fitting the train out just in time. We set off in a blaze of glory from Central Railway Station to the sound of a band and with good wishes from all the top brass of the state government and rugby league. We were waved off on our trek by Australian rugby league chairman, Ken Arthurson (a stalwart at Manly for years) and by the former Australian and Parramatta player, John Quayle. John was the new boss at the NSWRL. In total, the train took in 25 towns and travelled just under 10,000 kilometres of rail track.

Anyone who complains about a train journey lasting more than a few hours should think about our 16 week trip aboard the Rugby League Express Train. As a kid, I always wanted to drive a train and this was going to be my chance. Even if it was against the rules, I often jumped into the front driving seat and helped the Express towards its next destination. There's a kill button that the driver must hit within two minutes. If the driver fails to do this, the train automatically starts to apply the brakes. I got used to it and I enjoyed every moment up front.

Our first stop was Goulbourne, 300 miles from Sydney.

We travelled all night to ensure we were ready for the first rush. Bob Dawson brought me an early cup of tea and suggested I didn't look out of the window because it was pouring down with rain. It was throwing it down in stair rods. The train was parked at the station with a gale-force wind and not a soul in sight. It looked like our project was doomed on the first day. I gave the order to open the doors at 10.00 am sharp and told all the staff to cross their fingers. What we didn't know was that the railway officials had not allowed the fans to enter the station because it was too dangerous to stand exposed on the platforms. They had, unbeknown to us, steered the fans to the back entrance of the station. We couldn't see the fans but they could see us and hundreds of people poured through the train in the first couple of hours. We were on track to a huge success.

Most of the top rugby stars in Sydney have come from the breeding grounds of country football. It was a master stroke by the NSWRL to fly in the rugby heroes of each town we visited to meet the fans. The homecomings created huge interest in the local media. Local TV and radio stations fought to interview the league stars of the time. Unsurprisingly, all the major stations from Sydney (who had links with country stations) made a big issue over the fact an Englishman was running the train. I could guarantee the first question to be posed related to me being in charge of a train promoting Australian rugby league. Ron Casey, a leading radio show host, was inundated by listeners complaining about my appointment. To put it mildly, they were pissed off over my selection. Ron rang the first morning of the exhibition and posed the same question. I cut him short. I stated that it was my idea, most of the stuff on board belonged to me and that I'd got off my backside and helped the league bosses to launch the train. This should have shut them all up but it didn't. At each new town came the same old question. Not that it mattered. The publicity was good and the most important part was the excitement of the enterprise. The youth of the country started thinking rugby league again after a period where the city and country leagues just didn't see eye to eye.

Not all radio stations wanted to give us publicity. Alan Jones, Sydney's leading talk show host hardly mentioned it. I knew I wouldn't be getting a call from him either due to the way he publicly hung me out to dry over a story I once wrote in the *Sun* newspaper a few years earlier. I'd had an exclusive back-page lead indicating that Manly coach, Bob Fulton, had offered huge money to Canterbury Bankstown's hero scrum-half Steve Mortimer to join the Sea-Eagles. There was a massive outcry and people ducked for cover saying it was all rubbish. Suddenly nobody had spoken to Mortimer, never mind had offered him money. I knew I was right as Mortimer's agent had told me about the meeting at the Circular Quay Café close to where the Manly ferry runs. Mr Jones blasted me live on air for being irresponsible. He said he was surprised that a man of my standing could make up such a story! It was heavy stuff, but I knew I had my facts straight. Twelve months later Steve Mortimer wrote his life story. He revealed details in the book about the meeting with the Manly coach and the huge amount he was offered to switch clubs. I can remember making a copy of that page and sending it to Mr Jones by first class post. I never got a reply. I guess it must have got lost in the post!

What weren't getting lost in the mailbox were letters of praise about the train as thousands of people turned up. Coaches and players from yesteryear were on hand to help show the kids how to pass and tackle. The full Monty of league skills were there for all to have a go at and enjoy. The crew lapped it up. We certainly enjoyed the hospitality of the sponsors. One sponsor in particular, Tooheys brewery, dropped in a few cartons of beer for us the day before we set off from Redfern sheds in Sydney. I say 'a few' because the bloke who delivered it asked where I wanted the cartons putting. I waved towards the last storage carriage and dismissed him because I was busy and we were behind deadline.

'Listen mate, I don't give a shit but you want me to put it in that small van at the back?'

'That's right. What's the problem?' I replied.

He dragged me by the shoulders to show me one of the hugest trucks I've ever seen and declared proudly, 'That truck's full and it's all yours.'

One forklift truck and a few railway volunteers later, we finally loaded up no fewer than 500 cartons of beer. 12,000 cans! They were everywhere, stashed in cupboards, stacked under the beds. There was no space which didn't host a can. Even the chef contemplated clearing out one fridge to accommodate our new passengers on the trip of a lifetime. It certainly was the trip of a lifetime if you enjoyed the odd beer. Word soon got around that the train was a good venue to be invited to. We held a welcome party each night to fulfil our obligation to our sponsors: Tooheys, State Bank, FootyTAB and of course the NSWRL. Any top player worth his salt rang up and offered his services. Greg McCallum, the top referee and later the former boss at the RFL joined the crew. So did Joe Lydon who was playing for Eastern Suburbs. Even that great scrum-half from the 1940s, Keith Holman, came for one day and stayed four nights on board. The fact that Keith has never had an alcoholic drink in his life gives an idea what a great project it was. I could go on for ages naming all the stars at the time that came on board but two youngsters in particular stand out. Whilst in Canberra, the Raiders sent two blokes who were such a pleasure to have around and worked so well with the kids that it was obvious they would make it at whatever they turned their hand to. Ricky Stuart and Laurie Daley appear to have achieved a lot and they both still offer much experience to our game. The two days the pair was on board stay with me forever.

As the weeks went on the excitement rose even higher as word got around that the 'League Express' was coming to town. Such was the excitement that the fans in Sydney complained to the newspapers that they hadn't been given a chance to see the museum. The whole concept was to bring back some life into country rugby league after years of bickering between the head office in Philip Street, Sydney and the delegates from the bush. Like I said it was a master stroke from the NSWRL but, like most things in life, someone will complain about it. Even I didn't think the museum would reach such high profile.

After the designated 16 weeks on board visiting the country regions, we had no option but to offer the museum to the local fans in the metropolitan region of Sydney. The prospect of another four weeks added to the tour stretched us to the limit. All we wanted was a few good nights' sleep in our own bed and a rest from alcohol! It's hard to imagine after the episode at Redfern when the sponsor dropped off so many cartons that we could run out of beer, but we did after only eight weeks. It doesn't take Einstein to work out that the alcohol consumption was of a high degree. One telephone call later and the full-to-the-rafters semi-trailer was on its way yet again to restock us!

I hope the reader doesn't lose sight of what we were trying to achieve and think it was a 'booze tour'. We drank a lot but after working 10 hours a day with the general public, we found we needed a swift one from time to time. The bedrooms were comfortable but small and we had to use them as storage space for just about everything. We squeezed in boxes of t-shirts, jumpers and anything else you can think of and worked around it. Bob Dawson was a champion at arranging his room as his room was a bunk bed high up the wall. The height of his bed meant there was plenty of space below to fit no less than 60 cartons of beer for his own little pub (as he called it). He carved out a staircase from the cartons which would lead up to his bed, or what he called 'heaven'. He slept well each night and never took a sleeping pill once. We had a problem one night when the overnight driver ran into a cow on the track. It brought the train to a grinding halt. As I flew out of my bed, I heard an almighty crash next door and rushed in to find cartons of beer all over with poor Bob buried underneath. It took ages to dig him out and when he surfaced, black and blue, he had an open can in his hand! His dedication had to be admired.

I mentioned how much the young Laurie Daley enjoyed his time on the train. He was quick to inform us that when we got to Junee we had a treat in store as his father owned a pub there. Junee is a small railway town handling stock for all parts of the country. The town will probably ring a bell with league fans as it was the club that the great Mick Sullivan came to play with in the 1960s. The town had formed a side to play in a rebel competition. When Mick flew out, the RFL banned him from playing rugby league anywhere in the world. Not that it bothered Sully. In fact I can't remember anything bothering Mick on or off the field of play. He was a tough character and still is a joy to spend time with to this day. The impact Sully had had on Junee amazed me. The people there all remembered the great flying winger and even knew that I had been born in the same town.

Another amazing factor about the rail tour was the number of times we would ride into a town boasting just maybe 2,500 people, yet well over 3,000 people would come through the museum! Australia is a big country and after a while it was no surprise to meet people who had driven 200 miles to see the train.

Daley senior was a great character who wouldn't allow us to buy a drink. He kept the bar open so long that it was daylight when we struggled back to our beds for a couple of hours to reopen the train at 9.00 am sharp (well nearly sharp). The pub was packed and at midnight, the host suggested we needed music and proceeded to rig up a full set of amplifiers, guitars and a drum set. We all played the night away. Even I was forced to sing and play the guitar. I can do neither but instead announced I would play the instrument with my teeth. I took out my top set of teeth, strummed some kind of noise and lisped my way through

'*Love me Tender*'. The crowd loved it, proving beyond doubt that common sense goes out of the window when full of beer.

It wasn't all fun and games. We had minor problems with petty theft. One particularly bad day we arrived at one town to find the police waiting for me at the station. One of the two Sydney players the league sent to the train had played up badly the night before at the local Leagues' Club dance. One delightful chap had decided to drop out his old feller and urinate down the back of a waitress. The town was in uproar and was baying for his blood. The police had the culprit locked up and wanted to know what I wanted to do with him. Even though this bloke was six feet four inches and built like a brick shit-house, I gave him a dressing down and forced him to apologise. The police took him to the airport and sent him back to Sydney. It was satisfying to hear that a day later the club struck him off the playing register and he never played in NSW again. As this was the only major problem during the long trip, the officials at the league were ecstatic. They wanted to do the same thing the following season at the start of the year. The first train foray took place during the Aussie winter. Don't be lulled into thinking Australia is warm all the time. Up north in Queensland and in the Northern Territory it is, but NSW can get bloody cold in June and July.

The year after, we extended the trip to 20 weeks on the track. We even went into Brisbane in Queensland where we stayed for three days for the Maroons fans to enjoy an even bigger exhibition. The trip coincided with a new format where the big clubs played warm up friendlies against the top country teams. The games were played at venues where sometimes three matches were on show. The games were all a sell out and naturally the crowds flocked to the train in their thousands. It was by far the most rewarding moment in my life. Seeing the youngsters peruse over memorabilia and photos will stay with me for ever. Often a youngster would be lifted to look closer at the team photos and ask, 'Is that you granddad?' Tears of pride would stream down the face of a man re-living past glory with his grandson. Moments like these convinced me that one day I would open a permanent museum to tell the history of our great game.

Approximately 1,000,000 people have clapped their eyes on my collection. I knew it was my destiny to continue to convince the rest of the world our game really is the greatest game of them all. Little did I know it would be nearly 20 years later before my dream would come true.

19

THERE'S A POMMIE BLOKE ON THE PHONE

The sun was shining and I had my feet dangling in the pool. Life was good and my exhibition was still doing the rounds after I had signed a contract with the TAB (the NSW government arm of betting shops). FootyTAB had been introduced to quash illegal gambling in pubs and clubs. It created huge interest amongst the Sydney competition as thousands of dollars were wagered each weekend. To be fair, the betting shop outlets were very much aimed at males and not many women found their way into such establishments without feeling uncomfortable. I hit on the idea of taking a road show to all the big shopping centres around Sydney.

After seeing the interest in my rugby league show at the same venues, it was obvious it would be a good marketing ploy to run 'dummy' races on huge screens and allow people to have a free bet. This way they could learn how easy it was to fill out a TAB betting card. We dragged up obscure races from 10 years or so back, renamed the horses and dubbed over a brand new race commentary. Not even the biggest gambler could have remembered which race it was. The venture was a huge success as women doing their shopping were eager to take part. They couldn't win any money of course but huge prizes were on offer. If they selected a winner their betting card was entered into a prize draw for cars and holidays. Not only did we take the show to the big shopping centres, we installed it in some of the big leagues clubs that operate a huge turnover of members. We also took it to a few of the larger pubs.

The chance to win major prizes for nothing is one sure way to create interest. I took my band of 20 attractive women to each venue with a smile on my face ... wouldn't you? It was a great marketing ploy because women felt comfortable with another female showing them how easy it was to fill out a betting slip. I must confess that the TAB knew what they were doing when they requested I should be the one to interview all 100 candidates for the job. Someone had to do it so why not me? Reducing the team to 20 or so wasn't easy but I didn't fall for the trap of selecting someone just for their looks. They had to have character and be able to communicate with strangers. To be fair none were ugly either, let's put it that way. The team worked well and we all had a great time even though it was hard work.

I became close to all the staff and they were quite happy to dump some of their problems on my shoulders. At times I felt like 'Dear Doris' handing out advice about any number of things that even amazed me in the end. Two ladies actually found their true loves whilst working the shows and to my knowledge are still married to this day. Stupid, I am not. Cupid? Maybe. Either way, this particular day as I dipped my feet in the pool and caught a few rays of sun, only the clink of the ice in my gin and tonic kept me from falling asleep. I soon snapped out of dreamland when the phone rang. My wife Maureen shouted down that there was a pommie bloke on the phone who wanted to speak to me urgently. I didn't recognise Eddie's voice at first but sparked up when he enquired if I would be interested in travelling to England to cover the 1990 Australian Kangaroo Tour. Ten minutes later I awaited another call from the rugby league producer, John Davis. He headed the sport section for Champion TV. Champion TV was a company I had only heard of barely six months before when I flew over to watch the Wigan versus

Warrington Challenge Cup Final at Wembley that May. The deal was for eight weeks and even though I wasn't looking forward to the cold British weather, I was excited at the opportunity to get back into TV.

At the Wembley game I had been introduced to a fresh-faced Australian guy with tight curly hair. He had sunk all his money into producing a video tape of the history of rugby league and got scorched badly. Neville Smith is now my boss at Sky Sports' Rugby League department but on that warm summer's day at the twin towers, he left me in no doubt that here was a guy who lived for our game. He was rugby league mad. Neville was injured as a player in his youth and had become a referee down under. He took a huge gamble when he attempted to make his fame and fortune in the UK. I think I would be right in suggesting he had achieved neither at that point in time but we hit it off well and went out on the town in London after the game. The game was once again won by Wigan 36–14. I hadn't grasped at this point that Eddie had switched from the BBC in Manchester to join Champion TV and commentate on rugby league for the new satellite broadcaster BSB.

John Davis and I agreed the terms of the contract and he arranged for me to pick up a flight ticket at Sydney airport. I barely had time to pack as the first game of the tour was at St Helens six days later. My best mate, Glen Farrell, had arranged a barbecue the following day so it was turned into a farewell party. Just before it became dark, Glen's girlfriend remarked that a trip to England would do Glen a world of good.

'Of course, you can't beat travel for broadening your outlook on life,' I said more with tongue in cheek than anything else.

I thought she was just kidding, so did Glen. A few minutes later she produced shoe boxes full of money and started counting the notes on the kitchen table. Where this stash came from I have no idea, Glen looked stunned too as it was a most wonderful gesture. Twelve hours later I had a companion on the flight to London. Boy were we going to have a good holiday. There would be some hard work in between holidaying but I was eager to show Glen the nightlife of rugby league heartland.

I learnt much later that Champion TV tried several co-commentators alongside Eddie over the course of a few weeks before the kangaroos landed in England. They had thrown Brian Smith, Kevin Ashcroft, Neil Holding and Terry Flanagan into the studio but thankfully for me, none impressed enough to convince the production team. Mr Flanagan won't be crying over spilled milk as his shrewd telecoms business dealings over the past few years have made him a millionaire.

Eddie had worked alongside former Salford and Great Britain star David Watkins on radio for quite some time when he was at the BBC. He was disappointed he couldn't tempt him away from ITV's new *Scrum Down* rugby league show. David has often suggested he did the wrong thing in turning the job down. I'm glad he did.

With time running out in the race to find a co-commentator, Eddie noticed a *Big League* Australian programme sitting on his desk and noticed my name on the inside cover. As well as doing the exhibition, I was also selling the advertising for the magazine at the time.

'Bingo. Maybe we can persuade Stevo to come over?' suggested Eddie. The rest, as they say, is history. I honestly didn't want to go back to England to work full time and this trip was just going to be an all expenses paid jamboree doing something that kept me involved in the game. It also provided me with an extra bonus. When I walked into the London studios of Champion TV to sign the contract, I was amused to read in the small print that the amount I thought I was getting paid per week was actually the amount I was getting paid per game. The tourists were playing twice a week! Producer Davis looked puzzled when I smiled as I read through the legal papers.

'Something wrong?' he enquired.

'No, just checking it's all in order,' was my reply. I walked out of the studios far more pleased than when I went in thanks to having a few bob extra in my pocket. London's pubs got most of it that night as Glen and I did the town in an attempt to come down with 'drinkers elbow'. It was made worse when I had to close his mouth each time he paid for a drink in the London bars.

'How much?' Glen would cry in astonishment.

'Welcome to the world of the Big Smoke.'

Unsurprisingly we were eager to travel north and meet the 'real' people. Deep down, I knew this was a chance to re-establish my credentials again on live TV. With the words, 'too controversial' ringing in my ears, I settled down into the GNER railway seats to Leeds and vowed to myself: 'You haven't seen anything yet.' I make no bones about it. I think I have the best job in the world, especially now rugby league is played in the UK in summer. There is an overlap in October and sometimes in November. The restart in February and March can freeze players' wedding tackle at times but I fly back to Sydney during their hot summer. It's bliss. Not that I haven't had second thoughts. In the early years I missed out on summer in both hemispheres. When the great hulk of Mal Menninga trotted out onto the St Helens' pitch that cold night for the opening tour game, I shivered so much I could have jumped back on a plane to Australia straight away.

Sadly it looked like Great Britain would struggle against the Aussie might on that tour. It proved that way in the end. Great Britain had its moments when it frightened the boys in green and gold from time to time. Australia eventually proved too strong for the British lads in the end. The most important thing for me was that Eddie and I gelled again. I wouldn't have thought it had been over two years since we worked together on radio in Sydney. We started to enjoy what we were doing, and didn't take things too seriously. We tried our best to present our thoughts to the viewers in a straightforward way. We ribbed each other all the time and never knowingly lowered the profile of our game. Even now I still think we call it as we see it. Not once have we sat down and discussed what either person will say when the red light goes on in the studio. We don't use autocue, it's all ad-lib and I never think all that comes out of my mouth is the pure English language. I don't expect the viewers to agree with what I say either. I do try to be honest. Eddie of course often looks stunned at some of the stuff I say. He's not on his own either. I'm often amazed at what drivel comes out sometimes and my partner never lets me forget it.

Both of us have done our fair share of charity work and helped many junior and professional clubs raise much needed cash for benefits, injuries and old players who have a hard time. We are more than pleased to help where we can. It's not a chore but sometimes people don't realise how often we get asked to commit our time. Many get disappointed but we try our best to help.

Sometimes we can't win. I remember receiving one irate letter from a junior club in Bradford. The club blasted me for not turning up, disappointing the kids and ruining the night. I had no idea what they were talking about and I'd never had any contact with the club. It transpired later that the bloke who arranged to book me had forgotten to do the booking. Instead of owning up, he played out the entire evening as though I was coming.

Hate mail is another problem created by being on TV. Some letters are funny, others freak me out. One nice chap from Widnes sent me a delightful death threat claiming if he ever saw me on the street he would drive up the curb and run me over. He even added he would reverse the car backwards and forwards until I was dead. Being a fair minded bloke, I couldn't help myself from replying as he was kind enough to put his address and postcode on the letter. I requested he at least inform me of what type of car he drives, the colour and its number plate. A week later I received a photo of the car, signed, 'Yours in Sport'. The world's full of them. Of course such antics were not on the agenda in our early days because BSB was not the most popular broadcaster. Satellite TV was new and our square dish was hard to find. Not because it was small, which it was, but because not many households had bothered to buy one. There would be many days when Eddie and I drove around the north and exclaimed with much gusto when we spotted a squarial. On one occasion we could see three squarials on a long row of houses in Warrington. Most of the time finding a squarial was like searching for a needle in a haystack. I remember that at one charity night, Eddie introduced himself to a crowd of about 80 people. He indicated it was probably the biggest audience we had played to! Our viewers were pretty thin on the ground that first year. I refer to 'the first year' because after much discussion and negotiation with the powers that be at Champion, I decided to come back after the Kangaroo Tour and work the second half of the 1990–1991 season.

After spending Christmas in Sydney, I packed my woolly socks, hat, coat and thermal underwear and flew back into the freezing fog yet again. This time I had the confidence that I could make my relationship alongside Eddie work even better than before. It was the breath of fresh air I needed to get my TV career on song and this little birdie was going to be singing the right tunes. All that was needed now was for BSB to expand and convince the British public that satellite TV was something they couldn't live without. It was one thing to say it and quite another thing to make it work. The other media outlets didn't give us much hope of surviving as the whole concept was based around people paying. 'Pay for TV? You have to be kidding. We pay enough for the TV license.' Was the cry and as I mentioned earlier there were more dishes in a Chinese restaurant than there was people with our satellite dishes. It was a gamble and it wasn't the first time I had to weather a storm in life. We all stuck our noses to the grindstone and worked our butts off! Then a cloud of gloom and doom gathered over the company. There were rumours that BSB was losing millions each week and would go bust. This would have blown our contracts with Champion TV along with it.

'Bloody hell,' I thought, 'here I am 12,000 miles away from home trying to break back into top flight TV with the threat of the sack looming again.' These were nervous times and nobody knew what was going to happen. We bravely went from one outside broadcast game to another with fingers crossed.

I was staying with my parents at the time and mother came into the lounge to inform me that a David Hill was on the phone. My mind raced back to the boss of ABC in Sydney who had given me the elbow a few years ago. Rather aggressively, I snatched the phone ready to give him a good serve when I realised it was an Australian voice asking for Stevo.

'Yes, who's this?' I replied

'It's David Hill mate, the silver fox.'

I realised it was the top man who had made *Channel Nine* sports coverage in Sydney such a huge success. This was the bloke who introduced the clock to be displayed on TV screens on live games. He was the guy who displayed the cartoon duck on screen when dismissed cricketers failed to score a run. He was a man well ahead of his time. I'd had the fortune to work for David a couple of times a few years ago in the studio when Australia showed the Challenge Cup Final. I wondered why he'd called me. We all knew at Champion that David was in charge of sport at our opposition, Sky TV. Like us, Sky TV also found it hard to convince the general public that a dish on the roof was worthwhile. David and I chatted for some time about whether I was enjoying the league and who I thought would be the top sides. I suggested we met up for a drink the next time I was in London.

'When will that be?' he asked.

'I'm down on Wednesday to work in the studio,' was my reply and before I could suggest a meeting place he said I should drop into his new office.

'What's the address?'

'Never mind the address, it's right opposite where you and Eddie sit. Sky has taken over BSB. You're talking to your new boss.'

I was flabbergasted. Within days, Sky shifted people out never to be seen again. The media claimed it was a merger but it didn't look that way to us. It was obvious any dead weight was being thrown overboard quick smart. David landed the rotten job of downsizing the organisation.

David was quick to inform us that the rugby league team would be okay as it was a sport Sky would push heavily. This calmed our nerves but we still had the huge problem of making subscription TV work. It was not an easy task. It wasn't long before we moved into Sky studios' head office at Isleworth. This comprised a couple of small buildings and I think only 100 people ran the entire show. Nowadays there are somewhere around 3,000 staff, perhaps more. This success didn't come about without some hard graft and dedication from all concerned.

Working for David Hill was a joy. He knew how to get the best out of his team. We respected his leadership, especially when he encouraged us to ignore the bad press in the newspapers. The newspapers never lost a chance to snipe at our company and what it stood for. Even to this day when people ask what I do for a living and I inform them I work for Sky Sports, they often stick their noses up as though I've just farted in their face.

'Oh, you work for that Murdoch bloke,' they sneer.

'Best company I've worked with. It's a delight.' I bark back.

I've no doubt the influence from David Hill helped the company expand, even though in the early days he had to beg, steal and borrow certain sports to fill our schedules. Often Eddie switched from rugby league to host other sports. On one show, Eddie had decided to wear a nice knitted black and white cardigan. Hill bounced out of the office the next time he spotted Eddie and blasted him big time.

'Eddie if I want to hire a bloody panda to host a show, I will. No more cardigans.' I think we all got the message.

David was tough but fair and worked tirelessly to make our sport shows work. He was always open to ideas. Like I said earlier, he was ahead of his time and we all rubbed some of his magic into our productions. He had a habit of walking past without glancing at someone. Then he would suddenly stop, turn towards them and ask, 'Any problems?'

Woe betide the person who suggested there were any problems. We all quickly learned the answer had to be, 'Nothing we can't sort out ourselves.' He was good that way and encouraged people to make decisions, to think on their own feet, be inventive and not to be afraid to try something different. His office door was open most of the time. This was a sign that things were okay and we could walk in if we needed a discussion of some sort. When he closed the door, it was a serious business with people being grilled with a force that even Alex Ferguson couldn't match. He never held grudges and told staff the truth. This was hard to take at times but he always took time out to show where things had gone wrong. He was a true professional who has gone on to become a major player in the Murdoch organisation. He now runs Fox TV in America. This is a position he fully deserves. Not many in sports can tell superstars like Whitney Houston when to start singing at the half time of Super Bowl and gently guide them onto the stage! He has never forgotten his past either. One of our junior producers passed through

America a couple of years back and rang him to enquire if he could pop in and see how the Fox sport department worked. David arranged for him to be picked up at the airport by a limo and looked after the youngster as though he was one of the top directors!

One late afternoon, David bounced out of his office shouting across the room to me in a loud voice, 'Stevo get in my office. Quick smart. Now.'

The entire floor went deathly silent and people peeked behind desks and computers as I nervously set off. It was obvious to everyone I was going to get a blast from the boss. It didn't help matters when he shouted out even louder at me to shut the door. He pointed to the chair for me to sit down. 'Now then Stevo, I have just received a call to stand in for one of the top brass to give a speech and I want at least three good jokes.' I sank back with relief. After firing off my full repertoire of both bad and good jokes he asked me to leave, smiled and opened the door. I was barely half way back to my desk when David bellowed out, 'And don't you ever, ever do that again!' I have never told a living sole about what happened in his office that day until now. Some of the old stagers still refer to the day Stevo got the works.

We were all sad when he went to set up Fox Sports although an incident at the Christmas party probably helped make up his mind that escaping from Stevo wasn't such a bad idea after all. The drinks were flowing fast and furious at the Christmas party. Unfortunately the caterers had put some inexperienced staff on the bar. I was chatting away to David and two high flyers from the legal department. After a while, I asked the group what they would like to drink. When I reached the bar, the staff informed me they had run out of wine glasses. Rather foolishly, I suggested they put wine in whatever glasses they had left. I returned with four pints of Chardonnay! I was soon left standing on my own. I realised handing over pints of wine wasn't the best way to impress. Over the next hour I consumed the lot. When I joined in a celebration hokey cokey dance, I slipped and fell over, pulling at least 20 people to the floor with me, At this point, I realised I might be a touch over the limit! I couldn't for the life in me get up. Thankfully Neville Smith came to my rescue and escorted me to the safety of a spare office where I snored my way towards one hell of a hangover. I apologised to David the next day who took it in good spirit suggesting I had been in the grip of the grape. 'Happens to us all,' he said, but added it would be a good idea if I drank wine by the glass and not by the gallon in future.

Like I said he was a great understanding bloke. The guys at Sky and the wine industry miss him.

20

BOOTS 'N' ALL

Filling the boots of David Hill at Sky was going to be no easy feat. We all wondered who would be brought in to take over the ship. The ship, I may add was cruising smoothly and keeping its head above water. The general public was at long last accepting the fact that if it wanted good live sport it needed satellite. Our sport coverage was becoming second to none. Camera angles and replays gave the viewer an inside look at sport that had never been achieved before in this country. The subscriptions were building with pubs and clubs clamouring for Sky. They knew our live broadcasts brought in the punters. It did help that we now had the rights to televise football. In televising sport, we captured the nation's hunger for more and more games.

Unsurprisingly the man who stepped into Mr Hill's shoes was Vic Wakeling, a tough, experienced operator who had been in charge of football production since Sky merged with BSB. Not many outside the company knew him but he has steered our sports crew to bigger and better things since taking up the challenge. Hard work never does any harm and is the road to success. Those few words sum up Vic Wakeling. I shudder to think about the hours this man puts in each week. Through that fact alone he deserves to be called the most powerful man in modern sport.

Vic's a Geordie. Like most people from the north east, he has a wicked sense of humour. He's dry and a witty straight shooter who tells it to you straight. He's a man's man! I, like many others, was interested to know how he would handle the top job. When he was appointed, I was somewhat edgy due to an incident a few months before. Our Man of Steel Award Ceremony is an event at the end of the season. The entire bunch of power brokers, journalists and the usual hangers-on get together and celebrate the selection of the player of the year. For most of the time the event is held at the Midland Hotel in Manchester. Often the celebrations go on into the wee hours where there's much hilarity. Vic, being a football man, was intrigued over the impact of some of the tackles in rugby league and the often explosive manner in which rugby league players exchanged pleasantries. The conversation swung around to the 'Liverpool kiss' and whether it was different from the head butting technique that was favoured in and around Newcastle (an indication of the high standard of conversation offered at such functions). Laughingly, I suggested that the Liverpool version was aimed at the nose, whereas the Newcastle version made contact via forehead onto forehead. For added impact, I lunged my head towards Vic's head. He sadly moved forward towards me at the same time. I didn't miss and poor Vic jolted back slightly dazed. It was an accident and I was quick to point that out. Thankfully he knew it was an accident, but I caught him quite hard. He just shrugged it off as though a fly had hit him instead. Many weeks after this incident, I remember Neville Smith ringing me and asking if I had heard who had taken over David Hill's job.

'No, I haven't, who got it?' I asked.

'The bloke you head butted at the Man of Steel!'

It's always nice to get off to a good start with a new boss.

By this time we had started to introduce the first ever rugby league magazine show, Boots 'n' All. If Neville Smith hadn't badgered the power brokers for weeks, the show would never have got off the ground. We were all confident that it would attract a good audience, although the powers that be wanted to start with a blank dressing room style backdrop to give the impression of mud, grit, steam, blood and guts. Tongue in cheek, I suggested we may as well have a whippet sitting on our laps as well and, "ey up, it's grim up north' written on the wall behind us. Neville again changed their minds which resulted in leather chairs being added to the set instead. Our first guests were David Howes, who was at the time one of the big bosses at the RFL, and Ross Strudwick, the coach of the London Crusaders. Ross was a real character from Queensland with a typical Aussie sense of humour. He wasn't frightened to speak his mind. We thought it was the perfect clash and were confident Struddy would go for the throat as he had been critical in the press of the way the league had done very little to help the expansion of the game in London. I had known David Howes for quite some time and knew he would handle what ever was thrown at him as he was a trained journalist from Hull.

With much fanfare, Eddie opened the show, softly introduced both guests and started to turn the screw by asking Ross, 'What have the RFL done for rugby league in London?'

I waited for the bell to start ringing and the gloves to be off but Strudwick smiled and said, 'We all know what a good job the RFL are doing to help our club and the development of the game in London.' I was staggered. Eddie's jaw dropped and the debate fell flat as a fart.

Not many people realise what an effect a studio can have on people. The lights, cables, cameras, production teams, sound engineers and those words, 'Coming on air in 10 seconds,' can make the toughest of men freeze. It was obvious the character from Brisbane had dried up under the pressure. On live TV all the best laid plans can fall apart. Before the show, we tried to ease our guests into the mindset of the show by sitting down and discussing what we might say and what they might say in return. What's said over a coffee in the canteen doesn't necessarily mean guests will say it on air. We used Garry Schofield, the Leeds captain for a short period and I remember he gave me some lip in the make up room about how I had pulled Leeds down by suggesting there was a rift within the club. He was animated and this was exactly what we wanted on air.

'Okay Garry, my first question will be about the lack of team spirit at the club.'

'No problems,' was the reply. We quickly entered the studio. The lights went up and it wasn't long before I launched into my accusation of Leeds having no team spirit.

'Yes Stevo, you're right, we are a bit down at present,' wasn't the reply we wanted. Plenty of people have frozen on air and I have done it myself on more than the odd occasion.

We also had the great Alex Murphy on the same show as Fred Lindop, the leading referee at the time. Fred called us both the biggest cheats he had ever refereed! I thought Alex was going to hit him.

Interestingly, some guests provided us with solid suggestions about how the game could progress. Garry Heatherington whilst boss at Sheffield Eagles suggested that the top brass at the RFL should switch to playing in the summer. Other guests asked for full time referees and a better deal for the players. Many suggested a full time Great Britain coach. The ideas just kept flowing. This was back in the early 1990s when our show started. The early shows also included a certain Alan McClone, one of rugby league's first agents who handled the affairs of some of the top players, including Martin Offiah. Agents were a new thing in those days and the fans had no idea what part they played in the 13-a-side code. We invited Alan to explain the benefits to the players. Much to his credit was his reaction when I hit him with the question, 'A lot of fans think agents are a bit on the shady side, a bit dodgy. Are you?' He smiled and wriggled his way out of answering directly.

It was all good fun and the fans appeared to enjoy it. We certainly did, especially Eddie and I because we started to copy the Smith and Jones routine where they go nose-to-nose dressed in white shirts and talk rubbish. Take a look at the size of Eddie's nose and it's easy to see why it was difficult to get near him and to be fair to him, he had no idea what we would be saying in the scene. I had to write the so-called script and because of studio time restrictions, we had to record it within five minutes. He saw the script for the first time with just seconds to go before recording. It was usually a shambles and came out wrong, with more than the odd ad-lib saving the day. We had no idea what impact it had on the show or whether the fans liked it. We used to shrug our shoulders and have a couple of beers. One day a club official said in the press that the show was good but the bits at the start and finish of the programme with those two idiots was an insult to the game! Like they say, no publicity is bad publicity. It was a weird sight to see me racing around the office picking up props for the idiotic nose-to-nose section. Some people might not have liked it, but they were starting to talk about it! We started a show at Christmas in the dark. I wore a Santa hat with a bobble on the top flashing red. Eddie got the giggles, couldn't control himself and couldn't get the words out. He eventually spluttered, 'Is that you Stevo?' and laughed the rest of the time. That was it! The director said it was the best we'd done. It was a four-word classic. Before long all the fans gave us stick and the more they threw at us, the more we made the skits look and sound even worse. Eventually the young kids started to love it and shouted out to both of us at the grounds. People were watching the show. They also started to tune in to our outside broadcasts. The viewing figures were increasing and so were the crowds at the games. Letters even started to drop on our desks from outside the M62 areas. They came from Cornwall, the Isle of Wight, Devon, Sussex, Surrey, Scotland and Northern Ireland and even from overseas! Sadly, we had to drop the end bits as they became a bit repetitive to say the least but Eddie and I still laugh at those times. It was great fun.

The show still runs to this day. Like most things, it needs a revamp from time to time but the team at the Super League department strive to make the show interesting. I even changed into a Superman outfit in a public telephone box in Headingley and nearly got arrested when a woman threatened to call the police. She thought I was a pervert. We also flew to Paris to celebrate the introduction of Paris Saint Germain into Super League and did a skit in front of the Notre Dam. I walked past Eddie with a bundle of coats stuck up my back to impersonate the hunchback! Two gendarmes watched the filming and slowly raised their truncheons, leaving us to apologise and make a more than quick exit.

For a time when rugby league had switched to summer and became the Super League, we took the show on the road. Eddie and I filmed the links from all sorts of outside locations including the Yorkshire Sculpture Park just outside Barnsley off the M1. A new trophy was to be presented at the new Grand Final. This concept was based on the Australian competition. Nobody had any idea what the trophy would look like so we took the liberty to shoot an opener to the show beside an obscure Henry Moore sculpture. People wrote complaining to the RFL about the stupid design of the trophy! You have to love fans. Without fans we wouldn't have a game or a job. Without doubt Great Britain's league fans are the best fans in the world and I don't care which sport is mentioned, they can't match the way we mix together and enjoy the game for what it is … the best.

I mentioned earlier about getting nervous in front of the camera. That's exactly what happed to me when Super League was launched in Paris at the Charlety Stadium. Around 18,000 fans witnessed the French side PSG beating Sheffield Eagles. Neville Smith decided I should announce the teams from the touchline as they ran out. The atmosphere was electric and, after practicing the pronunciation of the French side for the umpteenth time, I thought I was ready. The light came on the camera and I started to talk when at the same time a bloody rocket whooshed past my ear with an amazingly loud bang. This was followed by five or six other rockets. I nearly shit myself. I was a bag of nerves. The first player I had to announce was the PSG full-back Lauren Luchaise and in a mixture of broken French, Aussie twang with a Yorkshire twist, I spluttered out something like 'Loreeen Lencasey' ... I was doomed. Not only that, the French guy calling out the Sheffield side got the names the wrong way around. He shouted with glee names such as, 'Senior Keith' and so on. To make things worse, we didn't know the dressing rooms were so far away from the playing area. After calling out three player's names on the PSG side, not one player had passed me!

Things deteriorated even further when we travelled to Oldham. Oldham took on the mighty Wigan at the Watersheddings. It could be said that this game was a letdown after the atmosphere in Paris. In Paris top entertainers had sung and danced to whip up the crowd into a frenzy. I don't mean any offence to the Watersheddings ground nestled up on top of the Pennines but it was a far cry from that modernistic all-seater stadium in Paris. The big catchphrase for the birth of Super League was that we would, 'Have entertainment that will be the envy of the sporting world.' The viewers may have been tickled pink over that PSG versus Sheffield game but what was on offer at Oldham that day fell somewhat short of the mark. An overweight Tina Turner look-a-like bashing out 'Simply the Best' with a huge hole in her black tights hardly set the pulses racing. It set mine going though when it came to calling out the Wigan side. Facing the camera I couldn't see who was running out of the tunnel and had to rely upon David Redfern, a former Great Britain international colleague who has been a floor manager for some years now to nod and inform me when the players ran out. Everything went well until I called out Martin Offiah. Instead Dean Bell ran past me. Again I called Offiah. This time Vaiga Tuigamala trotted past. The flying winger stitched me up big time before he did actually run onto the playing surface. I bungled my way through both sides and set off for the commentary position only to be stopped by one of the Oldham fans who suggested his home team had no chance against Wigan today. 'You never know,' I replied.

Before I could say anything more, he barked out to his mates around him, 'What chance have we got against a side that's got three Martin Offiah's playing?'

After four weeks of this sort of fiasco, we dropped it because other sides were also taking the piss. I can remember David Howes whispering in my ear that it was a waste of time because the players wanted to get onto the playing field quickly and get on with the game, not be stood in the tunnel hanging about! He was right, although the next time we went to St Helens to broadcast, David, who had become the CEO at Saints, copied the system. Before the game commenced, the announcer started to call the bloody players out one by one! You just can't win sometimes.

Howsie did a great job at Knowsley Road and had wonderful success. He not only helped guide the club to trophies, his PR and marketing experience sucked in the crowds, even if some of his promotional ploys were somewhat bizarre. One week he had posters in the style of Wild West cowboy movies plastered all over St Helens town. The posters had my bloody head displayed in the middle of a target with the words, 'Wanted Dead or Alive!' Evidently I had bagged the team over some issue or other and the entire town was gunning for me. A quick telephone call and a swift bollocking in David's ear did the trick. No more silly posters hit the streets. His use of former Great Britain scrum-half, Neil Holding, was a master stroke. Neil has a great sense of humour and his cheeky style over the microphone had the crowds in stitches of laughter. A few times he would go overboard and insult the visiting fans. It was all good fun but some complained to the club and he was told to tone it down a bit. Yet he still used to wind up all the supporters by pointing to the TV gantry and shouting out, 'If you all hate Stevo, clap your hands.' It was bad enough to get through the crowds in the first place without Mr Holding whipping up the fans to boiling point. Many younger fans took to tapping me on the head as I walked past them to the studio situated at the corner of the ground. The walk through was lower than the crowd barriers and by the time I got to the studio my bloody head was slapped red raw. On a cold night it left my exposed, bald skin stinging like hell. Most were friendly taps, but others slapped quite hard. I had no time to react other than force my way through quickly to ensure we came on air three minutes after the advertisement break. I tried wearing a hat but that ensured they hit me harder. Eddie laughed and said they were all fond of me deep down. It was their way of showing they liked me. I dread to think what would have happened if they didn't like me! Two years later a bunch of youths started to ruffle Eddie's hair as he raced towards the studio. Eddie went ballistic and demanded that from here on in we had to have security to protect us. I laughed so hard, I could barely splutter out the words, 'Come on Eddie they love you deep down.' Ever since that incident we have had police escort us to our studios and commentary positions. I felt this was going over the top but some of the spectators did get a little excited from time to time.

These days the fans at Knowsley Road are a joy to be with. After several years of crowd trouble, the new regime at Saints has stamped out abuse and racist chants from a small section of the crowd. The fans concentrate on watching one of the best open play sides in the competition. I always enjoy being invited into the boardroom at Saints where I can enjoy a quiet drink after the match. They make me feel welcome now, unlike the old board at Saints who actually sent a letter to Sky telling the bosses I was banned from the ground due to my comments on air. I'm not sure how the issue was resolved but I suspect a threat of a reduction in their TV money helped change the club's mind.

Even with protection it's difficult to force through the crowds. I'm not always sure what's going to happen. One security guard stood outside the studio listening to the half time chat. When I came out to be escorted back he turned to me and said, 'Hey, you've just given our team a right bagging, you can walk back on your own!'

The old Central Park was another problem ground for us as we had to race over 100 yards to the studio through the crowd at half time and then race back again at full time. A bunch of young kids used to hide behind the stand and lash out with their boots to try and trip us up. On a few occasions they clipped our ankles and raced away into the crowd. One bloke, who must have been 25 stone in weight, used to give me lip as I raced past on each Wigan home game. On one occasion he was trying to leave the ground and lifted his elbow as I ran past. He hit my shoulder although he had obviously aimed at my head. I was furious, stopped dead in my tracks and stepped back to confront him. He tried to force his way through the crowd but got stuck due to his weight. In retaliation, I launched an almighty boot up his backside. He never said another word after that episode.

Headingley hasn't been a happy hunting ground for me either as a player or a commentator. I never won a game at the ground, including the Challenge Cup semi final loss to Bradford in 1973. I used to dread going there. Thankfully the stairs to the gantry are now at the back of the South stand so we climb up with no hassle from the fans. Before then the bloody spiral staircase was a nightmare. It was situated smack bang in front of the crowd and we were open to abuse. The objects thrown were amazing. Coins were the major worry and I often feared for my eyes. It may have been funny to the fans but it wasn't for this little budgie. We had no protection as the spiral was so tight we had to climb slowly. This left us a prime target. The bottom few steps also left us easy prey for the kids. They tried to trip us up and the amount of sweets that came flying our way was amazing. One youngster waited at the bottom of the steps pretending to ask for my autograph. As I stopped to grab his pen, he threw a handful of midget gems into my face. One caught me in the eye and I was furious enough to say, 'Sod the half time chat, this little bloke's going to get a clip round the ear.' I chased him through the crowd and clipped his ear! The kid yelled out he would bring his dad to sort me out. I told him to make sure he was at the bottom of the stairs on my return and I would clip him round the ear as well! The boy's dad did wait for my return and offered me an apology. He forced his son to do the same. This encouraged my faith in society still providing a platform for manners.

In the early 1990s when rugby league was still played in winter, one freezing night, I tried to say Ellery Hanley's name with the emphasis on the 'H'. This is difficult for a Yorkshire man. My top set of teeth fell out, bounced off the table and disappeared into a mess of cables. It took me ages to find them and Eddie collapsed with laughter. Neither of us said a word for about two minutes over the broadcast mainly because Eddie was speechless! Two minutes is an eternity on TV and our executive producer, Neville Smith, was far from happy.

I wasn't filled with joy either a few weeks later when a guy threw a house brick at me as I was going into the studio. It just scraped the door as I closed it and I could hear the commotion outside as security and the police were called to catch the idiot. Eddie and I calmly went through our chat as though nothing had happened but there was a right ding-dong going on outside. I quickly peeked around the door to see if it was safe to race back to the gantry only to see two coppers arresting a bloke held on the ground. The prostrate man was swearing like a trooper and shouting abuse at me. One of the policemen asked me if I wanted to press charges and I just requested they throw him out of the ground. The policeman's response surprised me, 'We've already kicked him out once.' Amazingly this bloke had been shouting abuse at me from the stands throughout the first half of the game. He was thrown out only to pay to get in again with a brick in his coat pocket! That's how they swell the crowds in Leeds.

We stopped putting the studio near the crowd after that but even when we moved it upstairs, I still came a cropper. The old gantry at Leeds had a wire mesh door to walk through and as I rushed past it, I was unaware it had brushed my eyebrow. It was so cold I didn't feel a thing and went on air with blood streaming down my face! The blood dripped off the end of my nose, much to the delight of Eduardo. He was laughing again at this point. It was only when I looked at the TV monitor that I knew what was happening. I have a heart problem and take medication to thin the blood. When I break my skin, the red stuff flows like the Niagara Falls and it takes ages to stem the bleeding.

The episode on that cold Leeds night may have been messy but it was nothing compared to what happened at Knowsley Safari Park near St Helens. When the RFL decided to go for summer rugby league we had a short interim competition to ensure the switch was smooth. It gave us the opportunity to promote the new formation of Super League. The *Boots 'n' All* crew embarked on a tour of the area surrounding the clubs to entice visiting fans to sightsee in the daytime and watch the match in warm conditions afterwards. The Safari Park was an ideal place to film. The show opened with me walking five elephants through the car park. All five elephants were linked together and I felt like a character in the *Jungle Book*. It was tremendous fun and as I held onto the tusk of the leading elephant and looked into his beady eye, he kept sucking with his trunk on the top of my head. It was a strange feeling to say the least, although the park ranger suggested this big fellow liked me. Eddie wouldn't come within 100 yards of the elephants and despite my pleading; he refused to go any closer. We had to shoot a wide shot of him instead. He wasn't eager to join us on the back of the truck amongst the rhinos. I took great delight when one of the rhinos came on his blind side and tried to push him off. And so the day continued with us filming all the animals. We wondered how to close the show. About 15 ostriches were kept in a huge pen and I went inside the gate and tried to drag Eddie with me. He wouldn't come in. That particular day, I was wearing a red scarf and after a couple of takes, I realised the scarf was attracting the attention of the birds. The kept pecking at it.

I discarded my scarf and Eddie launched into the now famous words, 'Hope you enjoyed the show, as you can see Stevo's in with all the birds as usual ...' At that point one of the ostriches took a fancy to my right ear and proceeded to bite a big chunk out of it. Christ, it hurt. The blood didn't just drip from the wound, it spurted out like a fountain! It wouldn't stop bleeding and I rushed out past the gate whilst the ranger went inside waving a huge stick to keep the birds away. What I didn't know was that the cameraman, Murphy, was still filming.

Eddie lost control again, going into hysterics and shouting out, 'It's bleeding, look it's bleeding!'

'Of course it's bleeding ... the f****** thing just bit my ear off,' was my painful reply.

For those who may be interested, the beak of an ostrich is serrated in a similar way to a saw blade, fine and sharp. To this day I have the scars to prove it. After 10 minutes or so, Eddie composed himself enough to ask the ranger if we needed to take precautions and have a tetanus jab, at which point the ranger replied with a straight face, 'I'm sorry but I don't know which ostrich bit him.' Eddie set off into hysterics again whilst Mark Smith, the *Boots 'n' All* producer stopped me from strangling the man. I did have some revenge when my partner in crime, instead of looking where he was reversing, couldn't keep his eyes off my bandaged head. He smashed his beloved Jaguar into the car park wall. There was justice at long last.

Years later people still tell me they often play that video back when they need cheering up. It was funny but it was bloody painful. The battle to launch Super League was also painful. What should have been the start of global acceptance of our great game became a war that nearly resulted in an acrimonious split similar to our breakaway in 1895. It almost undid 100 years of pride and glory since the fateful day on 29th of August at the George Hotel which drove a wedge between league and union. This time infighting within our 13-a-side code would nearly bring the greatest game of all to its knees.

21

SUPER LEAGUE WAR

Super League should have been a huge boost to rugby league. Whilst everyone in the game could see the advantages, some people in Australia dug in their heels and took up the sword. Having played for many years in both countries, I knew what little reward an injured player received. If a player was forced to retire through injury they received virtually no compensation. This fact was the key to all the top players jumping onto the Super League bandwagon. Contracts were being offered to ensure they had an income for life if injured. Schemes were set out to entice youngsters into university as well as playing rugby league. This meant they had a future outside of the game. These schemes proved an attraction. Rupert Murdoch's backing offered a new dawn for both hemispheres and a chance to expand international competition at both country and club level.

Here in England, most of clubs struggled financially and owed millions to the banks. Many hung on by the skin of their teeth. Maurice Lindsay may have his critics but at least he realised this was one chance to wipe the debts clean and restart the code on a sound financial footing. Lindsay was the boss at the RFL at the time and no doubt his strong attitude ensured the vote went the right way. The British clubs accepted Murdoch's News Limited offer and Super League was born in this country.

The plan was to erase debt and provide the players with a

good living and give the fans a better deal. There would be new stadiums, junior development, better coverage on TV and there would be money available to ensure the plan got under way. Rugby league was in a win-win, situation. A fairy godfather had landed and waived a magic wand.

Rules and regulations were drawn up to ensure a percentage of the money the clubs received would go into development. The clubs looked at it in a different way. Thousands of pounds that should have gone to improvements went in the players' pockets instead as the fight for league prominence began. I don't want to bore anyone with the fine details of what was written in that Super League blueprint. Let's just say most of it was ignored when the battle between the game here in England and over in Australia exploded. Both sides were eager to secure the top names and so went about offering huge amounts of money to star players to stay with their respective leagues.

It was a blessing for the players' pockets and a huge, messy, ugly boil on our game. In some cases players picked up a cool $1,000,000 in Sydney to stay with the Kerry packer organisation which had leant its power to opposing the new Super League structure in Australia.

Our top stars were raking in the coin too, and agents flew around the world brokering deals and playing one organisation against the other for their client's signature. I don't blame the players for taking advantage of this war. Rugby league is a tough way to earn a living but some players didn't give a damn which side they played on. Loyalty is one thing but most of it was bought.

Coaches were also being bought up in a major scramble as the phones were red hot with offer and counter offer. Handshakes didn't count for anything. I know of one incident where a bloke changed his mind three times and no doubt the amount on offer changed too.

The sad part of all this was how it affected the people that count, the fans. Things were in turmoil as cheques were being thrown about with gusto. All the fans knew was that the toilets and beer standards at the grounds wouldn't change. It's only over the past few years that fans have seen a change in facilities. We are now able to watch our game in comfort and purchase a pie that won't break any dentures and have a cup of tea that isn't stewed. I remember taking Ken Arthurson to task over his campaign to stop Super League from being formed. Ken is a great bloke and has done heaps for our game but on this occasion I couldn't agree with his stance. His campaign where he hung huge signs around Sydney claiming, 'It's our game,' irritated me. Arthurson and John Quayle ran the show at the Australian Rugby League and New South Wales Rugby League respectively. The word 'our' indicated it was 'their' game. The game belongs to us all: the players, coaches, backroom staff and the fans, the hard working people who took it from grass roots level. The game does not just belong to a few administrators. It became a personal battle. Heated words were exchanged amongst fans, fighting broke out in certain areas, families were split and even I became embroiled in the hate campaign. Yes, I work for Mr Murdoch's company and enjoy doing so. This fact didn't entitle the kids at school in Australia to give my two daughters a hard time. They were threatened, pushed and punched because their dad worked for Super League. I don't actually work for Super League, I work for Sky but it didn't matter, I was associated with it such was the venom of this split.

It's only recently that the Australian game pulled together and decided what a futile war it was. The game lost millions of dollars whilst the legal boys sat at home and counted their fees. Nobody can actually give me an exact figure of how much went into the lawyers, players, administrators and coaches pockets but I know even a fraction of it would have provided a huge boost to the junior development of our game. It broke the ARL and the NSW leagues and left a bitter taste when the two warring parties made up. It created eventually the NRL as we know it today. At least in England we recognised what a blessing the advent of Super League was to our game. We had many detractors when Super League was first announced. The powers that be irritated the fans no end by telling them what would happen. Northern people didn't like being told what to do. The announcement that three clubs would merge and form Calder United (or some other obscure amalgamation) didn't go down well. They should have let the clubs weigh up the financial benefits of such mergers and work it out amongst themselves. Ironically, the RFL are going towards that idea in the not too distant future by bringing in franchises to apply for Super League. That's what should have been offered in the first place.

Another point that many fans overlook is the fact our game was on its knees. It was nearly broke and in danger of being wiped away from national exposure. The game would still have existed in small pockets with small crowds. It needed a shake up at all levels. Changing to a summer competition has attracted bigger crowds. The marketing of the Bulls, Rhinos, Warriors and other teams has given youngsters a mascot they can take to bed with them. Unsurprisingly, if you ask some of the younger fans about their favourite player, they often reply 'Ronnie the Rhino' or 'the Bull-Man'! Sky's audience figures for Super League go up each year. A survey last season indicated that just over 65 per cent of viewers are from outside the M62 area. Massive crowds at the grand final indicate the return to playoffs has been a huge success and it is now classed as one of Britain's premier sporting events. The return to Wembley for the Challenge Cup final is another jewel in our sporting history and since the advent of full time players; the standard of play is amazing.

How I wish I could have had that chance. It's the only thing I feel deprived over. If only I could have played the game I love without the problems of working a five-and-a-half day week, it would have been heaven. Many fans ask me about how I must hate these modern day players getting huge money. It doesn't bother me one bit. I enjoyed my time and my memories are a constant source of satisfaction. I'm not one of those old players who whinge about today and moan about how the old days were better. Nobody can claim they've heard me say things like, 'In my day' or 'When I played,' because it doesn't matter what I did. The fans are watching their heroes of today and that's how it should be.

So when the day came for Super League to be launched I was excited. So was Eddie. I must say we looked pretty smart too at the launch at London's Sports Café just off the Strand. Both of us had been with Patsy, our stylist (not for our hair). She had fitted us out with new suits, shirts, ties, the works and we decided it would be a good idea to invite her along to the launch that evening. It wasn't surprising that she accepted as we retired for a late lunch and celebrated our shopping spree with a couple of bottles of wine, or three!

Both Eddie and I knew we didn't have to officiate in any way so we let our hair down slightly. We waltzed into the Sports Café with Patsy at the same time as Linda Messenger, the page three girl. To the entire world it looked like we both had a busty girl on our arm. It was a coincidence that made its mark as journalists threw an envious glance our way. The photographers were quick to spot Ms Messenger. It isn't surprising to those who have seen the talented model work the press. She is one smart cookie who has made a fortune. She's no dumb blonde, that's for sure. The media obviously thought Patsy was another page three girl and flocked around both ladies like flies. We lapped it up as the cameras flashed away. Later that evening a bunch of us ended up in China Town when Chris Caisley, the Bradford Bulls chairman and director of Super League Europe, offered to buy us all a meal. We dragged poor Patsy along. By this time she was somewhat worse for wear (not that any of us were in great shape) but it became quite clear she had hit the brick wall when she fell asleep face down in the fried rice. We finished the entire meal, including the rice by slowly lifting Patsy's head, scooping the rice out and carefully placing her rather cute features back onto the plate. She looked so peaceful. Patsy, to her credit, rang me early the following morning and asked if I knew where her pushbike was. She asked where we had been that night. The poor girl walked around London for four hours before she found her bike locked and chained to some railings off Bond Street.

The opening game of the historic competition was to be in Paris. Naturally we got excited at the chance to sample the delights of the French capital. I've already mentioned my panic over announcing the teams at the stadium but I had to endure some frantic, if comical, moments at De Gaul airport. Sky chartered a plane to take all the team, including cameramen, technicians and producers and so on. When we saw the plane, we didn't feel entirely confident. It looked far from tip-top and shook all over the place on take off. To make matters worse, they announced they'd not had a chance to stock up with beer or spirits for the flight. Only the first three rows got the chance to purchase a nerve calmer. Three weeks later, the same plane had to crash land with the Leeds United football team on it!

We arrived at the airport and they sent us through a special customs' section. I was dying to go to the toilet, so as soon as we stepped off the tarmac, I bolted for the first bog. By the time I had finished my business, the entire crew had gone through customs. They had locked all the doors and I was stranded in no-man's land. Thankfully I could see through the glass windows and tried to attract the attention of our guys in the terminal. They appeared to ignore me a number of times, so I started to climb the glass partition … boy they didn't ignore me anymore. Two armed policemen came rushing towards me with guns aimed in my direction. My command of the French language is limited but I got the idea that I shouldn't move any further as they screamed at me. A few bows and scrapes later and a dozen attempts in 'Franglish' to say sorry, they finally opened the gates and let me in after frisking me all over. I really don't think I look like a terrorist.

For some reason it never runs smoothly when we hit Paris. There was the time one of our production staff dropped a bundle of Euros worth about £1,000 in the hotel foyer one night. Fortunately one of the team picked up the money, otherwise we would have had to buy our own meals. This time the same girl involved in the Euro saga had flown out in advance to arrange the coach to pick us up at the airport and take us to the ground. Unfortunately the girl and the coach were stood outside Orly airport as we arrived in De Gaul! To say she wasn't bright is an understatement and she didn't last long after arranging a hoist platform for a camera we didn't use anymore at a cost of hundreds of pounds. The final straw probably came when executive director/producer Neville Smith requested she put the lights back on because we still had interviews to do out on the pitch side.

Neville blew his top when she casually turned around and switched on the scanner studio lights in the truck!

'Not those bloody lights. The floodlights.'

Like most partnerships, the relationship between Eddie and I gets tiresome and tense at times. To say we've never had a cross word would be telling a lie. I know I've got up both Eddie's and Neville's noses at times and they have infuriated me but, apart from a couple of bust ups, things have gone pretty smoothly. Working with the same people all the time can be a strain so we try and keep a mocking tone throughout. Dishing out the odd abusive comment, joking with each other helps ease the tension. There's plenty when it comes close to kick off time and we go live on air.

Once, in the early years, Eddie and I were summoned to

a meeting where some whiz kid marketing guru started asking questions. He asked us why we thought doing studio work and commentary as well was a good idea. It didn't take long to see where this guy was coming from and where he wanted Eddie and me to be going to ... separation! We are the only ones at Sky that do this type of broadcast and we have done it for over 16 years. I wasn't going to let some bloke fresh out of college split the team and I told him so in no uncertain terms. We have all worked hard to get our broadcasts to the highest point and we strive to make it even better each year. We both agreed it was wrong to throw away all our hard work establishing a team ethic. I realise there are plenty who don't like our style. There are others who like it and a few who would think nothing of pushing both of us, or maybe just me, off a cliff.

Eddie is the most professional presenter and commentator I have worked with. It's a joy to sit at the side of him most of the time. I say 'most of the time' because on a couple of occasions we have fallen out. Once was after an article appeared on Phil Clarke's former web site called *www.rugbee.com* written by the ex-Salford coach Karl Harrison. Karl wrote a scathing article that claimed I was past it. He said it was time to go. He went on to suggest it would be a good idea that I be replaced of course by none other than Phil Clarke himself. I couldn't care less what anyone says about me, everyone has a right to voice his or her own opinion and Mr Harrison certainly had given his. I make enough comments about players and officials to realise I'm not immune to being slagged off. It's part of the job. What hurt me was the fact that Eddie and Neville tried to keep the information away from me. They contacted Phil and suggested it would be a good idea to pull the article quick smart. He did pull the article but it was too late. Several people had seen it and a few days later informed me about the content. Unsurprisingly our next discussion over the issue was somewhat heated. I made it clear that all I expect in life is honesty. I told them that I am big enough to look after my own battles without any help and disliked anyone making decisions on my behalf. I added that trying to hide things away from me was childish and foolish. All this, I may add, blew up just one hour before we went on air at Bradford. The air was blue but I said my piece and they said theirs and we went about our job like professionals. We had to. The show must go on.

Sometimes when presenting, I perhaps didn't feel too well, or a problem had arisen at home or in business. The viewers don't want to be bothered by this. They pay their money and expect a top production. Presenters have to put these obstacles to one side and smile down that camera. The hardest thing I have ever had to do was help co-host the Man of Steel awards just four hours after my father died. Dad had been in a home for over a year and was getting weaker each day. Although I knew he was slowly drifting away it still came as a shock, just as it did three years before when mum passed away. I arrived too late to see mum before she died. I flew from London in a rush, only for a traffic jam in Leeds to prevent me saying my last farewells. I was determined to be at dad's side when he left us.

Watching a parent die is a deeply sad moment. I realised all the tribulations and hardships he endured to make me what I was today. I wanted to hug him and tell him a million times how much I loved him and thank him. My father was a fighter to the end. After spending the last few days flat on his back, he managed to sit up at the last moment, looked to the heavens, closed his eyes and laid back down to take his final breath. My oldest daughter, Hayley, was by my side and we hugged each other and cried. Then she told me that granddad would have wanted me to carry on and go to work. She was right. Dad never missed a day off work other than for illness so I drove over to Manchester to join Eddie at the Midland Hotel.

Both Eddie and Neville wanted me to step down and let

Eddie do the entire evening. I wanted to do it for dad and they understood. Only the three of us in that room knew what had happened that day and I felt sure my old man was up there somewhere, looking over me and helping me through the night. My father got to know many of the Sky crew and enjoyed their company, especially Eddie. He thought Eddie had the neatest hair style, even neater than his own which was so slicked down it looked like he'd painted it on.

Dad was right. Eddie is one of the neatest blokes I've ever met, whilst I can only be classed as messy. Let's just say he likes luxury. Don't we all? There are times when we were forced to rough it. This happened whilst we were out in Australia for a Great Britain tour. We decided to drive 300 miles from Sydney to Parkes to watch Great Britain play the country locals. It was a warm up game that attracted thousands to this sleepy hollow and accommodation was impossible to find. Everything had been booked out for months. I had a mate who owned a chain of pubs and had just bought a dilapidated shack of a hotel in the town centre. A quick call ensured we could stay the night but he warned us the place had been run down and it wasn't going to be five stars. Boy, you could say that again. The new manager made us welcome and explained the beds were ready with nice clean sheets, so we settled in downstairs to enjoy a few ales before taking our cases upstairs. When we finally entered the bedrooms it was a real shock. There were no carpets and not much was left of the walls. There were holes all over the place. As it was an old country pub, the toilets were way down the landing and they didn't even have a door! Eddie refused point blank to stay there.

'I'm not staying in this dump,' he said.

I blew my top and suggested he bloody well drive to the next town and see if he could get a hotel there. It was 60 miles away. As the new manager downstairs had given us plenty of free drinks, I accused him of being an ungrateful snob. Common sense prevailed when he realised a nice, clean bed in any room, good, bad or indifferent, is a lot better than sleeping in a car. We shook hands and went downstairs to thank the new manager for his hospitality. We sank a few more beers. So many in fact that we all could have slept on a clothes line by midnight!

Eddie comments about our time together by suggesting you only get 10 years for murder. After 16 years together one shouldn't be surprised that both of us try to throttle the life out of each other from time to time. And I know he gets frustrated with some of the stuff that comes out of my mouth. Here are some comments that have left him dumbfounded:

'He hit him with all the might of an exercise missile.'

'He's got a smile as wide as Christmas day.'

'Got to the checkout and lost the trolley.'

'If you're going to put your foot in the water at least make sure you're on the beach and not in the car park.'

'The wheel's still turning but the hamster's left the cage.'

'If you lose your house keys you may as well break into your next door neighbours'.'

'Losing a game through one of your ex players makes you feel like you've divorced your wife and she wins the lotto the next day.'

'I've been itching down under to get back here.'

'It's more than five Eddie, It's in double figures. Nine.'

'I can't believe a referee can't count to six all he has to do is count on one hand.'

'Throw me off the train at Dewsbury and I land at Batley' (*explaining the momentum rule*).

Most of the time it's a blast working together and as I have explained, Eddie does get bemused at some of my outrageous sayings. He's dropped a few clangers in his time too. The biggest clanger was at Warrington when we came on air after half time and waited for the players to come out of the dressing rooms. For some reason they were delayed, so the cameras were set on the local cheer girls. One camera zoomed into a cheer girl doing a cartwheel so close it framed her legs. Eddie wasn't watching the screen and didn't realise how close we had zoomed in. He turned to me and said, 'Fancy having a bash at that Stevo?'

I struggled to keep a straight face and took a deep breath before replying, 'You mean the cartwheel?' Silence was golden before I broke down with laughter. I was reprimanded big time and had my knuckles rapped!

Presenters have to be careful about what they say these days and anything suggestive can be their downfall. There has to be no racist comments and we have to be polite throughout. Sometimes presenters tell the truth and it still lands them in hot water. For example one Saturday night Papua New Guinea was playing Wales in Swansea. During the first half, Eddie enquired what made the PNG side so fluent with their ball handling skills.

'It's all down to the coconuts. They play with them on the beach all the time,' I replied, which is true.

That same game I had some mates over from Australia and I got them some media tickets to enter the ground. I told them that they must not go to the press box but just settle in with the crowd where they could. We were just about to start the commentary when I spotted all four of them walking, or should I say stumbling, around the sidelines of the playing area where they were taking great delight in waving to the crowd as though they were important officials. Little did I know that instead of press passes they were given photographers' passes! I expected some international incident when they tried to sit in the PNG dugout. Fortunately one of them spotted a sign saying 'bar' and they climbed the fence and disappeared.

The gantry at Swansea is the highest of them all. A sheer climb up a ladder of 25 feet didn't deter one fan. He climbed up just before half time. He was pissed as a fart and tapped me on the shoulder whilst I was commentating and asked me for a light! I don't know why but I replied, 'Sorry mate I don't smoke,' before I realised the bloke was tanked up so high he was swaying in the wind holding his cigarette. Eddie sensed the danger and sent down the line to the truck a request for security. 'What security, we don't have any?' was the reply, and poor little Kirsty, the assistant producer, had to battle her way through the crowd, climb the huge ladder and more or less carry the drunk back down into the stands. It gained without doubt the biggest cheer of the night!

We often have trouble recognising players, especially ones from overseas. The PNG squad was no exception so we decided to go down and watch them train the day before the match. After 10 minutes of watching all the players running around in tracksuits, pom-pom hats and scarves, we decided to forget it. They all looked the same. Thank God for numbers. Eddie once called a player several times at Halifax and praised him for having such a great first half only to realise at half time there wasn't any such player. I once did a studio build up for the Australian Grand Final and had one second rower playing for the wrong team and another player I suggested could turn the game with his kicking prowess only to realise later he was out injured. The former Warrington props Gary Chambers and Mark Hilton look so much alike we both spent the entire game, yes the full 80 minutes, identifying them the wrong way around. It wouldn't have been all that bad but one had a below-par game the other played out of his skin. The viewers at home were given a different impression.

One hot summer's evening I arrived in a shirt, which to put it mildly was a bit on the flash side. It was all green and gold with huge flowers on it. I got so much stick that I changed into my dress shirt early only to find just before kick off that the drummer in the band out on the pitch was wearing my discarded flashy one! We went down to Bill Arthur on the sidelines to find he was wearing it. At half time a cameraman was wearing it and when we interviewed the injured Iestyn Harris at the end of the game he was wearing it too!

A hot summer's day is great for the fans. It's a problem for the players when it gets overbearing but it's not too good for me in the studio either. Being asthmatic is a problem in itself but when the studio lights go on the room is boiling. Even with air conditioning, I sweat like a pig. Out of screen I have to be covered by a huge, ice cold wash leather. This makes it a nightmare for Sue the makeup lady. Sue Goldstone is one hell of a nice lady who must cringe every time I sit in the chair. How she gets me to look good on TV is a mystery. Since we have gone high definition, poor Sue has to ensure all the hairs from my nose and ears don't show. Even the few hairs that sprout out of my bald head from time to time have to be removed. Looking up my nose that's been broken 13 times can't be very pleasant. Yet for the past 10 years or so she has done it with a smile on her face. We are lucky to have such a professional in our ranks. For years she made up the likes of Ena Sharples and Ken Barlow on Coronation Street. She's also 'put the gloss' on many other film stars, so I know I'm in good company.

The rugby league team at Sky are proud of our efforts. We all work hard, but others work much harder than Eddie and I. The production team is small but the amount of product we offer each week on the TV screen is a credit to everyone involved. Bill Arthur, Angela Powers, Phil Clarke, Chris Warren, Ben Proe and Rod Studd all offer their own style to our successful team of commentators and presenters. Executive director/producer Neville Smith has trail-blazed our sport to great heights. He is a man who brought to the fans the video screen and many other innovations that other sports now copy. Mark Smith, Producer of the *Boots 'n' All* show and faithful assistant to Neville is another team leader striving to capture the best of rugby league, week in and out. Kirsty Cottle, June Fairhurst, Melinda Farrell, Mathew Preece, Oliver Rice, Miles Hawthorne, Dave Ryan, Ian

Brash, John Murphy, Mick Miller, Martin Carroll, Paul Davies, Vicky Lewis, Andy Syres, Tony Robson and Richard Armstrong are names most people have probably never heard of. Without this team I would be nothing. There are a few others who have left the company but are certainly not forgotten. Mark Wallace was producer of our mid week show for a few years. He had a great sense of humour. At meetings he would often cry out, 'All pile on!' And we did, all over the boardroom table. How it held the weight of us all was remarkable. Mark had a great singing voice and toured the country with a group singing barbershop opera and I have never seen him without a smile on his face.

Another producer, Mark Lynch, was the same. He was laid back to the point where he looked capable of falling asleep in meetings. He liked Jazz and so do I, so we hit it off well and often 'breezed' through a Miles Davis number instead of getting down to hard work. He was such an easy going man! We had a Christmas party one year with another assistant producer, Chris Tate; we decided to go back to Sky's local drinking hole, the Grasshoppers Rugby Club after a long, hard boozy lunch. It was a big mistake. We were happy but rowdy and we started playing pool for money. When I potted the black, I turned to demand the £10 wager. They both gave it to me all right, but first they ripped the note into shreds before throwing it on the table. I scooped up the ripped note and demanded the barmaid change it for a brand new one! She rightly told me to get lost (or words to that effect) and I replied with added change and a few extra bob on top. Mary the barmaid was Irish, proud and strong and without pausing for breath she barred me from the club.

'Out now!' she growled.

I realised I was in the wrong and I tried to apologise. She stuck to her guns and demanded I leave there and then. Both Lynch and Tate were in no state to figure out what was going on so I told them we were all banned. We stumbled down the steps and caught a cab into town. I had drunk enough and hopped out at Kensington. I left the two others to go on to some seedy nightclub. I had barely walked 10 yards when I was crash tackled from behind. With my hands in my coat pockets, I hit the ground nose first and split it badly as we went sliding on the icy pavement. I struggled to get up and quickly swung a right hook at my 'mugger' and split his lip open only to find to my horror it was Chris Tate! 'You forgot to pay towards the cab fare,' he cried. We both looked a bloody mess. We burst out laughing and hugged each other, wished each other a Merry Christmas and set off home in different directions to clean off the blood and clear up the hangover. Chris still asks me for that cab fare to this day. I also informed both men years later that it was only me Mary banned that night!

It was fun working with the Sky team and still is. Our crew is special to me. I can't thank those people enough who make sure we get on air each weekend at the outside broadcast. I thank studio floor manager Dave Redfern, former Bradford and Great Britain star winger who each week drags me into position on time and ensures I have a pen. Pitch manager Brian Middlehurst is a bloke who can sniff out a story from nothing. I thank Chris Sandeman, operations manager, who makes me look like 'Twiggy' (which is probably the reason I like being in his company). Thanks to Ian Proctor, 'The Brain' who has the greatest knowledge of rugby league stats in the world. Ask him who won the Wembley final in 1946, or any other final for that matter and he'd rattle off the score, teams, referee and the crowd size without taking breath. I thank all the guys at Telegenic, our facilities company, and all at Sky Sports for giving me the chance to enjoy a job so much that I once rather foolishly said I would do it for nothing. If a loaf of bread wasn't so expensive these days I probably would. And of course to all those people who have helped me climb the ladder to my position in life, I thank them all for it's been one hell of a pleasure looking back.

22

HEROES AND VILLAINS

I know it's traditional for a sportsman getting towards the end of his life story to select his all-time-great team. In the time before I hung up my boots, I was fortunate to play with and against so many great players that it would be impossible to select my favourite 13. However, it would be churlish of me not to highlight a few.

Great full-backs are common in our modern game. Wellens, Webb, Briscoe and the recently retired Radlinski are something special but a player from the past who would readily fit into Super League is Paul Charlton. The former Great Britain and Salford star, 'Marra' Charlton was fearless to the point of stupid! I swear if a runaway tank had found its way onto the field of play, he would have tackled it. He had an unusual running style with head held high. He had an ungainly gait in full flight yet he read the game so well and was one of the major reasons we won the World Cup in 1972. He has a face only a mother could love and in all the years I've known him I still can't understand a bloody word he says.

Graeme Langlands was another delightful character I've spoken about earlier in the book. I couldn't fault his ability and will to win. He was a great player but I would think twice before inviting him to a barbecue. I bumped into him recently and he offered some kind of grunt as he shook my hand. This was something he didn't do in 1972!

Wingers Mick Sullivan and Billy Boston would make any select team over any era. They were tough, fast and ruthless in their quest to score a try. Mick and I come from the same town and he quite rightly is a legend in Dewsbury. Mick was a slim, fast winger at Huddersfield in his teens. He was a much bigger presence when playing for Wigan, St Helens, York and Dewsbury where his bulk became his trademark and forced him into the forwards late in his career. In his prime he was lethal and an incredible athlete who enjoyed using the 'ball and all' tackle with glee, much to the discomfort of his opponents! The opposition always kept a sharp eye out for 'Sully'. He once picked up a full bottle of beer that was thrown at him after scoring a try for Great Britain against Australia in the Ashes Test in Sydney. He flipped off the top and drank the contents in one gulp. It sent the crowd into a frenzy. He was magic!

What a man Billy Boston was. Without doubt, he was the most difficult player to stop. His upper body strength coupled with a huge step off both feet made him a firm favourite at Wigan during the 1960s. The fans often called him the human tank which is not surprising given the wake of destruction he left behind. Billy had played only a handful of games for Wigan before he was selected to tour. This was a remarkable feat. I love the story of when Reg Gasnier played in his first test against Billy. His Aussie team mates kept going on about how big Boston was and that the only way to stop him was to grab a lump of shit and throw it at the huge, Welsh born winger. Gasnier enquired as to where he would find such a thing on the field of play. 'Don't worry,' came the reply, 'when Billy starts running at you, you'll find plenty!'

I talk of Gasnier in the same breath as the others as he was a sensation. He scored a hat-trick on his Ashes debut and was hailed as the greatest centre the world has ever seen. He was blessed with speed, swerve, a side step and wonderful balance. I remember my dad taking me to see him play for the Kangaroos against Bradford in a floodlit game at Odsal on a cold mid week night. With his first touch of the ball, Reg changed direction twice, beat four men, raced towards the full-back and without changing pace chipped over the top and was waiting for the ball to come and land in his arms underneath the posts. He was amazing, a freak of a player.

Naturally, the Aussies were eager to undermine our British centres as not fit to lace Gasnier's boots. This was a little far fetched considering at the time we had a Mr Neil Fox and Mr Eric Ashton plying their trade. In my book, both are on the same level as Gasnier. They may have different styles but they were world class. Fox was an amazing athlete and played well into his 40s. His points scoring record surely will never be beaten. He scored 358 tries and kicked 2,575 goals for a total of 6,220 points. He was the most prolific rugby league scorer in history. He was a solidly built centre who later in life played in the pack. He started his career in 1956 and played his last top class game in 1979. He was difficult to put down and would often run many yards forward with would-be tacklers hanging onto his back. He also had a good sense of balance and was able to throw a dummy and twist his body through the slightest of gaps in defence but it was his left boot that marked him as a great legend.

Eric Ashton is without doubt the most stylish player I've ever seen or played against. He was tall and elegant and one thought he was on roller skates such was his ability to glide past players. He would throw a dummy with such perfection it was like watching him in slow motion. He created hundreds of tries for his winger over the years. He was a perfect gentleman who won the Ashes down under when captain in 1962.

There have been so many good players who have pulled on the Great Britain number six shirt. Quite a few decent number six players have come from Australia too. Andrew Johns, Brett Kenny and Roger Millward were sensational players. All had speed to burn and the ability to be in the right place at the right time. Millward was exceptional and even at a young age was taking on the responsibility to organise and plot the opposition's downfall. It was his speed off the mark that established him as a great, durable player. He made a mockery of that old tale that small ones don't make it in league. Roger did big time and it was a pleasure to have played against him and with him.

David Bolton was another solid stand-off and he made me welcome at Penrith when I signed there in 1973. Bolton made his name at Wigan and then took Balmain Tigers to success in the Australian Grand Final in the 1960s after he emigrated to Sydney. David's been in Oz for well over 40 years and still has the broadest Wigan accent possible. He may drop in the odd 'mate' now and again but it's that good old Lancashire twang that meets the ear. Bolton was tough and creative and tells the wonderful tale each time we meet about when on the 1962 tour. The Great Britain camp put the players on a special diet of fruit and salad as a build up for the first test. The players weren't too impressed with this especially as they were in a land where good quality steak was to be found. Just before kick off, the coach indicated to all the players that they should whack the first Aussie they got their hands on. It was a tense dressing room when Bolton raised his hand and replied, 'First bloody Aussie I get hold of I'm going to eat him, I'm bloody starving.' He was a true character with a face that would give Paul Charlton a run for his money.

For sheer class I have to say Bobby Fulton's the best. He was a classy speedster who wouldn't shirk taking on the forwards. His speed from a standing start made tackling him difficult. He was tough and durable with a great football brain on his shoulders and an attitude to winning that was second to none. I really believe he was the first real full time professional. He demanded the best and played like his life depended on it. He was a star both on and off the field at a time when TV was becoming big for sport. He was a magical player, one of the best. If anyone happens to bump into him in a bar in Sydney don't hang about too long, it's possible to grow a beard before 'Bozo' puts his hand in his pocket to buy a drink! He's tighter than me and that's saying something.

I don't know of many league fans that haven't heard of Alex Murphy. He's a maestro, a character with charm to match and an ability to get up people's noses. He can irritate referees, officials, the media and anyone else that cares to be around him at the time.

Murphy is larger than life but as a player was ruthless, like Fulton, in his quest to win matches be it with his skills or tough defence. I have never seen a more motivated player take the field. His goal was simple ... he wanted to be the best. He set out on a career that still makes him the most talked about character in our history to this day. Drama followed Murphy around like a bad odour but he just kept coming up smelling of roses time and time again. Listening to Murphy in the dressing room was a joy to behold and to say his speeches could be a little blue would be an understatement. The little step, the swerve, neat pass, high kick, little grubber, or just sheer speed, he had it all. He was also the smartest player to take the field. His jet black hair and his quiff never looked out of place. Lord knows what he put on his hair to keep it so stiff and straight. I once ruffled his hair and the next chance he had he hit me with such force in a ball and all tackle it nearly broke all my ribs. From there on in I left such things to his barber. Murphy has to be also the best ever player-coach our game has seen. What he did at Warrington and Leigh was amazing. I still chuckle at him telling me whilst tossing the coin in the Championship semi final at Wilderspool that our winger Greg Ashcroft was going to have a busy day!

Now Greg wasn't the best with his hands and one never allowed him to pour the tea from a bone china teapot. I suppose in these modern times he would be called Teflon as not much stuck. Everything stuck in that semi final as Mr Ashcroft defused at least a dozen bombs in the first half alone. He did much the same in the second half. Even to this day Greg admits he doesn't know how he had such a good day at the office. He didn't drop a thing.

I couldn't pass the half-back spot without giving a special mention to Dewsbury half-back Alan Bates. Like Murphy, Alan was a toughie and tackled well above his weight. Alan was a tyro who never knew the meaning of giving in. He was justly rewarded with his selection on the British Lions tour alongside his brother John in 1974.

As I was a hooker up front of the pack, it provided me with plenty of time to assess those charming gentlemen called prop forwards. The prop forwards are a race and breed all on their own. One would suggest they didn't hit their prime until they passed 30, which I suppose leaves them many years to refine their talents and try out new things on the opposing hooker, ie … me! Dennis Hartley would be the first bloke to help an old lady across the road and Terry Clawson would not be far behind him. Sadly our game's not played on the streets where little old pensioners need assistance to avoid the oncoming traffic, it's played on a rugby pitch. Believe me these two guys didn't understand the word, 'play'. Maybe they were deprived as children from getting their hands on the Plasticine at nursery. Both were hard as nails and played rugby with the same demented look as a mad scientist playing with acid. Neither took a backward step, but sure made a few forward steps, especially Mr Hartley who had size 13 boots! Dennis was from the old school, and I'm pleased such things are in the past. I would have loved to have played rugby in the present day as now they just lean at the scrum for a rest and I may have kept a few of my looks. Hartley was a master of offloading the ball in tight situations but he gets a degree from me for hand squashing.

Terry Clawson had the same attitude as big Dennis and could also slip out a neat pass for his support play. He had to be the calmest player in the world. Talk about relaxed, he was often found sound asleep minutes before kick off. He wouldn't take in one word from the coach's last minute speech. I shared a room with him before the World Cup final and his snoring was amazing. He could sleep at will, when he decided to sleep, it was just like turning a light off. Bang and he was in the land of nod. We all expected Australia to come at us hard especially after we had beaten them in the group match four weeks before. As expected, the first scrum erupted with fists flying all over the place and Terry laughing out loud whilst throwing punches for his life. To me this was serious stuff. For Mr Clawson it was a joke. How one could think this was amusing whilst the likes of Bob O'Reilly, John O'Neil and Artie Beetson were throwing haymakers is anyone's guess. When it all calmed down Terry just whispered in my ear, 'Bit hot in there aint it?' I shook like a leaf whilst he cracked jokes. I have the greatest respect for both men despite the pair having a long-term effect on my modelling career. They were great players to have on your side, but it wasn't quite as pleasant to face them.

Special mention must go to all those guys who protected me over the years. Players need help whilst putting their head in a scrum up front. The likes of Trevor Walker, Dick Lowe, Big Jim Naylor, Harry Beverley and Brian Taylor at Dewsbury and Tim Sheens, Bob O'Reilly and Terry Geary at Penrith gave their all to assist a hooker that was never good at striking for possession. He needed all the help he could get.

They often say when a hooker is born they throw the mould away. This could be the case with me and all the other charming chaps I've encountered in the scrum. Some were strong like Close of Huddersfield. Others were quick like Dunne of York whilst Tony Fisher of Bradford and Leeds holds a special place in my heart. I say that because that's about the only place of my body that Tony didn't hit! Boy, what a character he was. He delighted in meeting people and gave them an unusual handshake that could often leave a mangled thumb. His huge hand squashed the life blood from the wrist down. The former RAF Champion boxer took great delight in most things hard and tough. Once at a Welsh rugby league reunion, both Tony and Big Jim Mills got bored and allegedly started to head butt each other for some fun. They say it was a sight to behold which is not surprising as they both honed this delightful skill on me over the years. A confrontation with either of them (sometimes both) and players knew it wasn't going to be a pass the parcel party, more like a race to see which bloke's blood hit the turf first. Usually it was mine, so it's easy to grasp why I offered my thanks to those gentlemen who protected me over the years in the previous paragraph. Another Welshman gets my vote for being the best, a true gent called Tommy Harris from Hull who invented the modern style we see from hookers these days. I'm proud to say I copied this bloke's style because he revolutionised the dummy half play by running and offloading with guile and speed. Harris won the Lance Todd trophy for man of the match at Wembley when on the losing side and although taken off on a stretcher before full time had shown enough courage and skills to snatch the award. It wasn't a sympathy vote either. He was outstanding that day and I can remember saying to my dad after the match that I wanted to be just like Tommy. It was a sad day when Tommy died but I was glad to have been introduced to the great man. He didn't know it but he moulded my game and I was so happy to thank him before he passed away. Peter 'Flash' Flanagan is another tremendous hooker that's no longer with us. He was another great character we lost from the game. These men were great servants to league.

Dick Huddart was another player who changed our game. He became another three-quarter in many ways. Second rowers were rarely seen striding with speed out wide. Huddart proved devastating at St Helens and unsurprisingly was snapped up to join St George in Australia where he still lives. Big and strong with a high leg action, Huddart left players in no doubt they had to get their tackling technique spot on when facing his rampaging runs. Phil Lowe took up the same style in the late 1960s and early 1970s. He was also snapped up to play in Sydney with Manly. Lowe gave great service to club and country and, like Huddart, was a hard man to pull down. Bob Haigh could hold his own in this company too. He was a prolific try scorer and held the record for tries scored in a season by a forward for a long time. He was a crafty player with plenty of style which made him a pleasure to watch.

Last but certainly not least is the loose-forward, 'Gentleman' Johnny Whiteley, the Prince of Players from Hull. Whiteley would hit hard and fast but rarely resorted to anything close to foul play, hence his nickname. He was always a super fit athlete who still runs five miles a day. This is not bad for a bloke well past his 70th birthday. The Hull legend was a solid defender but it was his 'gliding' style of running that caught the eye. For such a big, tall man, his speed was incredible, especially whilst cover defending. He was a true hero on Humberside and I'm proud to know him as a friend. He also proved to be a good coach who never confused a player by asking for him to do something out of his reach. He made such a huge impact on me whilst taking charge of the Yorkshire County team. I will never forget his short speech where he requested we all do our duty and respect the selectors' confidence in the players they had chosen. 'You're the best, that's why you're here. Just play.' We did and won the Championship three years' running.

His words were simple but effective. Maybe some of our modern coaches could learn something from the past. Who knows? When they get old and sit down and write their life story, they might be saying the same thing. Life goes on but at times it's nice to look back.

23

MY DREAM COMES TRUE

It's hard to believe a cricket venue would provide the spark I needed to get my lifelong ambition off the ground. I didn't think it would take someone born in India to bring it to fruition. For years I glanced at the crates under my house in Australia packed with my collection of rugby league memorabilia. The collection had been stacked away only months after its two years of travelling on the train around Australia. I felt guilty it was not on show to the general public. I had worked in England for Sky TV for nearly 15 years and never really had the time to think about it. I suggested opening a museum to the RFL many times, but unfortunately this suggestion fell on deaf ears.

Eddie and I were doing a charity speech at a local cricket club in Huddersfield for the Giants Squad Builders Fund. I was introduced to a gentleman next to me on the top table who turned out to be the owner of the famous George Hotel. He was called Mr Umesh Ummat. Umesh looked somewhat surprised when I quickly claimed I had a great idea for the hotel and asked if I could get in touch later to discuss my project. He asked what the project was but I said I would explain in detail at a later date.

'I look forward to meeting up,' was Umesh's reply. I felt a sense of excitement at the man's interest. I found it hard to concentrate for the rest of the evening as I just felt I might have found a kindred spirit.

Even Eddie was intrigued, 'What scheme are you

conjuring up now?' he asked.

'Just a little something that could help our game,' I replied.

Within days I started to put together a profile complete with drawings explaining what I needed to get my dream off the ground. Ironically, I bumped into Umesh a couple of weeks later whilst comparing a Robbie Paul benefit night at the Queens Hotel in Leeds. He was quick to exclaim he hadn't heard from me about my proposition.

'Sorry Umesh but I'm not ready with my pitch or the correct plan of attack. Don't worry I'll ring you soon,' A few days later I called him. We arranged to meet at the George Hotel the following Thursday where I arrived armed with plans, photos, drawings and my mind full of ideas.

Umesh listened for just over five minutes without saying a word as I launched into explaining my dream. Before I could show him any plan, drawing or anything else, he looked at me and said, 'Great idea let's do it!'

You could have knocked me down with a feather. For three weeks I had been preparing my pitch. Here I was and my opening gambit about the museum and heritage centre was snapped up by one shrewd man within minutes. I couldn't believe my luck. Umesh had been born in India. He came to this country to further his education and set up a business. He knew little about our game yet could grasp the importance of giving the fans a chance to re-live and understand the history of rugby league. When others had turned down the project, this gentleman could see its advantages. Within 10 minutes we both went downstairs into the cellar and started planning our campaign. It was as simple as that. That was the easiest part. Financing the project was the hardest part. Talking is one thing, finding the cash to do it is quite an obstacle.

Umesh and I both invested a considerable amount to get started. I set out to find an exciting sponsor to help complete the deal. I decided to go to the top of the tree and approached one of the largest companies in the world, Gillette. I befriended a certain Tony Colquitt, the Sponsorship Director at Gillette and offered him the first chance to be involved. Within a week we had set up a meeting with all parties and the scheme was accepted after a two hour discussion in London.

I just can't begin to explain my excitement. For over 40 years I had been collecting league memorabilia and now I was bringing it all back to the place where our game was born, the George Hotel, Huddersfield. This listed building still has the room where the meeting took place on Thursday 29th of August 1895 when the split from Union was decided. I still get goose bumps each time I walk into the hotel and think about the fight for payment for players. They formed the Northern Rugby Football Union with a pledge to push forward without delay its establishment on the principle of payment for bona-fide broken time. So the rebellious Yorkshire and Lancashire senior clubs paved the way for what we now know is rugby league. It was a historic moment. In many ways that meeting with Umesh in the same room 111 years later was also a historic time.

Ironically, out of the 21 clubs that attended the meeting in August 1895, Dewsbury, my home town team, was the only club to refuse to join the rebels. The club soon realised its mistake and joined a few years later.

The Dewsbury club may have stuttered at the time but this Dewsbury lad didn't stutter and the hard work to get things underway began.

Umesh, Tony Colquitt and Gillette provided outstanding support and within two weeks the space downstairs was ripped apart and the designers moved in. I moved into the hotel and lived out of a suitcase for several weeks. I know some of the builders and designers became pissed off at my urgings but I realised it had to be finished to be opened around the time of the famous date of 29th August. To say I was on their backs day and night is an understatement. There were many tiffs between Adrian Smith from the design company, Touch Media Solutions and myself. We are still good mates and realise what pressure we were under. I must say he did a great job.

To my disappointment 29th August that particular year fell on a bank holiday Monday. This was not a good day to ensure good media coverage. Reluctantly I targeted 30th August instead. I have no regrets at the pressure I put myself and the builders under. The museum had to be opened. It was as simple as that. It meant I had to work non-stop in the final week. I often slid into bed exhausted at 3.00 am. I questioned my sanity at times and I admit I would talk to the walls and have discussions with the likes of Wagstaff, Lomas, Goldthorpe and Batten. These men were all time greats of our game who stared back at me from the exhibition walls. I didn't expect a reply as I'm used to that working with Eddie. He's ignored me for years. I don't really believe in ghosts but at times I felt 'they' were helping me! It sounds like I'm crackers but the job was finished on time. Just.

It was a proud moment on 30th of August 2005 when over 120 people turned up for the opening. The sponsors, print media, TV, Radio, RFL officials, fans, family and friends were all there. They witnessed three of our all time great players: Neil Fox, Billy Boston and Mick Sullivan, do the honour of declaring my dream open. We were all tickled pink at the reaction. We had good coverage from nearly all the media. Like most things involving rugby league, a few ignored it. They gulped down the free lunch, beer and wine and left with a grudge rather than a report. But that's life. It was a fantastic day and an even better night as we celebrated our achievements. The bar tab came as a bit of a shock but it wasn't everyday I fulfilled my dreams. Boston, Fox and Sullivan were fantastic. They were interviewed and photographed time and again. As the night wore on, the stories got better. Tries were recounted, breaks got longer, tackles more cruel and there were even suggestions that players kicked goals from 60 or 70 yards out! It was a special time when the Gillette Rugby League Heritage Centre was born. I had a blast.

After over 40 years collecting memorabilia, I feel happy that it now resides at the George Hotel and is on display for all to see. Since we opened the museum, it is amazing how many people have taken up collecting memorabilia. We often get people asking if we can find out the history behind what they have saved or purchased. No doubt many other collectors enjoyed re-living the events of yesteryear. Many ask questions about their collections and we are happy to help out with information where we can. Some visitors have realised they also want to show the fans some of their historic treasures. They have kindly donated items to the centre over the past 18 months. I thank them from the bottom of my heart for their tremendous gestures.

The centre could not operate without the wonderful help of two retired people who give up their time so generously to ensure it keeps open. Sam Morton was a former BARLA Great Britain coach and a tough player in his time. He played with the great Dewsbury Celtic side and spends hours researching the game's history. There cannot be many people in the world who know more than Sam about rugby league. Keith Burhouse is another man who loves the game and has been a great servant both to the Centre and his beloved Huddersfield Giants. He has supported and worked hard for the Huddersfield club since being in short pants.

My oldest daughter, Hayley, keeps the finances up to date and prevents me from dipping my hand in the till! Hayley's husband John also often helps out, together with my lovely granddaughter Holly. She is just old enough now to put her sticky fingers all over the display cabinets. This ensures the staff has plenty of cleaning to do.

I must congratulate the RFL for helping get the Centre

up and running. They have given me great support throughout and donated some outstanding photos and memorabilia to enhance the exhibition. I'm proud that they gave me the go-ahead to set up the game's 'Hall of Fame' within the George Hotel.

There are also many more people I should mention but it would take days to read if I listed them all. They know who they are and I'm humbled by the support they have provided.

My one wish is that through our Gillette Rugby League Heritage Centre we will give some youngster the spark to play our great game. What a tremendous day it would be if that same man were to walk back inside the Centre years later to see his own name up in lights. I remember on the day of the launch telling one journalist that it was a shrine to rugby league, and that everyone connected with our game should come and pray. I hope they do visit and I feel proud of being involved in the greatest game of all. Rugby league has come on in leaps and bounds with sponsorship, TV, new stadiums and full time players. The future looks rosy and no doubt will become even better. I notice now that some clubs are eager to open their own museum and celebrate their great history. That's great as we should never forget all those people before us who have given their time and some their lives in the quest to keep one of the world's toughest sports in the forefront of society. Often our sport has been ridiculed for its northern tradition. Its background of being a working man's game has also been ridiculed. Some have tried to smash the game into the ground. Others have simply tried to ignore it, especially some of the newspapers who through gritted teeth give us a few paragraphs from time to time hidden away amongst crown green bowling and squash. I'm proud it's a northern game. All league fans should feel that way too. We should celebrate even more the fact that those teams in 1895 had the nerve to break away and demand their rights for broken time payment. Many owe those people so much and I'm proud to have taken up what they set out to do. Hopefully I haven't let them down.

POSTSCRIPT

LOOKING BACK

Looking back has been a real blast for me and I hope it gave you an insight into what makes 'that bloke off the telly' tick. Most people know me only as Stevo. For this I can thank the Aussies. They quickly give people nicknames and when a nickname sticks, they have it for life. Not that I have any regrets about my life. Far from it. The fat, ugly, bald chap you see on TV (and often turn down the sound on) enjoys every minute of the media industry, be it TV, radio or the printed press. I like to think I don't beat around the bush. I call it as I see it. I know you may not agree with everything (or anything) I say but I offer my opinions with an honest approach and I don't make up things for the sake of it.

Away from the media, I'm quite different. I enjoy live theatre and good food and wine. Living in London offers me plenty of scope in that direction and of course, when the season's over, I fly out to Sydney and enjoy the summer months out there. I have no complaints.

Am I lucky? Maybe I am, although I tend to think the harder people work the luckier they become. I've had some hard times. But haven't we all? I don't think I'd change much in my life if I had the chance to start again.

Am I happy? I am. And I'll try my hardest to stay that way, although I do have to thank many people who have helped me along the way both in Britain and in Australia (and in a few other countries as well). I love the adventure of travel and the new friends encountered on the way. If I could weave a patchwork quilt out of those people I've met along the way, there wouldn't be many patches made of silk! There would be plenty of patches with lesser quality cloth and perhaps an odd patch of fine worsted. These people have been a mixed bunch of rogues and gentlefolk.

Sadly plenty of my good friends are no longer with us but although they may be gone, they are not forgotten. This was one of my motivations for opening the Rugby League Heritage Centre. We can all enjoy reading about those pioneers who have left us the legacy of the greatest game of all. I would have loved to have seen the likes of Wagstaff, Batten, Goldthorpe and many others display their skills. A number of those stars of the past that I did see have now passed on. Trevor Foster, the great Bradford player, was a wonderful man. I became a great friend of his in his later years. He was a gentle giant who was the game's first development coach. He was a proud Welshman. On the 1946 Tour down under, he slept on the luggage rack of a train for three nights from Perth to Sydney and played a game a day later. He was also the man behind the resurrection of Bradford after they went bankrupt in the 1960s.

Jimmy Ledgard is another who passed away to that great playing field in heaven and I can just imagine both him and Trevor discussing tactics. Jimmy was a great player for Dewsbury and Leigh and won the first World Cup in 1954 for Great Britain. He also gave outstanding service to Yorkshire. His house was just over the wall from Crown Flatt, Dewsbury's old ground and often after training he would advise us about what we needed to do to get to the top. Jimmy and I were both inducted into the first Dewsbury Hall of Fame ceremony along with my old playing partner Nigel Stephenson a few years back. Jim still had that fine head of black hair. Just months before he died, I had the pleasure of inviting him and his wife to the Rugby League Heritage Centre to show him some live footage of him playing for Great Britain soon after the Second World War.

It was an amazing scene to witness this great man seeing himself on screen for the very first time in his life with tears rolling down his face. I could see the pride bursting out. His wife suggested he was a good-looking man in those days. 'I still am!' was Jim's reply. Even at just over 90 years of age, he was still good looking. A few days later, he presented me with his jersey, badge, honour cap, boots, shorts and shoulder pads from his Great Britain Lions tour in 1950. The kit was all neat, clean and tidy. The look he gave me that day will live with me forever. His eyes were moist but sparkling with a smile that made his face come alive. It was as though I was looking into the eyes of a young man in his prime rather than a man in his 90s.

'I thought you might want to put these somewhere,' he said.

'Of course I will,' was my reply. At that moment I realised why I had set out on that long journey of collecting memorabilia years ago. People like Jimmy and Trevor should never be forgotten. I often watch both Trevor and Jim on tape. They were both remarkable men and great players.

Another former player close to my heart is Alan Lockwood, a former Yorkshire, Hull KR, Leeds and Dewsbury hooker who spent a lot of time teaching me the basics of striking for the ball in the scrum. He helped me on my way when I was a struggling young kid at Shaw Cross Boys club. Alan would wait for me after his training stints at Dewsbury and he supported me in my quest to make it to the top. Sadly Alan passed away earlier this year. He was a proud and fair man who gave his all for our game.

I still have friends in the north that I try to see from time to time, none more so than Pamela and Philip Robson. These two delightful people lived in the same street as me in my early days in Saville Town. Pam and Philip courted each other from the age of 12 or 13 and they have been together ever since. Whenever I need updating with the goings on in the north, Pam's the girl! Not much gets past Pam, who has a heart of gold and a husband that loves her to bits. Phil and I played rugby league on the hard streets as scruffy kids. He still has a great interest in our game through his involvement with Thornhill Rugby League Club, based in a suburb of Dewsbury. I can still see Pam and her mother, arms folded, stood on the steps of their house in Warren Street watching the world unfold with a fierce look on their faces. If Hitler had made it to Britain, Pam's mother, Mrs Chappell, would have made him turn back!

Michael Clift was another influence on my life mainly because he was the bloke who somehow could afford a real ball! Clifty was older than all of us by about six or seven years. He lived for rugby league and all the kids in the neighbourhood enjoyed playing alongside him. He had the worst bowlegs in the world and wouldn't have been able to stop a cow in a ginnel, never mind a pig! Clifty and I also went into business cleaning windows. We even had some cards printed. It earned us a few bob when times were hard until one day someone knocked off our ladders, buckets and cloths. The result of this was the end of the business. Michael wasn't the best looking bloke on the block but surprised everyone by pointing out an attractive girl working on one of the busses. He declared he'd marry her. We all laughed, but within a year he got the girl and to my knowledge they're still together. I bet he's still got that ball as well!

Tony Firth was another tough lad who was small in stature but big in courage. Boy he could throw a left hook with the best of them. How do I know? Because I copped most of the blows! Not that I didn't get my revenge. He took a few on the chin from my superb swinging right fist. The reason for this was that we found an old pair of boxing gloves on the tip and decided to box each other most nights after school. He chose the left glove, I chose the right glove. There were no electronic games or computers in those days. We made do with what we had. I still remember the Christmas day when we were about six or seven. We both ran out onto the street proudly displaying an orange and of all things, a banana! This was sheer luxury back then.

Many people have shaped my life and a lot of players helped me on the way. I was saddened when our Great Britain captain, Clive Sullivan, died at a young age. I couldn't write this book without paying tribute to this man. He was a superb skipper and an outstanding player. Sullivan was a quiet character that let his skills on the field tell the story. He had amazing speed and agility and overcame many injuries to become the best. Hopefully, through the hard work of Leeds Rhinos former operations manager Stephen Ball, a statue of the great winger will be erected on Clive Sullivan way near the Humber Bridge in the not too distant future. Clive deserves nothing less. His effort in the 1972 World Cup was magnificent. I remember that great length of the field try in the final against Australia where he raced 70 metres to score. It came at the right time, just before the break and lifted our spirits when it looked like the Aussies were getting on top.

Many people have helped me on the way and I hope I have helped a few to enjoy life like myself. It's impossible to name all these people but I thank the few hundred (or is it thousands?) who have thrown the odd pint down their throat in my company. I hope they enjoyed it as much as I did. I'm no shrinking violet when it comes to having the odd slurp and many is the time I have over indulged and paid the price. My nose has been broken 14 times, 13 times on the playing field and once when I fell out of my mate's car and smashed my nose on the pavement! I try to think I'm a much mellower person these days. I certainly have given up the two and three day 'benders' I had in the past. Some of the Sky camera men are hard to avoid, especially after the games on Friday and Saturday nights. 'Macca' is one who can drink for Britain and tells some of the best stories when the liquid is in full flow. He's a great bloke, like all those involved in the Sky Super League broadcasts.

Neville Smith, the executive director/producer, has had a huge influence on my career. His search for new ideas is a huge bonus for our team. 'Nev' is the bloke who brought the big screen to our game. He also introduced the video referee and a host of great ideas that have pushed Sky to the forefront of televised sport. In fact Nev loves our game so much and has been in England so long he shouts for Great Britain rather than Australia. This indicates his passion for British rugby league. He never stops trying to introduce innovative ideas. His understudy, Mark Smith, is another ideas man who directs the *'Boots 'n' All'* shows and does a great job. I've seen Mark grow into the job from being a young, spotty teenager. On more than one occasion I've taken him under my wing so to speak, not in work mode but by offering him a chance to see a bit of life! We've had more than the odd trip away to the likes of Tenerife. He soon settled into the 'have a good time' mode. I remember him telling me on the flight out that he was not going to drink and wanted to sit in the sun all week. I showed him the beach as soon as we arrived early in the morning and told him to take in the view and run the soft sand through his toes.

'Why?' he asked.

'Because that's the last time you'll have a chance,' I replied. Two hours later he was drunk! I rest my case.

Mark rarely drinks these days as he's a fitness fanatic. He's now married and has turned into a decent chap who will do anything to help you. He's the sort of bloke you would like to marry your daughter. He's an all round good egg! See I helped him in some way.

Talking of help, our make up lady, Sue Goldstone, is without doubt the most important person on our Sky team. Sue has the job of making me look presentable to the viewers. It's not an easy task and she sighs each time I sit in her chair. I thought at one time that she sighed out of admiration. It turns out she sighs out of desperation! Putting make up on my melon is probably one of her worst jobs, although she used to make up Ena Sharples on Coronation Street! Sue is such a nice lady. She's a real professional. How she puts up with the antics in our mobile home (which doubles as a work station and dressing room) is anyone's guess. Not only does Sue apply layer upon layer of foundation and powder (or maybe Polyfilla), it falls on her to trim the hairs in my ears and nose as well. Like I said, she's a real pro!

Another group of people I admire and call friends are those guys who rig our outside broadcasts. It's not an easy job and they work in all types of weather at an amazing speed. I arrive at the outside broadcasts about five or six hours before kick off. These guys arrive at the grounds at the crack of dawn, lay down over five miles of cables, and prepare the studio and cameras. They then un-rig it all when the game's finished and are away before midnight! It's an amazing feat of endurance and they are all great guys.

Fellow Great Britain player, Dave Redfern, is our studio floor manager. This is not an easy job as he has to control myself, Eddie, Clarkie and our guests. He's like a mother hen pushing us here, there and everywhere. He does his job as professionally as he did whilst wearing his country's colours.

Brian Middlehurst is 'Mr Quiet', the man who looks after things in and around the dressing rooms. He gives the signal for the referees to allow the kick offs and without his input, we wouldn't know what was going on in the engine room. Poor Brian has to listen to all the complaints from players, club officials and those merry whistle blowers. He handles everything with a smile. In fact the entire Sky rugby league team are a wonderful bunch. The team is made up of John Kidd and son Paul, Shirty, June, Kirsty, Ben, Heidi, Ollie, Pip, Andy, Steve, Vicky and of course Phil Clarke and Bill Arthur. Bill gets the rough end of the pineapple at times as he has to sit on the sidelines in all sorts of bad weather. He rarely grumbles. Clarkie continues to amaze me by dragging up stats that no one would dream of such as, 'It's been 1,080 minutes since so and so has scored a try!' It's magic stuff. I also feel both Phil and Bill have created their own good style of broadcasting when they combine for the national league matches and the Challenge Cup.

There are many other people I should thank. For all those people I've missed out in name I can assure them that deep down, I respect them for helping me through life. Of course this would never have come to fruition without the support and help from my family; my wife Maureen, son Craig and my three lovely daughters Hayley, Kayley, and Alyssa. Even my brother Derek and his wife Jackie said they would put their hand in their pockets and buy the book! Such loyalty cannot be underestimated.

And finally, it just wouldn't be right for me to not thank Eddie for doing the foreword for this book. It's still a great pleasure to sit alongside such a professional. He's a great mate and an all round good egg. I look forward to many more years of us working together. He's neat and tidy to the point of distraction and despite what people think, he does know a hell of a lot about our great game. So I say a huge thank you to a man who starts the month with jet-black hair that amazingly goes light brown before 30 days are out. Maybe it's the sun?